Library of
Davidson College

THE
DREAM
THEOPHANY
OF SAMUEL

Its Structure in Relation to
Ancient Near Eastern Dreams
and Its Theological Significance

Robert Karl Gnuse

UNIVERSITY
PRESS OF
AMERICA

LANHAM • NEW YORK • LONDON

222.43
G572d

Copyright © 1984 by

University Press of America,™ Inc.

4720 Boston Way
Lanham, MD 20706

3 Henrietta Street
London WC2E 8LU England

All rights reserved
Printed in the United States of America

ISBN (Perfect): 0-8191-3717-0
ISBN   (Cloth): 0-8191-3716-2

All University Press of America books are produced on acid-free
paper which exceeds the minimum standards set by the National
Historical Publications and Records Commission.

89-11494

To Margaret Elizabeth Gnuse

(1915 - 1981)

iv

ACKNOWLEDGMENTS

The present work represents the revision of a dissertation presented to the Graduate Faculty of Vanderbilt University in partial fulfillment of the requirements for the Ph.D. degree in Old Testament. Special thanks must be given to my dissertation director, Douglas Knight, for his guidance and encouragement in the creation of the dissertation. Thanks also go to Walter Harrelson and James Crenshaw for their assistance in reading and providing insight throughout this process.

As this work now appears in its present form I wish to express my gratitude to University Press of America for their willingness to publish this work.

Robert Gnuse
Loyola University
New Orleans, 1983

vi

TABLE OF CONTENTS

Page

ABBREVIATIONS.................................... ix

PREFACE... xiii

Chapter

I.   INTRODUCTION........................ 1

Ancient Near Eastern Parallels..   2
Anthropological Observations....   3
Dreams and Psychology..........   5

II.   DREAMS AND THE ANCIENT NEAR EAST... 11

Ancient Attitudes toward Dreams.   11
Categories of Ancient Near
   Eastern Dreams..............   16
Dreams in the Various Cultures..   23
Negative Attitudes in the Ancient
   Near East toward Dreams......   33
Dream Incubation...............   34
Later Developments in the
   Dream Pattern...............   39
Conclusion....................   44

III.   DREAMS IN THE BIBLICAL TRADITION..   57

Epic Literature................   63
Dreams in Historical Literature.   79
Prophetic Attitudes toward Dreams.   85
Joseph and Daniel Dreams.......   88
Allusions in the Psalms.........   101
Wisdom........................   102
Later Literature...............   104
Conclusion....................   105

vii

IV.	ANALYSIS OF I SAMUEL 3...............	119
	Text Criticism..................	119
	Form Criticism..................	130
	Genre Criticism.................	133
	Content Analysis................	152
	Theological Meaning of I Samuel 3...................	156
	Conclusion......................	157
V.	ANALYSIS OF I SAMUEL 1-3..............	179
	Form Critical Units.............	179
	I Samuel 1-3 as a Unit..........	193
	Conclusion......................	202
VI.	THE SAMUEL TRADITIONS.................	215
	History of Research.............	216
	Conclusion......................	219
VII.	CONCLUSIONS..........................	247
BIBLIOGRAPHY..		253

ABBREVIATIONS

AB	Anchor Bible
AJSLL	American Journal of Semitic Languages and Literature
AnBib	Analecta biblica
ANET	Ancient Near Eastern Texts Relating to the Old Testament
AnOr	Analecta orientalia
ARW	Archiv für Religionswissenschaft
BAR	Biblical Archaeology Review
BASOR	Bulletin of the American Schools of Oriental Research
BBB	Bonner biblische Beiträge
BHK	Biblia Hebraica, Rudolf Kittel, editor
Bib	Biblica
BibS(N)	Biblische Studien (Neukirchen)
BJRL	Bulletin of the John Rylands University Library of Manchester
BO	Bibliotheca orientalis
BWANT	Beiträge zur Wissenschaft vom Alten und Neuen Testament
BWAT	Beiträge zur Wissenschaft vom Alten Testament
BZ	Biblische Zeitschrift

ix

BZAW	Beihefte zur Zeitschrift für die alttestamentliche Wissenshaft
CBC	Cambridge Bible Commentary
CBQ	Catholic Biblical Quarterly
CBQMS	Catholic Biblical Quarterly Monograph Series
CQR	Church Quarterly Review
EHAT	Exegetisches Handbuch zum Alten Testament
EncJud	Encyclopaedia Judaica
EvT	Evangelische Theologie
ExpTim	Expository Times
FBBS	Facet Books, Biblical Series
FRLANT	Forschungen zur Religion und Literatur des Alten und Neuen Testaments
HAT	Handbuch zum Alten Testament
HKAT	Handkommentar zum Alten Testament
HTR	Harvard Theological Review
HUCA	Hebrew Union College Annual
IB	Interpreter's Bible
ICC	International Critical Commentary
IDB	Interpreter's Dictionary of the Bible
IDBSup	Supplementary Volume to Interpreter's Dictionary of the Bible
IEJ	Israel Exploration Journal
Int	Interpretation
JAOS	Journal of the American Oriental Society
JBL	Journal of Biblical Literature
JBR	Journal of Bible and Religion

JNES	Journal of Near Eastern Studies
JPOS	Journal of the Palestine Oriental Society
JQR	Jewish Quarterly Review
JSS	Journal of Semitic Studies
JTS	Journal of Theological Studies
KAT	Kommentar zum Alten Testament
KHAT	Kurzer Handkommentar zum Alten Testament
NorTT	Norsk Teologisk Tidsskrift
Or	Orientalia
OrAnt	Oriens antiquus
OTL	Old Testament Library
ORTG	Old Testament Reading Guide
OTS	Oudtestamentische Studiën
PEQ	Palestine Exploration Quarterly
RB	Revue biblique
RevQ	Revue de Qumran
RGG	Religion in Geschichte und Gegenwart
RSO	Rivista degli studi orientali
SANT	Studien zum Alten und Neuen Testament
SBLDS	Society of Biblical Literature Dissertation Series
SBLMS	Society of Biblical Literature Monograph Series
SBT	Studies in Biblical Theology
SJT	Scottish Journal of Theology
TDNT	Theological Dictionary of the New Testament

TLZ	Theologische Literaturzeitung
TSK	Theologische Studien und Kritiken
TZ	Theologische Zeitschrift
UF	Ugarit-Forschungen
UT	Ugaritic Textbook
UUA	Uppsala universitetsarsskrift
VT	Vetus Testamentum
VTSup	Vetus Testamentum, Supplements
WMANT	Wissenschaftliche Monographien zum Alten und Neuen Testament
WO	Die Welt des Orients
ZA	Zeitschrift für Assyriologie
ZAW	Zeitschrift für die alttestamentliche Wissenschaft
ZDMG	Zeitschrift der deutschen morgenländischen Gesellschaft
ZDPV	Zeitschrift des deutschen Palästina-Vereins
ZTK	Zeitschrift für Theologie und Kirche

PREFACE

The primary focus of this work is to evaluate I Samuel 3 in its total literary and theological context. Scholars have defined this text in the past as a prophetic call narrative, but this author maintains that it should be viewed as an ancient Near Eastern message dream theophany. Ancient Near Eastern dream reports are evaluated and compared with this biblical text in order to establish that point. The author has sought to present this thesis in previously published material -- "A Reconsideration of the Form-Critical Structure in I Samuel 3: An Ancient Near Eastern Dream Theophany," ZAW 94 (1982): 379-390. This present work offers a fuller evaluation than that brief article.

Taken by itself such a thesis would not merit an entire book. But this work offers more than just a detailed analysis of I Samuel 3. Dream reports throughout the Old Testament are evaluated with the use of ancient Near Eastern categories. No other work combines the thorough study of Biblical and ancient Near Eastern dreams. Hopefully, the reader also may find some value in the study of ancient Near Eastern dreams in their respective cultural contexts and the review of the traditio-historical development of dreams in the Biblical tradition. Furthermore, this work offers an evaluation of how this new understanding of I Samuel 3 affects the Samuel traditions as a whole. The author offers a summary of recent scholarship on the traditions in I Samuel 1-15 and some of his own conclusions. Hopefully, the reader may find the history of scholarship in Samuel studies equally useful as the study on dreams.

CHAPTER I

INTRODUCTION

The small boy hears his name called in the darkness of the sanctuary. In his innocence he does not perceive that it is the voice of the Lord. But the Lord prevails and the child must bear an ominous message of judgment and doom for the established leadership at Shiloh and the nation of Israel. The story is charming but deadly serious. It comes as a climax to stories about corruption in the holy shrine, and it brings divine justice against those so worthy of it. The small boy is none other than Samuel, the great prophet, priest, judge, mediator, and leader of Israel. How appropriate that the great Samuel be the one to bring the message to the house of Eli. Even as a small boy he functions as the great messenger of the Lord.

I Samuel 3 serves as a climax to the Shiloh history in I Samuel 1-3, but it is also the beginning of Samuel's ministry. The chapter is a sensitive story which contrasts the innocent boy with the old impotent man. It brings the dramatic confrontation of the Lord and the boy in that very shrine which has brought divine wrath. It contains the pathos of a loyal child who must inform the dutiful old man of his impending doom, and with his last shreds of dignity the old man accepts his fate as just. This artfully created narrative has theological purpose, for it justifies the fall of Eli's house, the loss of the ark in battle, and the demise of Shiloh in favor of Jerusalem.

Not only the narrative style but also the form in which the story is cast is intriguing. Though commentators often fail to mention it, this narrative account centers on a revelational experience that appears to be a dream. Any doubt about the experience's definition as a dream is dispelled when ancient Near Eastern dream reports are observed. The similarity between the narrative account of Samuel's experience and ancient Near Eastern message dreams is great.

A primary purpose of this work will be to determine the genre of this text and its classification as an ancient message dream. This will be accomplished by a close consideration of those ancient dreams and a comparison with I Samuel 3. Motifs of ancient Near Eastern dreams will be compared with the com-

ponent parts of I Samuel 3 to show the evident parallel pattern found in the Samuel experience. The chapter will be considered text critically and form critically in this comparison. Traditio-historical analysis will be used in evaluating this text and the greater context of I Samuel 1-3, for which the theophany in chapter 3 is the climax.

We have concluded that I Samuel 3 is a late literary creation cast in the form of an ancient Near Eastern message dream theophany. Care will be taken to establish the date of the text. Furthermore, if this segment is a late literary creation meant to serve theological purposes, the question of Samuel's historical role is raised. The development of the Samuel traditions will be evaluated in the light of the attribution of this dream theophany. The figure of the historical Samuel will be considered under the premise that I Samuel 1-3 is a literary creation.

Ancient Near Eastern Parallels

The comparison of biblical material with ancient Near Eastern material is fraught with danger. An extreme often exhibited is the discovering of parallels between biblical and ancient Near Eastern material no matter how tenuous their relationship. Many so-called parallels have been adduced on the basis of superficial similarity. Certain phrases, expressions, or aspects of literary forms may coincide, but the essence of the material may be totally disparate. These do not constitute authentic parallels. Instances where there is a similar use of language for different purposes with different meanings are questionable parallels. The Israelites were Semitic as were many of their neighbors. Similar concepts and attitudes may have developed out of this common environment, both physical and intellectual, which have no direct relationship with each other. Such examples are not authentic parallels. We must seek to avoid such avid parallel hunting and search for only legitimate ancient Near Eastern influence on biblical material. The text must show more than coincidental development out of the same Semitic milieu. Ringgren has stressed that frequently literary forms have been utilized by the Israelites. He offers examples that illustrate such a practice. These examples have more than a word or expression in common with their ancient Near Eastern counterpart; an entire literary structure or genre is adduced[1] with many points of similarity, both in expression and purpose.

This work will offer such an example. The ancient message dream is a literary genre with several component parts. I Samuel 3 is also a literary genre with comparable component parts. The comparison between the two will be on the basis of

genre structure and of the individual parts. For this purpose we shall carefully evaluate ancient Near Eastern dreams to perceive their form, function, and content; then we shall analyze the form, function, and context of I Samuel 3. The commonality between the two is to be found in form and content. The relationship is not one of superficial similarity. This will become evident with the fuller explication of both sets of material. Further biblical material in the other books of the Old Testament will be reviewed to indicate that I Samuel 3 is not an isolated instance.

Anthropological Observations

An initial observation of how dreams are understood in the ancient world, including Israel, tempts the scholar to make a comparison with similar views among primitive peoples. Although there are many discontinuities between ancient and primitive people in regard to dreams, nevertheless some insights may be gained from their points of commonality.

Dreams are communications from another realm, the world of the dead or the gods. The dream world is more real than this world, which is but a mere shadow of the other realm whence dreams originate. Visions and dreams are contact with that other realm for the purpose of receiving a message, increasing the strength or courage of the dreamer, and seeing the future.[2] The dreamer's experience is often one which is shared by the community. The dream will give direction and courage to the community in regard to their future actions. For this reason both ancient and primitive people saw dreams as important guidelines in life. The messages of the gods or deceased individuals and bizarre visions enabled them to respond in daily life for survival. Dreams and myths both perform a socializing role, for they enable the dreamer and his or her contemporaries to cope with reality. But there are differences. Myths are universal symbols of an entire society which seek to express the meaning and purpose of the cosmos and the relationship of people and society to that cosmos. Dreams are individual experiences of specific persons, they are neither exemplary nor universal. They will give direction to one or more people, but they are not universal symbols with lasting significance. Dreams are experiences of the sleeping state, whereas myth is a category which is experienced by the whole person. The projections of the myth encompass all the living experiences of humanity. Dreams will draw upon the motifs important to the mythic matrix, but they cannot function as myths.[3]

During sleep the dream process could occur in several fashions. The other realm could come into contact with the

3

dreamer, and a god would speak or a scene would be enacted before the dreamer. At other times the soul would be taken from the semi-conscious body and he or she would go to the other realm or a distant place in this world in order to see or enact dream visions. The Chinese believe there are two souls, the P'o or animal soul, which never leaves the body, and the Hun or spiritual soul, which travels during dreams. [4] The Eskimos believe that the soul visits a special dreamworld. [4] A very common belief is that if the dreamer is suddenly awakened, the soul will be lost.

Many people believe that the dead can be contacted in dreams. Dreams can be proof of the afterlife. If a primitive person sees a departed friend in a dream, that friend is alive somewhere. Some scholars believe that the belief in immortality may have arisen from seeing departed friends and relatives in dreams. [5]

Primitive people must react to dreams as though they were part of real life. Among American Indians what is dreamed must be attended to in real life. Snakebites in a dream must be cured when the dreamer awakes. [6] Among the Shilluk in Africa the god Nyakang will appear in a dream and demand a sacrifice, and the king must fulfill this request. [7] When a member of the American Plains Indians dreams he is possessed by a female spirit, he must thenceforth live as a woman. [8] Dreams are taken to the elders or a special diviner for interpretation and advice as to what action need be taken.

In certain societies care was taken to induce dreams. Indian tribes like the Areharas and the Gros Ventres would induce dreams in special ceremonies. [9] The Iroquois and the Hurons had a festival of dreams wherein people would run about the village destroying personal property and tormenting people until someone had guessed what they had dreamed. [10] Even in Medieval Europe there were various "Fire-Festivals" in England, Ireland, Sweden, and Germany where unmarried boys and girls would gather ivy or flowers to place under their pillows at night or creep through briar patches while invoking the name of the devil or druids. The youths would dream of the person whom they were to marry that night. [11]

The work of folklorists like Frazer, Stith Thompson, Anitus Aarne, and others has brought collections of material together for use by anthropologists, sociologists, and psychologists. Significant patterns have been discerned in this material that have given insights in all these fields. Established patterns have been noted in the nature of dreams and their reporting. These patterns have been shaped by cultural patterns in the society and environment of the dreamer. The dreams of non-settled peoples tend to be more

fluid with a wider range of symbols and interpretations, whereas the dreams of settled peoples tend to be more controlled, with established symbols and regulated patterns of interpretation. The reporting of dreams also followed established cultural patterns. Laufer has noted that inspiration dreams have a similar pattern among Chinese and American Indians. In both cultures these dreams will foretell the future by allowing the dreamer to experience future conditions.[12] However, some patterns may not be due to cultural links, but the unconscious may provide similar dream symbols and structures for all people. Eliade observes that dream motifs of flying, ascending, or climbing are universal symbols of breaking free from a situation. Ascension is symbolic of going to heaven and the staircase is a symbol of passage from one mode of existence into another, a "rite of passage."[13] Dreams are dependent upon the mythic mind for images to serve the needs of the dreamer in every society.

The observations made by anthropologists and sociologists are fascinating, but they could lead us far from our main topic. This brief overview serves to illustrate some of the views held by both primitive and ancient people about dreams. With our modern era, however, new understandings have developed.

Dreams and Psychology

In our modern era dreams are no longer seen as communications from another realm or the transfer of the soul to a hidden realm. Dreams are seen as creations of the mind brought about by the mental and physical conditions of the dreamer.

The first scientific study was undertaken by Maury in 1861. He advocated the physical stimulus theory; dreams were caused by things that physically occurred before or during sleep. Sudden movements, muscle twitches, muscular pains, and outside disturbances caused dreams. He personally dreamed that he was being guillotined, and he awoke to discover that a bedpost had fallen on his neck while he slept.[14]

Sigmund Freud was the first psychologist to analyze thoroughly the dream phenomena. By 1895 he theorized that the purpose of dreams was to fulfill repressed desires by allowing the Id to communicate to the Ego, or the conscious mind. The Id sends overwhelming urges upon the sleeper's mind during sleep, for it is then that the Superego is no longer in control. These urges are converted into a creative story, or a dream, by the Ego in the process called Dream Distortion. This is a protective device, for every dream is an attempt to put aside a disturbance of sleep by the Id. When the Ego

cannot contain the impulses sent by the Id, it wakes the dreamer, and this is called a nightmare. The Ego is a censor which disguises the latent content of the dream with a manifest content. Freud's analysis seeks to discover the latent content with its infantile wishes and libidinal desires. Each dream symbol represents a hidden desire, and the symbols include linguistic constructs, childhood memories, and archaic ancestral experiences. Symbols are created in five different fashions: 1) condensation -- several latent meanings are compressed into one image, 2) displacement -- emotional charge is imparted into a symbol or object, 3) dramatization -- concepts are expressed with concrete images, 4) symbolization -- one object is represented by another object, and 5) secondary elaboration -- the dream is ordered to recall an image. Dreams are signs of psychosis, for they reflect past problems left unresolved, and the Ego is trying to handle the raw impulses of the Id left over[15] from the unresolved tension. Dreams are symptoms of illness.

Carl Gustav Jung built upon and revised Freud's thought. Jung emphasized dreams as part of a series, and the single symbol was part of a complex and interrelated scheme of meanings. Dreams were the product of a healthy mind, images brought to the conscious level for positive consideration. To dream in one's sleep is natural. Jung's contribution is his study of the "collective unconscious" and "archetypes." The collective unconscious is the myth-forming structure in every human psyche responsible for the dreams and fantasies in which inhibited activities of the dreamer can be expressed. Herein primitive humanity pushes into the conscious mind, and our ancient ancestors act out their primal urges. Thus people experience mythological motifs when they have no formal knowledge of the old mythology. They share with all people a collective unconscious within which there are the archetypes, those images and motifs found in all tales, fantasies, dreams, and myths everywhere. Archetypes recall the mythic world of our ancient ancestors. Motifs include the "shadow," "wise old man," "primordial mother," "child," or "hero-child," "animal," and "maiden." The maiden motif can come in many different forms, including "girl," "whore," "saint," "good fairy," "witch," "mother," and "goddess." Archetypes appear in myths, rites and dreams with a positive purpose. They express hope for the future on the basis of the past. They are the language of the unconscious[16] speaking to the conscious in spontaneous and universal terms.

Wilhelm Stekel was a student of Freud who expanded the analysis of dreams to include religious symbolism. For him dreams often contained a mixture of religious and sexual symbolism. The God figure was a hidden and threatening figure of authority, the fisherman represents the last judgment, and as such was an expression of guilt over sin. In

interpreting his patient's dreams Stekel looked for recurring motifs or patterns that applied to the individual's chief problems in life, background, religion, and dominant goals.[17]

Alfred Schutz evaluated the impact of the dream on the total life world of the individual. The dream belongs to the private world of the dreamer, and it occurs without an intersubjective experience with other people. Dreams occur when the mind is withdrawn from reality, and the mind then experiences the spontaneity of the imagination. However, dreams can influence the conscious state of an individual by giving spontaneous ideas. Dreams are an experience of the ego, and the same structures of consciousness are operative in the dream world as in the intersubjective or waking world. These include memory, imagination, and perception. Dreams are an experience of the ego and therefore real to the dreamer, they are simply not experiences shared by other individuals.[18]

Today psychologists view dreams as the result of a multiplicity of factors interacting with each other. Dreams are personal experiences of unique individuals, they are a manifestation of a specific life style of a person. Dreams deal with the individual's attitudes and often they ignore the greater social and political scope of the surrounding world. Dreams are seen as the attempt by the unconscious mind to communicate with the conscious mind, while the conscious mind tries to make sense out of these messages.[19]

The most important advances in dream analysis have come in the area of scientific psychology. In 1953 Nathaniel Kleitman and Eugene Aserinsky at the University of Chicago observed dreaming periods and periods of rapid eye movement (REMs) in sleeping patients as opposed to periods with no rapid eye movements (NREMs). Their work was later confirmed by W. C. Dement of the University of Chicago. During periods of REM patients would be awakened, and they could vividly recall their dreams. There were three to five REM periods for about ninety minutes out of every eight hours of sleep. The first REM period was five to ten minutes in length, the next ones would be correspondingly longer until the final one was thirty minutes in length. Infants had more REM time than adults. When patients were awakened to avoid REM periods, the patient would have additional REM time the next night. A particular EEG brain wave and pulse are associated with these REM periods. All people dream, and everyone has REM periods; this is a physiological necessity.[20]

The modern views of dreams often isolate them from the total reality for the sake of scientific study. Their impact upon life is carefully analyzed. Ancient and primitive people were not so careful in their scrutiny. For them dreams were a real

experience, a message from another realm. Dreams were heeded and feared. Modern people can no longer empathize with that understanding, and that sets them apart from both. Modern scholars often seek to study the phenomena of dreams among primitive people, almost seeking a past they have left behind. But a problem arises. The conscious mind forms the images of the subconscious into an acceptable set of images. When the dreamer retells the dream he or she often reforms the image again, as it is told in a dream report pattern acceptable to the customs of society. Thus the dream has gone through two filtering processes. It is the second filtration which hampers the modern scientist in the attempt to study the dreams of ancient or primitive people. He or she confronts a literary form instead of psychic phenomena and must call upon the aid of folklorists and anthropologists in evaluating the dream.

The review of modern psychological, sociological, and anthropological views is necessary for reason of comparison. Ancient and biblical dreams must be set in the perspective of a larger study of the dream phenomena. Many of the categories of modern study cannot be applied to ancient and biblical dreams, because the disciplines are often concerned with real dreams, whereas the latter are literary creations. The disciplines are helpful, however, in evaluating the context of dream reports, their use by society, their role in religion and politics of a given society, and their use by the storyteller. We can analyze the role of the dream report and some of the universal symbols, but we cannot analyze individual dreams of the ancients. Psychologists cannot reach beyond the grave to analyze the dreams of the departed; we can speculate only about the general use of symbols by a given society in their dream reports. But this introductory study is necessary in order to gain a perspective on the meaning of what a dream is and how it functions. We can now turn to a more narrow consideration of the literary dream reports of the ancient Near East and the Old Testament.

CHAPTER I

FOOTNOTES

[1] Helmer Ringgren, "The Impact of the Ancient Near East on Israelite Tradition," Tradition and Theology in the Old Testament, ed. Douglas Knight (Philadelphia: Fortress, 1977), pp. 32-40.

[2] John Neihardt, ed., Black Elk Speaks: Being the Life Story of a Holy Man of the Oglala Sioux (New York: Morrow, 1932; reprint ed., New York: Simon and Schuster, 1975), pp. 17-39, 154-158, 205-206.

[3] Mircea Eliade, Myths, Dreams, and Mysteries, trans. Philip Mairet (New York: Harper and Brothers, 1960), p. 16.

[4] Berthold Laufer, "Inspiration Dreams in Eastern Asia," Journal of American Folk Lore 44 (1931): 210.

[5] James George Frazer, The Golden Bough: A Study in Magic and Religion, 12 vols., 3d ed. (New York: Macmillan, 1935), 8:261.

[6] Ibid., 1:172.

[7] Ibid., 4:25.

[8] Ibid., 6:255-256.

[9] Ibid., 3:161.

[10] Ibid., 9:127.

[11] Ibid., 10:242, 11:52-54, 292-293.

[12] Laufer, "Inspirational Dreams," pp. 211-213.

[13] Eliade, Myths, pp. 116-119.

[14] The New Encyclopaedia Britannica Macropaedia, 1974 ed., s.v. "Dreams," by Wilse Webb, p. 1011.

[15] Sigmund Freud, An Outline of Psychoanalysis, trans. James Strachey (New York: Norton, 1949), pp. 46-50, 56-61, and The Standard Edition of the Complete Works of Sigmund Freud, vol 4-5: The Interpretation of Dreams, ed. and trans. James Strachey, Anna Freud, Alix Strachey, and Alan Tyson (London: Hogarth Press, 1953), pp. 356-357.

[16] Avis Dry, The Psychology of Jung (London: Methuen, 1961), p. 148; Carl Gustav Jung, Psychological Types or the Psychology of Individuation, trans. Godwin Baynes (New York: Random House, 1962), p. 581, and "The Psychological Aspects of the Kore," Essays on a Science of Mythology, trans. R. F. C. Hull (New York: Random House, 1949), p. 219.

[17] Wilhelm Stekel, The Interpretation of Dreams: New Developments and Techniques, 2 vols., trans. Eden and Cedar Paul (New York: Livergith, 1943), 2:72-73.

[18] Alfred Schutz and Thomas Luckman, The Structures of the Life-World, trans. Richard Zahner and Tristram Engelhardt, Jr., Northwestern University Studies in Phenomenology and Existential Philosophy (Evanston, Illinois: Northwestern University Press, 1973), pp. 28-34.

[19] Encyclopaedia Britannica, 1972 ed., s.v. "Dreams and Dreaming," by David Ballin Klein, pp. 667-668.

[20] Ibid., pp. 665-665a.

CHAPTER II

DREAMS IN THE ANCIENT NEAR EAST

The mind set of ancient people has been variously described as pre-logical or mythic.[1] Comparison with modern primitive people is sometimes undertaken, but it is not without its difficulties. Ancient civilized people with their technology and art are often quite different from our primitive contemporaries. The ancient world often demonstrated a range in attitudes from the naive to the sophisticated in the same historical periods. Plurality was evident, even if not in the custom with which we are familiar. Yet for the purposes of our study certain accepted generalizations will have to be utilized.

Among ancient humanity there was no clear distinction between reality and appearance. "Whatever is capable of affecting mind, feeling, or will has thereby established its undoubted reality."[2] In the era before the rise of Greek philosophy people did not critically distinguish the categories of reality. No distinction was made between the various forms of perception. Cosmogonic myths simultaneously related the origin of the universe and the recurring cycle of events that permeated the surrounding world, because for ancient humanity there was no difference. All perceptions were received and related to the not always consistent cosmogonic world view.

Ancient Attitudes toward Dreams

Dreams were no less real than impressions received during the waking state. They were not considered to be inner psychological experiences, as we view them; they were the external experiences of sleep, they were real. Dreams often contained the bizarre and the fantastic, and it seemed to ancient people that they were in contact with another realm, the numinous realm.[3] This other realm was the realm of the gods or the dead. Dreams were an attempt by someone or something to communicate to the dreamer,[4] and the dreamers were intermediaries between two realms. Gaster gives one of the best definitions for both biblical and ancient Near Eastern dreams:

11

Dreams are visions of things actually transpiring on an ultramundane plane, where persons are not bound to bodies nor events to specific moments and places. This plane is indistinguishable from that of the gods (or God), and dreams are therefore[5] considered to be divine communications.

Dreams are unlike myths because they are manifestly the experience of individuals in specific situations, whereas myths are universal archetypes, the common experience of all people projected into a universal story. As a result dreams related more closely to other divinatory experiences, both accidental and deliberate.

The ancients endeavored to perceive divine advice or the direction of their lives in a host of ways. Hepatoscopy, the removal and investigation of animal livers and entrails; libanomancy, the pouring of oil on water; lecanomancy, the observation of smoke patterns; astrology, the observation of astral bodies, the flight of birds, seismic disturbances, the weather, strange births, deformities, and a host of things could constitute the various omina. The omina were decoded and interpreted by specialists in these respective fields, and they could give advice for those interested in heeding the signs of the universe and moving with the flow of the cosmos. The predictive nature of omina was also augmented by oracles, which could be given by deities to the priests or uttered through the mouths of ecstatics.

Dreams constituted a minor form among these various omina revelations. Dreams blur the distinction between oracle and omen, but then we are not too sure of how the ancients might have made such a distinction, if at all.[6] There was no "sharp distinction among dreams, hallucinations, and ordinary visions," and the result is a rather complicated overlap of the different modes of revelation.[7] It is difficult to differentiate a dream from a vision. The only criteria are the stylized formulas that denote a dream as being such. The gods communicated to people in various channels, by signs and portents, by oracles, and by various types of dreams.

Dreams were experienced in different manners according to the ancients. The soul might leave the body and visit distant places in order to see bizarre visions, which would constitute a symbolic dream. The god of dreams might bring dreams, or a specific god might bear a special message for the dreamer, and this would be a message dream. Fears and hopes could induce dreams; this too, was perceived by the ancients, but such dreams were not worth recording. We call these the

12

psychological status dreams. In this last category are included dreams brought by divine wrath, angry gods, or disease. They often dealt with sexual or taboo matters, and nightmarish features typified these experiences. Their interpretation had to be undertaken lest a curse come upon the dreamer for failing to interpret the dream.[8] Similarities with modern dreams may be perceived in this latter category of psychological status dreams, and Freudian interpretations can be discerned in the ancient dream interpretation books. But we stand too far distant from the ancients to psychoanalyze them. The recorded dreams of the ancients are distinguished[9] from modern dreams by the reference to divine epiphanies. A dream in which the deity spoke demanded action no matter who received it, although usually kings, priests, and professional dreamers were the recipients. The common person experienced the nightmarish dream unworthy of recording, and he or she attributed the experience to evil spirits.[10]

Assessment of ancient dreams by modern standards offers many difficulties. The language of the texts is vague, reports are terse and under restriction of form, mood, and content. The censorship exhibited by the ancients reduced dream reports to a small number of types. Restriction due to fear and awe of recording the sacred encounter between the human and the divine led to increased stylization. The individuality of the dreamer is removed from the records, for the reports mention neither the physical and the psychological state of the dreamer, nor his or her needs, hopes, or conflicts. Human personality is never observed in the official dream reports. The sparsity of dream symbols makes psychoanalysis difficult. Their own strict interpretation of symbols is meaningless to us except for a few universal symbols. The interest of recording dreams is for the sake of the future, and the records are to be read by later kings and the gods. Finally, the evil dreams or psychological status dreams would be of greatest interest to modern psychoanalysts, but their contents are taboo and they are never recorded. We learn about the possibilities of what such dreams contained by the listing of various omina in the dream interpretation books. Whereas modern people unravel dreams therapeutically in order to find out about the dreamer's personality, the ancients unraveled dreams ritualistically in order to discover the message from the gods or the dreamer's ritual status.[11]

Though this sounds negative, some positive observations can be made. The ancients did perceive that evil dreams might proceed from a bad mental or physical status of the dreamer. But they viewed dreams as conveying a more important function for their society. The ancients emphasized something that modern people no longer accept: that dreams are a point of contact with another realm, an avenue of revelation. Dream

records and message dreams are a literary device, and stylistic procedures take priority over the actual content of the dream. In this fashion kings could undergird their particular choices in the affairs of state. The dream was a religious and political literary device.

As a phenomenon which offered an omen to people the dream had to be interpreted. Dream books were created to facilitate this process. Compiled on the basis of past experiences and the association of certain actions, dream analysis attempted to predict the future course of events.[12] Dreams were often interpreted to the reverse of their apparent meaning. Dreaming that the god cursed you implied blessing, catching a bird meant loss of possessions, and a woman kissing her husband signified ill fortune.[13] The texts endeavored to reduce the data to the form of short maxims. However, the concept of causality fails to be found; instead, an impersonal divine intent permeates the various observations. The relationship between omen and meaning often eludes us.

From a later era Byzantine and Arab dream books reflect for us the basic structure in its fullest form. They are either topical or alphabetic with the motifs and their respective meanings. Three ancient dream books remain extant, one from Assyria and two from Egypt, a demotic and hieratic copy. With a dream book ancient oneirocritics, or dream interpreters, could ply their trade. Throughout most of ancient Near Eastern history oneirocritics were considered to be a lower class of diviners and often had to function without official sanction. This was due to the lower esteem in which dreams were regarded when compared to other forms of divination.

A dream is dangerous until it is interpreted. The utilization of the dream book by the oneirocritic is for a therapeutic interpretation of the dream on behalf of the dreamer's well-being. There are three types of interpretative guidelines that we perceive. Some dream omina are based on puns. For instance, "If a man eats a raven (arbu), income (irbu) will come."[14] This is common in the hieratic and demotic dream books of Egypt. Other dream omina are based on symbolic associations. For instance, urination refers to the procreation of many children, or a stolen seal means that a child will die. Finally, some dream omina are simply incongruous; they operate with principles culturally alien to us. For instance, if you "eat your hand, your son will die; if you eat your foot, your daughter will die."[15] A number of the omina are concerned with the dreamer's eating habits.

Dream interpreters were qualified for their profession by a number of factors. Intuitive perceptions could turn one into an oneirocritic, or a particular combination of normal human

14

characteristics, whether it be sex, age, social status, or some charisma. A scholar with mastery of the dream book could also qualify. Finally, a dreamer who dreams a second time in order to interpret the first dream also becomes an oneirocritic.

There are several different traditions as to who were the earliest interpreters. Women served in the interpretative role in Mesopotamia's early epic literature. Gilgamesh and Tammuz had either their mother or sister interpret their dreams. But the goddess Gatumdug interpreted Gudea's dream. Futhermore, there are references to a lú.sag.še.na.a priest who can interpret dreams by entering the cella of the god to incubate a message dream, which can be used to interpret the prior dream.[16]

In Akkadian there is the common title for professional interpreters, the ša'ilu priest or ša'iltu priestess. This office was higher than the bārû priest, who also divined dreams. Documents in Old Assyrian indicate that the ša'ilu priest took difficult dreams directly to Ashur for interpretation. This priest also called upon the underworld for assistance, and this element of necromancy frequently brought discredit upon the profession. There may have been a particular mode for each type of priest. In the Ur III texts and in Old Babylonian sources like the Hymn to Shamash the ša'ilu priest may use libanomancy, oil patterns on water, to assist in dream interpretation. The bārû priest may have used lecanomancy, rising smoke patterns from burning incense.[17]

The word for interpret is pašāru in Akkadian and bur in Sumerian. These words are used in varying contexts to mean "recount or retell," "transfer the evil power from the dream to an inert object," "transfer symbols into words," "be unfolded or explicated," or "be removed." Oppenheim uses the definition of "solve, dissolve" to cover the entire range of p.t.r. in Hebrew, p.š.r. in Akkadian, p.š.r. in Aramaic, p.s.r. in Arabic, wh^c in Egyptian, and woh in Coptic.[18]

Ritual purification had to accompany all dreams, especially in Assyria. Meaning was found, but the danger had to be removed by additional action. This might often involve sacrifice. In cases where a second dream was incubated to interpret the first dream, those sacrifices might have functioned as atonement and purification for the first dream. Evil dreams made the dreamer impure until the dream was interpreted and dispelled. If the dream could not be interpreted, the power or curse of the dream was transferred to a lump of clay, which was then cast into water where it would dissolve.[19] All dreams carried the curse, whether they were divine message dreams

received by kings and priests, or whether they were the nightmares experienced by common people.

Surviving dream accounts do not abound, and they are limited to certain historical periods: the reigns of Hattushilis of the Hittites, Ashurbanipal of the Assyrians, and Nabonidus of Chaldean Babylon. Dreams are located in certain epic literatures, the Gilgamesh epic, Hittite epic material, the tales of Dan'el and Keret from Ugarit, and the Elohist in the Old Testament. There is no answer why surviving records are so limited. It may be that the texts from other eras are lost. From 625 B.C. to 539 B.C. there was a decline in the astrological omina due to the rise of a more sophisticated astronomy. Astrology as we know it began to evolve, and the predictive nature of the stars became more fixed with less flexibility for the interpretation of specific events. Thus royal figures turned to dream omina for the affairs of state.[20]

Categories of Ancient Near Eastern Dreams

Classification of ancient dreams by modern scholars is somewhat artificial. But the reports appear to fall into two major categories, the simple message dream and the symbolic or ambiguous dream.[21] The first type seldom needs the assistance of the oneirocritic; the message is auditory and clearly understood by the recipient. The second type may be auditory, but it usually has visual imagery instead. This visual imagery lends to the dream that ambiguity which requires interpretation. Occasionally this category may be divided into two more groups, the symbolic and the mantic.[22] The distinction between these last two categories is difficult. Symbolic dreams are simple with one or two symbolic statements, gestures, or a single visual image. The dream may be interpreted by the dreamer. The mantic dream is a more complex vision, usually visual, not auditory, which has many motifs and symbols with their own respective meanings. Usually a professional is needed to interpret these dreams. The dreams in the book of Daniel would be classic mantic dreams. The vision entails many symbols, and often there is involved action, whereas simple symbolic dreams might have only one unmoving visual apparition. There is, of course, the broad category of psychological status dreams, which includes nightmares and evil dreams. But these do not constitute a literary category, for they are never converted into dream reports. Thus we are left with two major literary categories for ancient Near Eastern dreams: the simple message dream and the symbolic message dream, with the latter divided in simple symbolic and mantic dreams.

Format of Dream Reports

Stylistic conventions determine the manner and format of the dream reports. They are recorded as a message to an important leader in society. Censored, properly interpreted, purified from cultic impurity, and cleansed of the irrational, they may be inscribed on a building. This sets them apart from all evil dreams. The message dream is a "literary category based on transformed actual dream experiences."[23] It is difficult to ascertain whether the dream was transformed by the literary convention or the dream experience was standardized by cultural conditioning.[24] We shall probably never be able to analyze ancient people to discover the actual relationship between real dream experiences and official accounts. Only occasionally, as with some of the dreams of Nabonidus, may we be approaching the truly authentic dream world of an individual. At other times we suspect that we are confronted with contrived dream reports meant to justify royal activities, as with Hattushilis the Hittite.

The dream frame in which dreams are reported is a format found from ancient Sumer down to the Hellenistic era where it received its fullest elaboration. The first part of the frame is the setting. This includes the person who experienced the dream, when the dream happened, the place of the occurrence, and under what conditions the dream came to the person. The second part of the frame is the actual content of the dream itself. The third part is the formal conclusion of the dream and the initial reaction of the dreamer. Last of all, there may be testimony to the fulfillment of the dream prediction, if there was one; or a statement may indicate how the dreamer carried out the mandate of the dream.[25]

In the first part of the dream frame the person is said to be deeply asleep. The phrase may be the Assyrian word utullu, "to be in bed," "he was sleeping in his bed," or "his majesty rested."[26]

The time of the dream was not so specifically limited in the ancient Near Eastern world as in the later classical era, where dreams came right before dawn. The only specific references to time in the ancient Near East are the noonday dreams of Thutmosis IV and the early morning hours for dreams in Ludlul-bêl-nêmeqi. Morning hours may have been understood as the time when the dreams came, but it is not recorded. Usually the reference to time in the texts is the report that it came in the night or at the time of sleep. Morning hours have been viewed in various societies as the best time for dreams.[27]

There is scientific plausibility in this, for dreams customarily occur in the lightest period of sleep, which is in

17

the morning hours, they are the longest dreams, and they are most easily remembered by the dreamer upon waking so shortly afterward.[28]

The dream content often stresses the actual presence of the deity, especially for auditory message dreams. The deity comes and goes rather suddenly. Assyrian texts use the word erēbu, for the entrance of the deity, and aṣû and ana aḫīti for the departure.[29] The movement of the deity is sudden and usually startles the dreamer into an awake state. Later classical sources stress the coming of the deity by having a physical object left behind as a testimony to the divine presence.

The dream figure of the deity is quite distinctive. The deity may be of gigantic proportions. Gudea's dream figure reached the top of the heavens. The figure is sometimes described as being very beautiful. The twin motif of size and beauty becomes standard in later classical texts. The dream figure or deity usually stands at the head of the dreamer. Eannatum's dream states that the deity "stood," Ludlul-bēl-nēmeqi records that the deity "entered and took his stand," Khnum "was standing over against me" says Pharaoh Djoser on the Egyptian Hunger Stela, "the Lord came and stood" for Samuel, in several Assyrian dreams the word to describe the action of the deity is zâzu, "to take one's stand," and even Homer has the stylized phrase epistanai kata in his dream reports.[30]

In the reception of the dream there is the emphasis upon the awakening of the dreamer. This verified the veracity of the dream and the received message. The dreamer may be awakened for the reception of the message, he or she may awaken with a start after the dream is over, and sometimes there is a reference to both awakenings. Pharaoh Djoser states that after the dream "I awoke refreshed," and likewise Gudea "woke up with a start, it was but a dream." Others who are awakened during the dream process include the priest of Ishtar, who was awakened in order to receive the message for Ashurbanipal, and Samuel who was awakened three times. The Akkadian word is nēgeltû, "to wake with a start." In later classical sources Hermes wakes Priam in the Iliad, Athena wakes Odysseus in the Odyssey, and other Greek texts use the standard phrase of introduction by the deity, "Are you asleep, NN?"[31] In these cases the awakening is done either as a prelude to the divine message by putting the dreamer in an awake or semi-conscious state, or it is the formal conclusion to the dream. In both instances the awakening motif affirms the veracity of the dream.

18

These are the basic elements of form that are found in almost all the ancient dreams. There are formal stylistic peculiarities that belong to specific dream types.

Auditory Message Dreams

In these dreams the deity comes and delivers a particular spoken message to the dreamer. The auditory message dreams seem to come exclusively to men, for the few women who receive dreams experience symbolic dreams. The men are usually priests and kings.

The messenger is easily recognized, for he or she is almost always a god. The distinction between this kind of experience and a theophany becomes vague; perhaps, the message dream is an outgrowth of the theophany.[32] Rarely is the messenger a deceased person from the realm of the dead as in later classical dreams. Nabonidus sees Nebuchadnezzar and Gilgamesh sees Enkidu, but these are the only instances.

The relationship between the messenger and the recipient is formal. Occasionally there is dialogue, and when it occurs, it is very pious. Examples of such dialogue include Thutmosis IV, the priest of Ishtar, Solomon at Gibeon, Nabonidus in the temple dreams, and Abimelech in Genesis 20. Seldom does the messenger do anything physical. El touches Dan'el in the Aqhat epic, but the text is vague at this point. In an Assyrian dream one supplicant reports the deity touched his hand, in an Egyptian dream Merneptah receives a sword, and Judas Maccabeus receives a sword from Jeremiah. By the Greek period this motif is even more common, for tokens are often left by the gods as a proof of their presence.

Symbolic Message Dreams

Symbolic dreams come not in clear words, but words veiled in mystery, gestures, and actions pointing to a hidden meaning. The dreamers are still passive[33] recipients of this message; they take no part in the dream. But the message needs to be interpreted. Repetition of these dreams in slightly altered form can be the clue to initial interpretation. So the recipient may decode the dream or receive another dream for assistance. In Mesopotamia another form of divination might be used to assist in interpretation, and this might include the incubation of another dream, as with Gudea. In Egypt and Mesopotamia a dream book could be used. Because of their occasionally bizarre images the dreams may have been more strictly censored than simple auditory dreams.

As with simple auditory message dreams, the gods often were able to communicate with human servants. But whereas auditory message dreams would present clear words of encouragement, promises of action by the deity, and imperatives upon which the human servants had to act, symbolic dreams were often limited to the predictive category. Thus the individual could take a certain course of action knowing the outcome was fixed and affirmed by the gods. In Egypt Prince Bekhten saw the golden falcon flying to Egypt, and Tanutamon saw two serpents. Both dreams were clear to the dreamer, no professional interpreter was needed, and they enacted the course of action implied by the dream. In Mesopotamia symbolic dreams predominate in epic literature. Gilgamesh has a dream concerning his own fate, Enkidu has his own death dreams, and Tammuz dreams his own fate. Likewise among the Hittites symbolic dreams are in the epic literature, as Kessi observes his fate in several dreams. These are the dreams which women interpret for the men, Gilgamesh goes to his mother, and Kessi goes to his sister for help in interpretation. Ludlul-bél-némeqi has the sick person experience three symbolic dreams to foreshadow his return to health. Gudea's dream, which commissioned him to rebuild the temple, was symbolic and enigmatic to him at first.

The typical dream frame is often modified. The component parts may be replaced by the truncated form of "he lay down to sleep," or "he had a dream."[34]

It may very well be that the ancient Near East recorded few symbolic dreams because the simple auditory message dream was demanded on the public inscriptions. The deity would not speak to a divine or semi-divine representative, be he king or priest, in anything less than clear words, for these words were the epiphany of the deity to his or her servant. Symbolic dreams are reserved for epic literature where they can be used in a literary fashion.

Mantic Dreams

Closely related to the category of symbolic dreams are the mantic dreams. They differ from symbolic dreams by deviating more from the message pattern. In symbolic dreams the deity may still act out the scene or give an enigmatic message to the dreamer, but in mantic dreams no such clear cut message may be given. These dreams contain cryptic scenes laden with symbols, which the dreamer passively observes. These visual scenes are always prognostications, which the wise person can unravel, interpret, and take heed in preparation. This prognostication differs from the earlier two types of dreams, where the element of prediction is connected with commission.

But the division between mantic and symbolic dreams is still vague, and particular dreams sometimes are difficult to classify. For instance, Oppenheim considers the dreams of the Joseph cycle to be symbolic while the Daniel dreams are mantic.[35] Most scholars would consider both to be in the same category, usually mantic. The only operating criterion for distinction is the degree to which bizarre imagery is utilized. The mantic dreams are more bizarre, contain more images, and are far more likely to require a professional interpreter.

Psychological Status Dreams

These dreams lie beyond the pale of a discussion of dream formats, because they are never recorded for us, but a discussion of such dreams is necessary for the sake of comparison. These dreams are an indication of the physical and spiritual health and also the cultic success of the dreamer. They reflect the degree of protection the deity has afforded. The Assyrian Dream Book and Old Babylonia texts see a correlation between evil dreams and a poor state of health: "If (a person) says, 'My dreams are fine!'" (it means) the guardian of the health of (this) man (takes care of him)."[36]

Psychological dreams can be good or evil. The good dreams are šunāte damqate, "pleasant," and evil dreams were limnu, "unpleasant," or pardu, "confused," or aḫû, "strange," or eklu, "dark," or šašu, "confounded," according to Akkadian texts. The emphasis was upon avoiding those evil dreams and seeking the good dreams.

When the motifs of such evil dreams are given in the dream book, no specific dream is recorded, no one is named as the dreamer, for that would be an impure act. These dreams are dispelled only upon interpretation and if the prayers to the gods are favorably accepted, thus countering evil with a more potent magic. Since evil dreams frequently coincide with sickness, both phenomena are seen as punishment, curse, or desertion by the god of the sufferer. This requires propitiation by the sufferer, sacrifice, prayers, and other ritual actions. When the evil dreams cease, it is a sign of the deity's reacceptance of the dreamer and the forgiveness of those sins which caused the illness and nightmares. Many of the Akkadian hymns of lamentation reflect the pious believer's attempt to motivate the god to restore health and remove bad dreams.

Particular examples of such evil dream motifs are recorded in the dream books to enable the interpreter to make a predictive analysis of the dreamer's fate. A good example is:

21

> If a man -- when he is asleep -- the town falls repeatedly upon him, and he cries (for help) and one does not hear him (this means): this man will have attached to him a protective angel and a (good) spirit. If a man -- when he is asleep -- the town falls repeatedly upon him, and he cries (for help) and one hears him (this means): an evil spirit will be attached to him.[37]

These psychological dreams belong to the common person, whereas message dreams come to priests and kings. Our knowledge of the former comes not from dream reports, but from the types, symbols, and examples placed in the dream omina collection. They would intrigue the psychoanalyst, for they are the legitimate dreams of people unaltered by literary and stylistic conventions.

Non-classifiable

An apt testimony to the artificiality of our modern analysis and reconstruction of the apparent dream structure are those few dreams which remain outside the pale of the categories already enumerated. Several of these non-classifiable dreams have parallels with later established classical dream patterns, however, so we may have a different type of a format and too few dreams to discern a distinct category.

Certain dreams demanded that a votive offering be made to the deity. Hattushilis, Nabonidus, and Ammiditani, the third successor after Hammurabi, all had to offer such gifts in accord with a dream mandate. These dreams were not reported in the dream format, and the third was not recorded in any fashion. Though these dreams function like message dreams, often a simple visual image communicates the command to give a votive offering, which is more comparable to a subtle symbolic message dream. When the offering is then presented by the ruler in reality, the action is done according to the "dream of his majesty, NN."[38]

Inspirational dreams gave the recipient the pattern by which to create a work of art. Hattushilis and Muwatallus received such dreams and subsequently dedicated the object to the deity. The Akkadian "Epic of Irra" was received by the author in a dream. The "Institutions of Amen-em-het"[39] came to the dreamer from his deceased father in a dream. One is reminded of how Jacob received instruction from God on how to raise sheep, and perhaps of Solomon who received instructions of building the temple in a possible dream.

Two of the auditory message dreams are recorded in a strange fashion, which deserves mention, for they are rather removed from the stylized dream report format. Nabonidus has a dream wherein he sees a deceased individual and is addressed by a third person mediator. A dream at Mari in the Old Babylonian period is recorded without the dream pattern, many irrelevant details are included, and it contains the unusual facet of the dreamer's physical transportation to a distant shrine. It is a manufactured dream designed to enhance the priesthood at the shrine of Terqa. The strange style of this dream may be due to the fact that Mari is on the fringe of Mesopotamian culture at this time, and it has not yet adopted the accepted pattern of dream reporting.

A few indirect message dreams are also reported. In the Gilgamesh Epic Enkidu is allowed to observe the gods debating his death. Another close parallel is in later Egypt. Petesi, the hieroglyph carver of Pharaoh Nektonabos, overheard the god Onuris complaining to the god Isis about the unfinished work. Finally, when Ea addressed the reed hut rather than speaking directly to Atrahasis, he may have given an indirect message dream revelation.

These examples serve to illustrate the artificiality of trying to categorize neatly all of the dreams from the ancient Near East. Were we allowed to discover more such dream accounts, our outline and categories might take on a more complete outlook, and we might also discover more types and patterns into which some of the above unclassified examples would fit.

Dreams in the Various Cultures

Consideration of the dreams in various ancient Near Eastern cultures will give us insight into the variations found between different societies and will also provide a chance systematically to list the dream reports available.

Babylonia

The oldest dream reports come from ancient Sumer, and we find both symbolic and auditory message dreams. The greater number of the dreams are found in the epic literature. In the epic of "Lugalbanda and Mt. Hurrum," Lugalbanda, the servant of Enmerkar, falls asleep while on a journey. Utu, the sun god, commands him to kill a wild bull and sacrifice it. In an early account of the deluge from Nippur there is mention of the dream which Ziusudra induced at the shrine. Ea delivered a message to a hut in the Atrahasis Epic, and the

23

text describes it as though it were a dream theophany.[41] Dumuzi, the so-called dying and rising god of vegetation, had a dream which foreshadowed his fate. Upon seeing a series of plants and animals experiencing misery, he recounted the dream to his sister who then interpreted the dream as foreboding evil for Dumuzi.[42]

In addition to the accounts from Sumerian epic literature, there are accounts from Akkadian literature which go back to early Sumerian originals. The Dumuzi account has a counterpart in the Tammuz cycle. The Gilgamesh Epic has several dream experiences. There are three series of dreams in the cycle which symbolically foreshadow the unfolding of future events. They thus function as a literary device to heighten the suspense of the developing plot. In the first series of dreams Gilgamesh has two dreams wherein he is struck by a kisrum, which may be a bolt from Anu, and then an axe falls into the middle of Uruk and no one can move it. The mother of Gilgamesh interprets both dreams to mean that Gilgamesh would meet a powerful man, who would become his closest friend. Enkidu comes and fulfills that dream. The second series of dreams occurs in the forest of Humbaba. Gilgamesh has three dreams, only two of which are preserved. In the first dream the mountain puts him to sleep in preparation for another dream. In that following dream the mountain falls upon him. Enkidu interprets both dreams to mean that they would finally overcome Humbaba in a fierce struggle. Enkidu then dreams about flashing lightning and a falling sky, and when Gilgamesh is asked to interpret the dreams he perceives the ill omen for his friend.[43] The third series of dreams is the death of Enkidu, and they are two in number. In the first dream he sees the council of the gods trying to decide whom to punish for the death of Humbaba, whom both Gilgamesh and Enkidu have slain. In the second dream he sees a horrendous beast carry him off to the house of darkness where he sees all the great kings of the earth, who have died and now live in dust. Both dreams foreshadow his death.

The earliest recorded historical dream accounts come from the Sumerian period. Gudea of Lagash received a message from Ningirsu, who desired to have his eninnu rebuilt. Gudea perceived this in a symbolic message dream, wherein he saw a large man speaking in unclear phrases. He went to the shrine of Nanshe or Gatumdug, who was the ensi or priestess to the gods in the art of interpretation. She explained through the medium of an auditory message dream that he had seen Nindub, the great architect. As Gudea awoke from both dreams, it says, "he woke with a start, it was but a dream."[44] Eannatum records his dream experience on the Vulture Stela. Though the text is incomplete, we perceive that it states the deity came and

stood by his bed in order to deliver a message to him in his sleep.

In the Old Babylonian period there is the account of Dagan's indirect communication to Zimri-Lim of Mari through an official. A muḫḫum messenger comes with a word from the god to Itur-ashdu, the royal governor of the city.[45] The messenger tells how a man of Sagaratum was transported in a dream to the city of Terqa to a small shrine of Dagan. Here the god asks if the sheiks of Benjamin have made peace with Zimri-Lim. He then asks why Zimri-Lim has not made a report to the shrine and deposited a report of the year's activity. Finally, he promises victory over the Benjamin for Zimri-Lim, if he would only make an official appearance at the shrine.[46] The dream report was given in order to enhance the prestige of this little shrine.

In other literature from this period Ludlul-bēl-nēmeqi, "The Poem of the Righteous Sufferer," the hero sees a series of three symbolic dreams predicting his return to health.

In general, the Babylonians were more receptive to dreams than their neighbors to the north, the Assyrians. However, dreams were always a secondary form of divination. Most of the dream reports come from epic literature, and the symbolic dream predominates in this early material. But it is false to generalize that the symbolic dream is more important than the auditory message dream, as Lichtenstein does,[47] for there are significant message dream reports in this early period also. Dreams recorded in the historical texts were concerned with matters of national policy, such as the rebuilding of temples, which was a significant religious and political concern.

Various terms are given to describe dreams. In Sumerian the word ma.mú means either dream or sleep. In Akkadian the word is šuttu, which comes from šittu, the word for sleep. Other phrases include ḫiltu and the poetic phrase tabrīt mūši. Dreams are "seen," which is amāru, naṭālu, or naplusu. The word ma.mú can also denote a god of dreams. This is equivalent to the Akkadian zaqīqu, which may come from z.u.q., which means "blowing of the wind," or zāqu, which refers to demons who slip into the house through a crack in the wall. Zaqīqu or Zakar can refer to the souls of the dead, the carrier of a message, or swift and dangerous dream demons who come from the netherworld where dreams originate. Hence, Zaqīqu is a dream god who moves swiftly like a demon of the night, and he brings dreams to people. A third name is an.za.qar or an.zag.gar.ra, which refers to a tower (z.k.r.) and may be connected to the masseba of the Old Testament.[48] If so, one could speculate that the dream god was a pillar god.

The message dream formula is not clearly developed in the dreams of the epic literature. Historical texts, however, betray a more fixed structure and reflect the pattern more clearly. Epic literature tends to contain symbolic dreams and historical texts record the auditory message dreams.

Hittites

The Hittites have dream accounts in their epic literature dating from the Second Millennium. Like the Mesopotamian examples they are not developed message dreams; they are symbolic dreams used as literary devices to foreshadow the future and increase the suspense of the narrative. The significant epic is "Kessi the Hunter." Although the conclusion is lacking, the dreams may foretell the conclusion of the tale. If so, it may be seasonal myth, or it may parallel the Dumuzi-Tammuz accounts. Kessi the hunter has a number of strange dreams which apparently predict his descent into the underworld. He finds himself before a huge and unmovable door, witnesses a large bird carry off a girl at her chores, sees a bolt of lightning strike a man in an open field, meets his departed ancestors around a warm fire, discovers himself bound with women's ornaments, and encounters a dragon and dangerous harpies standing at his door. As in the other epic literature a woman interprets his dreams, for Kessi took them to his sister. Gaster believes these seven dreams reflect a standard list of portents upon which an ancient story teller could draw for the creation of his narrative. Given the repetitive nature of oral tales, he also assumes a close correspondence between the dreams and the actual events that have been lost at the end of the account.[49]

Among the historical texts the dream chronicle of Hattushilis (1290-1250 B.C.) is the most important. In his autobiography the usurpation of the throne is legitimated by declaring to the people that his mandate came from Ishtar. His autobiography is unique in the ancient world, for it was given wide circulation and was not meant to be read only by kings and gods on building inscriptions. He lists nine dreams, six of which he experienced and three which his wife experienced. She is the only significant woman in pre-classical sources to receive message dreams. Later a Hittite princess, Gushuliya, is said to have experienced evil dreams, but they were not recorded. The dreams of Hattushilis all have the same basic content. The goddess gives the promise of continued protection to the king and the hope of an enduring kingship. Each specific dream has the god or goddess giving specific direction to the king or queen in regard to future actions. In one dream Hattushilis sees the image of his brother, an image sent by Ishtar. Since his brother was alive, this parallels the example

26

of Zeus sending an image of the living Nestor to Agamemnon in the Iliad. In this same dream Ishtar acts with the deceit of a Greek goddess, as in later classical dreams. The dreams of Hattushilis can be seen to parallel later Greek dreams in several respects.[50]

In the Hittite language the word for dream is tešhaš, which also appears as zašhai or zazhi. The deity is said to appear, tešhanna. Hittite dreams parallel later Greek dreams in several respects, false images, women receiving dreams, the giving of votive offerings, and the duplicity of the deity. The Hittites may be a cultural link to the development of later Greek dream formats.[51]

A significant passage comes from the plague prayer of Mursilis. It is not a dream, but it is the request for a dream or some form of revelation to explain why plague ravages the land. Mursilis says,

> . . . either let it be established by an omen, or let me see it in a dream, or let a prophet declare it. . . . Let all the priests find out by incubation whatever I suggest to them. . . . the priests learn about it by incubation, or let a man see it in a dream.[52]

The king considers dream divination to be equal in status to the priestly oracles and declaration of prophets. It is not an inferior form of divination as in Mesopotamia. Here, too, one is tempted to think that the king is distinguishing between two types of dream divination. The incubation by priests would be a deliberate form of induced dream revelation, whereas the last reference to dreams might refer to a dream received by anyone throughout the realm to whom the god might care to speak. But the prayer might simply be repeating the same thought for rhetorical effect, or the difference might be between the incubational dreams of priests and the possible dream he might receive in the royal palace. It is interesting to compare this reference to one in the Iliad where Achilles calls for a prophet (mantis), or a priest (hieros), or a diviner of dreams (oneiropolis) during a plague.[53] This may be another testimony to the link between the Hittites and the Greeks in dream reporting.

Egypt

Egyptian dreams occurred as early as the Middle Kingdom for at least three pharaohs, but the earliest accounts we have come from the New Kingdom. Thutmosis IV experienced a

rather extensive dream at noon in the shadow of the Great Sphinx. The time is unusual, since message dreams of this sort usually come at night. The god promised him the kingship of Egypt in a rather lengthy speech. After this Thutmosis IV returned to the city to announce his affirmation by the god.[54] Thutmosis IV recorded this dream in an inscription meant to validate his kingship, and he utilized the format that his Middle Kingdom predecessors utilized in those dream reports unavailable to us.

Later dream reports by pharaohs were not as extensive or as spectacular. Pharaoh Merneptah saw the god Ptah standing before him. The god comforted Merneptah and gave him a sword, a highly unusual act in early dreams, for only in later classical sources does this become common. Tanutamun saw a very simple symbolic dream: a serpent lying on either side of him. It was obviously indicative of the fact that he was chosen to rule both lands of Upper and Lower Egypt. Prince Bekhten saw the god in the form of a falcon flying home to Egypt indicating his own homesickness. So the prince went home. Pharaoh Djoser received a message dream from the god Khnum, who promised prosperity and his continued presence. There are also a number of dreams given to Ptolemaic dynasts, but they use the later Greek format in their reporting.[55]

Dreams were more popular and more positively received in Egypt than anywhere else in the ancient Near East. This may be a reflection of the more positive state of mind found among the Egyptians, a result of their climatic regularity, geographic security, and social stability.[56]

The word for dream is rswt, a state that lies between wakefulness and sleep. The word means "to awaken," and it is drawn with the picture of an open eye. This implies the consciousness of the recipient, which enables him to see the vision from the other realm or to hear the spoken message of the deity.[57]

The Egyptians were noted for their ability to interpret dreams. An academy entitled "the house of life" trained young men to interpret dreams, most likely for the purpose of interpreting royal dreams.[58] When Esarhaddon of Assyria conquered Egypt in the Seventh Century, he took back dream interpreters to Assyria, for this was a rare art in his land. This might explain, in part, why dreams became more popular in the royal court during the reign of his son, Ashurbanipal.

Dream omina were collected already in the Twelfth Dynasty. Although collections in Mesopotamia may have begun at the same time, the Egyptians took greater interest in it. In Egypt dreams were the chief omina to be listed, whereas in

28

Mesopotamia dreams were just one of many omina. We have two dream omina collections from Egypt. The early Hieratic collection originating from the Middle Kingdom lists omina in two categories, motifs for the gentle Horus men and motifs for the rowdy Seth men. The Egyptians distinguished between types of men and dreams received by them. The second omina listing is Demotic and dates from the Second Century A.D. It moves away from the earlier topical arrangement and shows a great deal of Mesopotamian influence. Dream interpretation was based on puns, logical associations, or merely the relationship of good dreams with good results and bad dreams with bad results.[59]

The dreams of the Egyptians can be classified into three major categories. These are unsolicited dreams, solicited dreams in response to a human question, and dreams of warning. The unrecorded ones available to us fall into the first two groups. Unsolicited dreams include the dream of Thutmosis IV under the Great Sphinx, Ptolemy Soter's instruction to bring the statue of Serapis to Alexandria, Tunatamun's dream of two snakes, Shabaka's dream ordering him to retreat with his army into Ethiopia, and Prince Bekhten's vision of the golden falcon flying back to Egypt. Solicited dreams are exemplified by Merneptah's vision of Ptah at Karnak and the dream of Sethos at the temple in Hephastus. In both of these dreams there was a distinct pattern. The text records that the dreamer went into the temple, he prayed, the deity's name was invoked, the dream vision came, the deity appeared, then "the God NN spoke to him saying . . .," and finally, morning arrived.[60] This is the classic pattern of incubation dreams in Egypt. However, no actual text remains to us from the older period; this reconstruction is possible from incubation dreams in the later Hellenistic period. The older dreams are recorded in a similar but abbreviated form.

Dreams could also be invoked by magicians outside the temple. The magician would induce a dream for someone else by drawing a magical picture and reciting sacred words. One ancient text preserves this procedure:

> To procure dreams: Take a clean linen
> bag and write upon it the names given
> below. Fold it up and make it into a
> lamp wick; and set it alight, pouring oil
> over it. The word to be written is this:
> "Arimuth, Lailamochouch, Arsenophren-
> phren, Phtha, Archentechtha." Then in
> the evening, when you are going to bed,
> which you must do without touching food
> (or, pure from all defilement), do thus:
> Approach the lamp and repeat seven times
> the formula given below, then extinguish

it and be down to sleep. The formula is this: "Schmu . . . epaëma Ligotereënch: the Aeon, the Thunderer, Thou hast swallowed the snake and dost exhaust the moon, and does raise the orb of the sun in his season, Chthetho is thy name: I require, O Lords of the gods, Seth, Chreps[61] give me the information I desire.

The Egyptians did not believe that dreams were caused by soul separation from the body like many other people in Africa, but they felt that the sensitive nature of the dreamer enabled the reception of dreams. He or she was contacting the sphere of Nun, the netherworld. Dream motifs centered on eating, drinking, and copulating. They were free from many of the modern dream motifs which indicate sexual repression.[62] The Egyptians did not suffer from evil dreams like their counterparts in Mesopotamia. Rather, their dream life was happy, wholesome, and completely accepted by them. This positive attitude may also be seen in other aspects of life compared with the pessimistic attitudes found in Mesopotamia.

Ugarit

Ugaritic epic literature dates from the late Second Millennium, and here we have two significant dream reports. They are particularly helpful for describing incubation procedures. They also display a degree of influence of the message dream pattern.

The Aqhat Epic begins with a long section wherein Dan'el prepares himself in the shrine by praying and sacrificing to El in a request for a son. Eventually El appears and in a lengthy address promises him a son. The beginning is very helpful in observing an incubation ritual.

In the Keret Epic there are two references to dreams. In the beginning the king goes through an incubation process and is weeping on his bed while praying for a son. The motif of the childless petitioner seeking a son is common in both Ugarit and the Old Testament. The second dream involves a woman, Queen Horaya. Since this is epic material, it can still be maintained that the Hittite queen is the only historical woman to have received a message dream. Queen Horaya addresses the assembled nobles and tells of a dream message which recounted the impending death of Keret and subsequent mourning by the nobles.

The Baal cycle contains a symbolic message dream. The goddess Anat receives a dream after she has stolen Baal's corpse from Mot. She sees the dry river beds filled with honey, while formerly dry skies rain oil. She interprets the dream to mean that Baal is alive somewhere, for the dry rivers and skies had been a result of his death. The dream foreshadows the future event of Baal's return and restoration of fertility in the land. The myth may be a seasonal myth reflecting the dry and rainy seasons in north Palestine, or it may represent cycles of drought and plenty over a number of years. Several similarities with Mesopotamian epic literature lead us to believe that there is a connection between the epic literatures of these two cultures. This would then explain the similarity in function of the dreams, for they serve as literary devices to heighten the suspense of the story.

The texts of the Ugaritic material are sometimes vague and difficult to reconstruct. When El comes to Keret the text may be interpreted as though El touched Keret, but the translation is disputed. Lichtenstein takes this disputed text and then generalizes to say that all ancient Near Eastern dreams had such corporeal revelatory experiences. This becomes a starting point for his argument that corporeal and non-corporeal revelation can be intermixed in the same text, and hence the distinction between the anthropomorphic revelation of the Yahwist and the transcendent revelation of dreams in the Elohist are not sufficient categories to warrant a division between these two literary sources.[63] In reality, the ancient Near Eastern dreams indicate there probably is a distinction between corporeal and non-corporeal revelatory experiences, since the ancient Near Eastern dreams avoid physical contact between deity and recipient. But the incorrect deductions made by Lichtenstein illustrate clearly the dangers of working with the texts and trying to derive too many conclusions from them.

Assyria and Chaldean Babylon

It is in the First Millennium that many of our historical texts offer us message dream reports. In the reigns of Ashurbanipal and Nabonidus several royal dreams were recorded.

In Assyria dream interpreters were considered to be of low standing; they were often necromancers, sometimes women, like the witch at Endor, who were not accepted by official sanction. Assyrians were the most superstitious of all Mesopotamian people, and they indulged in many forms of divination. But oneiromancy was rare, and oneirocritics in the Assyrian court were usually hardibi, foreigners. After

Esarhaddon's conquest of Egypt Egyptians functioned as dream interpreters in the Assyrian court. Thus by the reign of Ashurbanipal dream reports emerged as an acceptable form of divination. Ashurbanipal even records a dream experienced by his grandfather, Sennacherib, wherein Ashur praised his wisdom. Perhaps the dream was not publicly recorded until the time of Ashurbanipal because of the low regard given to dreams in Sennacherib's day. Ashurbanipal experienced several dreams. The most significant occurred during the war with Elam. He stood before the image of Ishtar, crouched at her feet (akmis šapalša), prayed, and cried. That same night a šabrû priest had the same dream, or noctural vision (tabrit mūši(ša) . . . ušabrûšu), as did he, in which Ishtar came in (erēbu) and later went out (aṣû ana aḫiti).[64] She came in and spoke to a vision of the image of Ashurbanipal and ordered him to stay were he was, eat, drink, and be merry, while she went out to fight against Elam. In reality, Ashurbanipal did delay before attacking the invaders from Elam. In that same war with Elam the Assyrian army feared to cross the Idide River. A night dream came to the entire army encouraging them to pass. This is the only Semitic example of a mass dream. A fifth dream so carefully described the future victory of Ashurbanipal over Šamaššumukin that it was obviously composed after the event. Finally, Ashurbanipal recorded a dream that came to Gyges, king of Lydia, which encouraged Gyges to submit and ally himself with Ashurbanipal. Gyges saw a nibit sumi, that is, a phonetically transcribed version of Ashurbanipal's name into Hurrian. That same day Gyges sent a messenger to Assyria. These six dreams are the sum total of recorded Assyrian dreams, and they come only from Ashurbanipal's records.

The only dream book from the Semitic world comes from Assyria, perhaps because the lack of familiarity with the various dream omina demanded they be written down for reference. The book may have been compiled under Ashurbanipal's reign, but some of the omina come from the Old Babylonian period.[65] The book offers rituals to cleanse the dreamer from the dream's impurity. The omina are listed according to the dreamer's activity, eating, traveling, and a multitude of diverse actions. Some of the images correspond with the universal archetypes of Jung and symbols of Freud.

A century later the Chaldean king of Babylon, Nabonidus, records a few dreams. His dreams are concerned with rebuilding temples in Harran and Sippar primarily. We do not have all of the dreams intact, however. We have three dreams in which he is commanded to rebuild the temple of Haran. Once Marduk appears, once Sin appears, and another time both Marduk and Sin appear. In two of these he enters into dialogue and declares that Harran is surrounded by hostile

32

Medes and he cannot get through. But his arguments are in vain, and the gods persist. This kind of dialogue is rare in message dreams, and it is never found in symbolic dreams. Nabonidus also records a brief dream giving him instructions on his journey to Harran. In an entirely different type of dream Nabonidus sees the deceased king Nebuchadnezzar. He had to be formally introduced to Nebuchadnezzar by a third person, according to the standards of court etiquette. After meeting this deceased king, whom he never met in real life, Nabonidus awoke refreshed and happy. It is dangerous to psychoanalyze the dreams of a person dead for millennia, but we are tempted to believe this dream represents deep-seated guilt feelings by Nabonidus. Given the fact that Nabonidus was deeply pious and that he unwillingly had to seize the throne by killing Nebuchadnezzar's son, this dream may be recorded without restriction and may actually represent a true dream experience of Nabonidus. Being formally accepted by the deceased king indicated to his subconscious that he was forgiven for the regicide. The dream was a tremendous relief to his guilt-ridden psyche, and Nabonidus records his relief with the indication that he does not know why he is refreshed and happy.[66] The dream is also unusual in recording the presence of a deceased person in an ancient Near Eastern dream, for this is found only in later Greek dreams.

Negative Attitudes in the Ancient Near East Toward Dreams

Despite the positive attitudes toward dreams as a source of revelation, there were reservations. This is not in reference to psychological status dreams, or evil dreams that plagued the common man, but actual message dreams could also be called into question. Oneiromancy was often held in low esteem in Mesopotamia, especially Assyria. Even when dreams were viewed with respect there was some distrust. As Oppenheim states,

> A deep seated distrust of dreams and their messages speaks out of the perpetual desire for confirmation. The objectivity of a "sign" activated by the god himself is clearly preferred to the[67] subjectivity of the dream experience.

Frequently the dream interpreter had to utilize another form of divination either to confirm or to explain the dream. The dream as a form of divination was inferior to other forms of divination; it placed impurity and a curse upon the dreamer which had to be removed, and the interpretation of the dream was often seen as a dissolution of the curse. Even among the

33

Egyptians where dreams were highly regarded, there is reference to the ephemerality of dreams. In the wisdom text, "Instruction of Ptahhotep," there is the phrase "in the manner of a dream," which indicates shallowness.[68] One is reminded of Job 20:8, "he shall fly away as a dream," and Psalm 73:20 where the fleeting images disappear upon awaking, which are criticisms Israel may have inherited from Egypt's wisdom.

Dream Incubation

Despite the low esteem frequently attributed to dreams, there were times when individuals deliberately sought to receive a message from the gods by way of a dream. Several of the dreams mentioned were obtained by individuals seeking to receive such a dream, and occasionally we have reports of incubation and the actual dream is omitted.

Dream reports are not lucid in their description of the incubation procedure, nor do they inform the reader if the process did occur. The author apparently did not see fit to record what was common knowledge at that time. Our best examples, the Ugaritic dreams, are not helpful, so our real understanding comes from later Greek accounts.

Dreams could be induced by individuals who went to shrines in hope of receiving divine affirmation or directions for important decisions in life. A well known Akkadian psalm records the believer's plea for a dream from the deity:

> Send me that I may see a favorable
> dream. The dream I see, may it be
> favorable. The dream I see, may it come
> true. The dream I see, turn in favor.
> May my omens be satisfactory, may my
> dreams be favorable, the dream which I
> see make favorable.[69]

The earliest examples come from Mesopotamia or areas within the Mesopotamian cultural sphere. Here the practice would be for the priest to go to the sancturay, sacrifice, pray, and sleep in the cella of the god from whom he desired the dream. This might occur while sleeping at the base of the statue of the god. The incubant would hear the divine message and glimpse a vision of the god. In Sumerian literature we have the example of Ziusudra, who "prostrates himself in humility . . . in reverence. Daily (and) perseveringly he stands in attendance (at the shrine)."[70] Gudea had a second dream incubated in order to ascertain the meaning of his first symbolic message dream. An early Akkadian text records the incubation of a dream by Naram-Sin, although the dream is not

recorded. The text reads: Na-ra-am Sin-aš Šu-up-pí-ia-aḫ-ḫa-ti šu-up-pa-ia-as GišNa-aš še-eš ki-iš-ki-u-ua-an da-a-iš DINGER^meš-ŠU da-ri-ia-nu-ut nu DINGER^meš-ŠU mu-ki-iš-ki-u-an da-a-i." The translation of the text is as follows: "Naram- Sin purified himself, undertook incubation of his bed, cried to the gods, and began to complain to his gods."[71] Here ritual weeping is part of the incubation process, and the petitioner cries for the gods to appear. In later Assyrian material the goddess Ishtar refers to the previous incubation of Ashurbanipal when she says, "Inasmuch as you have lifted your hands in prayer and your eyes are filled with tears, I have mercy."[72]

There is evidence of other incubated dreams in the ancient Near East. Ashurbanipal's priest incubates his dream, and possible incubations might include one of the dreams by Hattushilis and the dream of Solomon at Gibeon. Hints of such activity may be found in other texts. The Safaitic inscriptions use the phrase t.l.l, which may refer to incubation. Likewise the word n.m in the proto-Hebrew inscriptions at Serabit al Hadim may refer to incubation.[73]

Some dreams may fall into a special category of unintentional incubation dreams. Such a dream would be induced by the mere presence of the dreamer sleeping overnight in the shrine without the explicit intention of trying to receive such a revelation. In such a case, the recipient would have undergone no special preparation for the purpose of inducing the dream, and he would be surprised by the reception of the dream. We speculate when we include possible examples, like the already mentioned dream of the priest of Ashurbanipal, and perhaps the dreams of Jacob in Genesis 28 and Samuel. However, the category of unintentional incubation dreams may be our own modern creation imposed upon brief literary accounts before us. It is difficult to call any dream an incubation dream when it lacks the deliberate intent of the dreamer and any preparation.

The best examples of incubation dreams come from Ugarit. The epic literature records two incubation experiences, one by Dan'el and one by Keret. A caveat must be uttered, for although these are our most complete reports, the authors are not concerned to describe the incubation process in detail, for the listeners were well acquainted with that process. The experience of Keret reads as follows: KRT A:I, lines 26-30:

26. y^crb bḫdrh ybky   he enters his room and weeps
27. bṭn rgmm wydm^c   while repeating his words, he cries

35

28.	tntkn udm^{c}th	he pours out his tears
29.	km ṭqlm arṣh	like shekels toward the earth
30.	kmḫmšt mṭth	as "pieces of five(?)" on the bed.

Translation notes:

30. The word kmḫmšt is problematic. This author concurs with Gray's translation, whereas Driver and Ginsberg interpret the last line to refer to soaking the bed with tears.[74]

Like Naram-Sin and Ashurbanipal Keret also undergoes ritual weeping in the incubation process. Even more thorough is the incubation account of Dan'el in the Aqhat Epic. The text reads as follows: 2 AQHT I, lines 3-18:

3.	uzr ilm ylḫm
4.	(uzr yšqy) bn qdš yd
5.	(ṣth y^{c}l) wyškb yd
6.	(mizrt) ynl hn ym
7.	(wṯn uzr) ilm dnil
8.	(uzr ilm) ylḫm uzr
9.	(yšqy b)n qdš ṯlṯ rb^c ym
10.	(uzr i)lm dnil uzr
11.	(ilm y)lḫm uzr yšqy bn
12.	(qdš ḫ)mš ṯdṯ šb^c ym uzr
13.	(ilm) dnil uzr ilm ylḫm
14.	(uzr) yšqy bn qdš yd ṣth
15.	(dn)il yd ṣth y^{c}l wyškb
16.	( ) mizrt pyln mk bšb^c ymm
17.	(w)yqrb b^{c}l bḫnth abynt
18.	(d)nil mt rpi anḫ ǵzr

3. he gave food and drink offerings to the gods to eat,
4. he drank the food and drink offerings of the holy ones, he put
5. ṣth (?), and went up and lay down, he put
6. his clothing, and he sleeps. Behold, another day
7. and a second, food and drink offerings to the gods of Dan'el,

8. he eats the food and drink offerings of the gods, the food and drink offerings
9. of the holy ones he drinks, a third and a fourth day,
10. food and drink offering of the gods, the food and drink offerings
11. of the gods Dan'el eats, he drinks the food and drink offerings of the
12. holy ones, a fifth, a sixth, a seventh day, the food and drink offerings
13. of the gods, the food and drink offerings of the gods Dan'el eats,
14. the food and drink offerings of the holy ones he drinks. He puts his ṣth (?),
15. Dan'el puts his ṣth (?), he goes up and lies down.
16. (He puts) his garment and sleeps. Lo, in the seventh day
17. Baal draws near in pity for the wretchedness of
18. Dan'el, the man of Rapi, for the sighing of the hero.

Translation notes:[75]

6. The word, _mizrt_, is supplied only by Driver and Obermann.

2-14. The word _uzr_ is problematic. Obermann relates the word to Hebrew _nezer_ and translates it as "votive offering." Driver translates it as "nectar," and Ginsberg has "oblation."

4-14. The author concurs with Driver against Obermann and Ginsberg on the translation of yšqy. The latter two have Dan'el "giving" the _uzr_ to the gods, rather than having him drink it. Ultimately, Dan'el had to consume the material himself, for the gods did not do so; that would have been a theophany in itself. The normal meaning for the word is "drink."

5 and 14. The ṣth is problematic. Driver calls it a "covering," Ginsberg calls it a "couch of sackcloth," Obermann calls it a "cubicle" and loosely translates yd ("hand" or the verb "to put" in this context) as "besprinkles." He feels that yd may be from ndy, an imperfect like the Hebrew nzʔ. ṣth is then a room, like the Arabic waṣid. For Obermann, this sprinkling is seen as an important part of the incubation process.

In summation the basic components of the incubation process can be seen. The incubant spends the night in a sanctuary, perhaps a special room for such activity. Sacrifices are offered to the deity; here they are called _uzr_, a form of food and drink offering.[76] Special preparatory rites, perhaps

purification, are undertaken. The recipient does something to his clothing; he either puts it somewhere or sprinkles it. Finally, there is the element of weeping, which was evident in the Mesopotamian incubation rituals. These four elements appear to be constitutive parts of the procedure, but we can state this only in a tentative fashion.

The Old Testament accounts lack a clear reference to any incubation procedure. If there were such a process, it is hidden in the text. Possible incubation texts include Genesis 15, 28:10-19, 46:1-4, I Samuel 3, and I Kings 3. But none of these texts gives the clear indication of being an incubation dream in the manner of the ancient Near Eastern models. Only in I Kings 3 do we find Solomon going to a shrine, giving sacrifices, and lying down to sleep. Ehrlich may have made a correct observation that incubation occurred at sacred shrines outside of Jerusalem, which caused the Deuteronomistic redactor[77] to tone down any such reference to incubation in the text. In Genesis 46:1 Jacob offers sacrifice before receiving his vision of the night, and the activities of Abraham in Genesis 15 may constitute incubatory sacrifice prior to his bizarre vision, but that one motif is too little to make a conclusion. As with the Deuteronomistic history the patriarchal material might have had any reference to incubation removed, perhaps because it would have been seen as an effort to manipulate God, who freely chose to reveal Himself to the patriarchs.

The best examples of the incubation process come from the Greek period, and in particular from the cult of Asclepius, the god of healing. Incubants went to his shrines in Cos,[78] Trica, Pergamum, Lebedena, and Aegae. The Greek incubation appears to differ from earlier ancient Near Eastern counterparts by virtue of the fact the incubants not only seek a message but physical healing.

There are other Greek incubation dreams besides Asclepius cult dreams. A number of late Egyptian incubation dreams are available to us, which display the basic Greek pattern.[79] Deubner records a number of early Christian incubation dreams. The format of these incubation dreams remains unchanged from the original ancient Near Eastern pattern. The recipient goes into a shrine or temple, conducts certain rites in preparation for the dream theophany, falls asleep, and an image of the god appears.[80]

38

Later Developments in the Dream Pattern

Greek, Roman, and Hellenistic Dreams

The Greek dream format was more highly developed than the ancient Near Eastern, although it was descended from it. We have far more material available on this subject; major primary material includes works by Artemidorus, Macrobius, Pseudo-Augustinus, Ionnes Saresberiensis, and Nicephorus Gregoras.[81]

Here as in the ancient Near East the difference between dream, vision, and ecstasy is difficult to define. The dream was a mode of divine communication, as were those other experiences, and a clear differentiation was not made.[82] According to Macrobius and others there were three types of dreams: the symbolic dream, the vision, and the oracle.[83] The dreamer was usually the spectator, but here unlike the situation in the ancient Near East, he or she could become an actor. Dreams belonged to the spatial and temporal peripheries of the cosmos, and they came to the recipient in a semi-conscious state, for to lapse into a deeper sleep would cause the loss of connection with the other realm. Dreams came in the early morning hours. Double dreams or repeated dreams were common, for they are attested in sources like Dionysius of Halicarnassus, Livius, Pausanias, Tacitus, Apuleius, Aelius Aristides, Josephus, Eusebius, the Acts of John, the Acts of Thomas, and the Acts of Barnabas.[84] The earlier critical attitude that the Greeks held toward dreams because of a lack of established forms for interpreting them gave way in later Hellenistic times to a wide acceptance, perhaps because Near Eastern dream interpretative models became available.[85]

Several differences between the ancient Near East and the classical world deserve mention. The classical world repeated message dreams, whereas the ancient Near East repeated symbolic dreams. Only Cicero and Tacitus attest to the repetition of symbolic dreams. Repeated dreams may have been those with which the society was least familiar, and the repetition was needed to assure the veracity of the dream.[86] Dreams had meaning in the Near East because the gods or evil spirits brought the dreams, but in the classical world the cognitive ability of the sleeping soul or the ability of the soul to leave the body sometimes underlay the rationale for receiving the dream message. Cultic dreams predominated in the ancient Near East, but in the classical world the dreams were predominantly political. Caesar dreamed of victory, Hannibal and Hamilcar received battle plans, Pericles' mother dreamed she bore a lion, and Xenophon had political success in his. These dreams were often recorded after the fact to indicate the individual had divine providence on his side.[87]

39

Davidson College Library

Homer's epics contain the earliest dreams. He distinguishes between two types of dreams; those from the "gate of ivory," which are[88] false, and clear and significant ones from the "gate of horn."[88] Dreams come from the gods, but they are not always beneficial or even true. It is interesting to note that in[89] the Iliad dreams come to men, in the Odyssey to women.[89] Dead personages, deceiving gods, and physical contact are among the various characteristics of dreams.

The philosophers also spoke of dreams. Plato felt that only insane men have dreams and only wise men can interpret them. During sleep[90] normally repressed feelings and actions were able to surface.[90] Aristotle wrote Parva Naturalia, which had three chapters on the study of dreams: "On Sleep and Wakefulness," "On Divination through Sleep," and "On Dreams." He was critical of dream revelations, for they were fantasies produced by emotions, physical ailments, and residual sensory perceptions. Dreams can be precognitive because human emotions are involved with future possibilities, and the dream can be an incentive for future actions.[91] The attitude toward dreams was divided, for while Aristotle and the Epicureans rejected dream revelation, the Pythagoreans, and many Stoics believed in it, and Hippocrates wrote a treatise on dreams wherein we perceive some of the rationale for Greek incubational procedures.[92]

Roman thinkers also displayed positive and negative attitudes toward dream revelation. Lucretius was almost Freudian in De Rerum Natura about seeing[93] dreams as a wish fulfillment of bodily needs and desires.[93] Cicero was very critical of dreams in his De Divinatione. In a world where divination was esteemed by all he maintained there was no connection between dreams and the divine realm; rather, "there is nothing too preposterous nor too monstrous that cannot be dreamed," and it was unreliable to expect the gods to communicate through them.[94]

The Hellenistic world saw an increase in the popularity of dreams. Plutarch gives advice on what foods to eat so as not to have confused dreams.[95] In Egypt individuals would sleep in tombs to induce dream visions from the gods, and Christian ascetes would live in tombs and not sleep lest the pagan gods bother them. The most significant Hellenistic phenomenon was the cult of Asclepius. He was the god of the sick. The infirm would go to his shrines, undergo dream incubation, and await his coming. The cult dates back to the days of Aristophanes, but it peaked early in the Christian era. It rivaled Christianity for a time, but Christians declared the superiority of Christ, not only because he could heal, but because he could also cast out demons. Much of the actual healing was performed by physician priests. In the theophany the god

would come and touch the patient, often performing regular medical work with normal instruments. All the accounts stress how the god was calm, gentle, and happy in his appearance. The patient had to offer sacrifices, undergo purification, and avoid strange activities before and after the healing.[96] It all sounds like good medical practice with the guidance of a physician acting the role of a god.

The Hellenistic era saw the creation of several dream books and commentaries. The commentary by Macrobius on the dream of Scipio Africanus comes from the Fourth or Fifth Century A.D. The dream itself is short, but the commentary is twenty times the length of the dream, and is a Neo-Platonic commentary of the political rise of Scipio Africanus.[97] The most famous of all dream books are the five books of the Oneirocritica by the geographer Artemidorus Daldianus, who wrote under the reign of Commodus (180-192 A.D.). He called himself Artemidorus of Ephesus, but he lived in Daldis, whence comes his popular name. His total writings fill twenty-two books, and much of his work still remains today.[98] He tried to bring a degree of reason and evidence into consideration rather than quasi-religious belief and superstition. He warned against interpretations that are too logical and too facile. Babylonian, Egyptian, and Greek sources were utilized by him in the compilation of this work. Without his efforts we would have totally lost the work of other men like Antiphon of Athens, Aristander of Telmessus, Demetrius of Phalerum, Antipater of Tarsus, Alexander of Myndus, Phoebus of Antioch, Artemon of Miletus, Panyasis of Halicarnassus, Nicostratus of Ephesus, and Apollodorus of Telmessus. But above all he seems to be dependent upon the Assyrian Dream Book. He divided all the dreams into five categories: dreams, visions, oracles, fantasies, or vain imaginations, and apparitions. He also studied the land of a dreamer's origin to discover hidden meanings of symbols. Many dreams were evaluated in the light of the activities of the previous day.[99] He is considered to be the greatest oneirocritic of all time.

Dreams performed a certain social function in the Hellenistic world. They preserved the basic fabric of society by preventing individualism from destroying the established institutions. In dreams and the interpretations an individual found meaning and a place in society. "The interpretation of dreams depended on external authority," and this perpetuated a cycle "within which men of antiquity were confined" so that there was "the promotion of the community without regard for the individual."[100]

41

Judaism and Christianity

Judaism and Christianity were both heirs of the ancient Near East and especially the Old Testament. Their attitudes toward dreams contrast with the surrounding Hellenistic world.

Philo considered dreams to be empty, but he granted that God does send knowledge of heavenly things to the pure soul in dreams. For Philo there were three types of dreams: direct messages from God found in the Old Testament, dreams caused by immortal souls in the air (Genesis 28 and 31:11), and dreams that come from the soul's own power of divination, which are exemplified by Joseph and Daniel.[101]

Josephus had no criticism of dreams, for he took all of the Old Testament dreams and adds a few of his own. These extra dreams include those of Moses' father Nathan. In postcanonical history he mentioned the dreams of Jaddus, Theopompos the gentile, Hyrcanus, Herod the Great, Archelaus, Glaphyra, the daughter of Archelaus, and Monobazos of Adiabene. In fact, Josephus even received and interpreted dreams himself, one of which encouraged him to join the Romans.[102]

Rabbinic Judaism had a number of new and traditional viewpoints. Valid dreams came from angels, invalid ones from demons. Ramael was the angel of dreams. A given dream never was fulfilled completely for the dreamer. By the opinion of some rabbis only experts could interpret dreams, but others maintained that common people could do so, while another group declared the whole process to be unfruitful.[103] Freudian motifs have been found in the Talmud according to some, especially where the Talmud equates the sexual motif to the meaning of dreams.[104]

Dreams occur in the New Testament, but they are not important as a mode of revelation. Matthew records five dreams: Joseph's dream in 1:20-25, the wise men in 2:12, the commands to go to Egypt and return in 2:13-20, and the dreams of Pilate's wife in 27:19. Their occurrence in the infancy narratives and stereotypical formulation may point to their legendary character. The other dreams, which are more like visions, occur in Acts, where the Lord appears in 18:9 and 23:11, a divine messenger in 27:23, and a man in 16:9, which may be the most authentic vision in the New Testament.[105] The greater concern with visions rather than dreams is attributed to the eschatological stress on the transformation of the world, for the risen Lord is breaking the established patterns of revelation inasmuch as He is the new revelation.[106] There is no interpretation of dreams in the New Testament, for God does not speak ambiguously to His people. Thus

42

Christians were basically critical of dreams, especially Gnostic dreams. Paul makes no reference to any dream in his letters, even though Acts attributes them to him. The New Testament dreams give comfort, consolation, and guidance; the fear and superstition found in ancient and Hellenistic counterparts is lacking, for this lack is sign of the new kingdom.[107]

The post-apostolic era saw the dreams of Christians coincide in style with the Hellenistic world. A greater emphasis upon dreams arose, and even Tertullian could write essays like, "No Soul is Exempt from Dreams."[108] Martyrs like Polycarp and Perpetua had dreams that foreshadowed their deaths. In the Fourth Century the neo-Platonist, Synesius of Cyrene, was converted to Christianity and became a bishop. He refused to retract his views on dream divination, which he articulated in "Dreams take the Soul to 'The Superior Region,'" a work full of eclectic ideas from diverse philosophical schools of thought. Written as a defense of his strange views in the face of orthodox criticism, the work gradually became a standard of orthodoxy in an age of ecclesiastical syncretism.[109] Whereas earlier New Testament dreams maintained continuity with the Old Testament, patristic dreams became very Hellenistic in form and content.

Later Near Eastern Developments

The Byzantine dream book of Achmet is dependent upon Islamic sources and the old Greek work of Artemidorus. It begins with Joseph and Daniel as the great paradigms, but it relies heavily on Indian, Persian, and Egyptian sources for its theology.

In Islam dreams played an important role in Mohammed's life and later Islamic theology. Since the Koran relies upon the Old Testament, it inherits several dreams. The Joseph account is very similar to the account in the Koran, except that certain theological insights have been altered.[110] Islam believes that Gabriel brings the true dreams and the false dreams come from demons. The time of a dream determines its validity; again true dreams are early morning dreams. Ad-Damīrī, a zoologist, compiled the first systematic treatment of dreams; and his creation built upon the work of Artemidorus, Muhammed ibn Sirin, Ibn al-Muqrī, the Persian Jamāsb, and others.[111] Later medieval theologians of Islam place dream interpretation among accepted theological disciplines.

The influence of the ancient Near East can be traced to India, where the great dream book, the Jagaddeva, displays its dependence upon the older Brhadāranyaka, the Fifth Century Atharvaveda, and the Assyrian Dream Book.[112] The epic

43

literature surrounding the life of Buddha foreshadows every major event with a dream, like epic literature in the ancient Near East. The audience perceived the difference between these literary motifs and the "real" or "subjective" dreams of others.[113]

Conclusion

In the ancient Near East dreams were seen to have great significance. Good dreams sent by the gods or from another realm contained a message of importance for the dreamer. Even evil dreams were important for indicating the health or cultic status of the recipient. In either case the dreams had to be interpreted, or evil would befall the dreamer. For this purpose there were professional dream interpreters and dream books, even though the entire discipline was often viewed with little respect. Because dreams had numinous power, their recording had to conform to particular forms. We have been able to note two basic types of dream accounts, the clearly understood auditory message dream given by a particular deity often upon request or incubation, and the symbolic dream, a visual experience requiring professional interpretation. The literary frame for reporting these dreams maintains a basic format with occasional variations throughout the ancient world. It served as a prototype for the more fully developed Greek forms. From there the ancient Near Eastern dream pattern can ultimately be traced to many cultures.

Dreams in the ancient Near East tend to be short and simple. Symbolic dreams use a few symbols in communicating their message, and the god comes to deliver a short but important message in the auditory message dreams. Epic literature tends to use symbolic dreams, and historical texts tend to use auditory message dreams. Symbolic dreams function as foreshadowing devices in the developing narrative, whereas auditory message dreams serve as mandates for leaders of society by virtue of the clarity and divine authorship. Symbolic dreams in the literature appear to be earlier than the auditory message dreams; they lack the formal structure of the historically recorded auditory message dreams. This might imply the evolution of a structure for recording these auditory message dreams that arose in the Second Millennium. The auditory message dreams of Ugarit come from an epic literature which is late, and the developing structure of the auditory message dream may have made its impact upon them.

Restrictions placed upon dreams because of their lowly status and ritual impurity have left us with few dream accounts and often stylized forms beyond which we cannot perceive the original human experience. The early epic literature with its

symbolic dreams shows the most varied use of symbols; later auditory message dreams that have the greatest significance for us, because these dream accounts show the greatest formal similarity with I Samuel 3, and there are indications that the biblical text has followed the format of ancient Near Eastern models.

CHAPTER II

FOOTNOTES

[1] Eliade, The Myth of the Eternal Return or, Cosmos and History, trans. Willard Trask, Bollingen Series, vol. 46 (Princeton: Princeton University Press, 1974), pp. 3-137; and Henri and Henrietta Frankfort, "Myth and Reality," Before Philosophy, ed. Henri Frankfort (Baltimore: Penguin, 1966), pp. 11-36.

[2] Frankfort, "Myth and Reality," p. 20.

[3] Andreas Resch, Der Traum im Heilsplan Gottes: Deutung und Bedeutung des Traums in Alten Testament (Freiburg: Herder, 1964), p. 4.

[4] Edouard Paul Dhorme, L'evolution religieuse d'Israel, vol. 1: La religion des Hebreux nomades (Brussels: Nouvelle Societe d'editions, 1937), p. 233.

[5] Theodor Gaster, "Dreams: In the Bible," Enc Jud, vol. 6, ed. Cecil Roth (Jerusalem: Keter, 1971), p. 208.

[6] Morris Jastrow, The Religion of Babylonia and Assyria, Handbooks of the History of Religions, vol. 2 (Boston: Ginn, 1898), p. 351.

[7] Frankfort, "Myth and Reality," p. 21.

[8] A. Leo Oppenheim, "Mantic Dreams in the Ancient Near East," The Dream and Human Societies, ed. Gustave Edmund von Grunebaum and Roger Callois (Berkeley: University of California Press, 1966), p. 346.

[9] Carl Alfred Meier, "The Dream in Ancient Greece and Its Use in Temple Curses," Dream and Human Societies, p. 311.

[10] Jastrow, Religion, p. 350; and Isaac Mendelsohn, "Dream," IDB, 4 vols., ed. George Arthur Buttrick (Nashville: Abingdon, 1962), 1:868.

[11] Oppenheim, The Interpretation of Dreams in the Ancient Near East: With a Translation of an Assyrian Dream

Book, Transactions of the American Philosophical Society, vol. 46 (Philadelphia: American Philosophical Society, 1956), p. 185; and "New Fragments of the Assyrian Dream-Book," Iraq 31 (1969): 153-165. His position is antithetical to Resch, Traum, passim, who uses modern psychoanalytic categories to analyze biblical dreams. Thomas Thompson and Dorothy Irwin, "The Joseph and Moses Narratives," Israelite and Judean History, eds. John Hayes and Maxwell Miller, OTL (Philadelphia: Westminster, 1977), p. 189, concur with Oppenheim from their perspective in considering the Joseph dreams.

[12] Jastrow, Religion, p. 404.

[13] Sandra Shulman, The Interpretation of Dreams and Nightmares (New York: Ottenheimer, 1973), pp. 18-19.

[14] Oppenheim, Interpretation, p. 219.

[15] Ibid., pp. 241-242.

[16] Ibid., pp. 221-224.

[17] Ibid., pp. 217-219, 222-223.

[18] Ibid., pp. 220.

[19] Oppenheim, "Mantic Dreams," pp. 346, 350. Sometimes the dream would be told to the lump of clay, and it would be thrown into the river to dissolve.

[20] Oppenheim prefers the former theory, Interpretation, p. 187; while Jastrow offers the second theory, Religion, pp. 151-152.

[21] Murray Lichtenstein, "Dream Theophany and the E Document," Journal of Ancient Near Eastern Society (Columbia University) 1/2 (1969): 49; and Mendelsohn, "Dream," p. 868. Biblical dreams fall into these two categories: Genesis 20, 31:11, 24, I Kings 3:5-15 are "announcements in plain language," and Genesis 37, 40, and 41 contain dreams "resolved by professional interpreters only," Mendelsohn, "Dream," p. 868.

[22] Oppenheim made such a distinction in Interpretation, pp. 206-217, 237-245, but in "Mantic Dreams," passim, he uses the simple category of symbolic to encompass both categories.

[23] Oppenheim, "Mantic Dreams," p. 348.

[24] Dreams can be culturally conditioned in a society. Berthold Laufer has noted patterns of inspirational dreams

among various groups like the Chinese and American Indians. He sees a cultural connection in establishing these patterns of prediction dreams, Laufer, "Inspirational Dreams," p. 210. H. R. Hayes has noted, "When it comes to the actual content of the dream . . . the established pattern of the culture comes into play and the spirits or communications which come to the dreamer may be shaped by his environment and his economy," In the Beginnings (New York: Putnam, 1963), p. 528. Two German anthropologists lived among the aborigines in the South African veldt to study their life style, and during their residence they began to experience the same dreams as the people around them, dreams of hunting animals and being a hunted animal; noted by Jacquetta Hawkes in History of Mankind: Cultural and Scientific Development, vol. 1, pt. 1: Prehistory (New York: New American Library, 1963), pp. 207-208. Since dream experiences seem to be conditioned by one's environment and experiences, this may imply that a society could induce its people to dream in certain accepted categories. The religious strictures for recording dreams may have induced people to dream in that same format.

[25] Oppenheim, Interpretation, pp. 186-187.

[26] Ibid., p. 187.

[27] Ernst Ludwig Ehrlich observes this to be the case among Hindus in India, Arabs, and the classical tradition even down to Dante, Der Traum im Alten Testament, BZAW, vol. 73 (Berlin: Töpelmann, 1953), p. 75.

[28] In 1953 Nathaniel Kleitman and Eugene Aserinsky observed the dream phenomena at the University of Chicago. They discovered that periods of dreaming occur regularly throughout the night, but periods of dreaming increase in duration and intensity as the night progresses. The first period of dreaming would be five to ten minutes in duration. Successive periods would be longer, until the final period in the early morning hours would be thirty minutes out of an hour. A dreaming period would come every hour, but the later ones were more intense. People deprived of their sleep one night would have increased frequency the next night, Klein, "Dreams," pp. 665-668. The implications are that the ancients also perceived this phenomenon and realized that early morning dreams were the most intense and easily remembered. It gradually became part of the literary convention to attribute any significant dream to the early morning period.

[29] Oppenheim, Interpretation, p. 188.

[30] Ibid., p. 189; and James Pritchard, ed., ANET, 3d ed. (Princeton: Princeton University Press, 1969), p. 32.

[31] Oppenheim, Interpretation, pp. 189-191; and ANET, p. 32.

[32] Oppenheim, Interpretation, p. 192.

[33] Ehrlich, Traum, p. 123.

[34] Oppenheim, Interpretation, p. 212-213.

[35] Ibid., p. 206.

[36] Ibid., p. 229.

[37] Ibid.

[38] Ibid., p. 192.

[39] Ibid., p. 193.

[40] Samuel Noah Kramer, "Heroes of Sumer: A New Heroic Age in World History and Literature," Proceedings of the American Philosophical Society 90 (1946): 124.

[41] Alexander Heidel, The Gilgamesh Epic and Old Testatment Parallels (Chicago: University of Chicago Press, 1949), p. 109.

[42] Bendt Alster, Dumuzi's Dream: Aspects of Oral Poetry in a Sumerian Myth, Mesopotamia, Copenhagen Studies in Assyriology, vol. 1 (Copenhagen: Akademische Forlag, 1972), passim.

[43] The text is confused and fragmentary at this point. Gaster reconstructs the second series of dreams to be two in number, one by Gilgamesh and one by Enkidu, The Oldest Stories in the World (Boston: Beacon Press, 1952), p. 28. Heidel reconstructs three dreams and attributes them to Gilgamesh, Gilgamesh, pp. 46-48. Oppenheim sees four dreams; the first three belong to Gilgamesh and the last one belongs to Enkidu, Interpretation, pp. 247-248. Gaster and Oppenheim divide the dreams between the two characters on the basis of a tablet division that places the last dream of the second series with the third series of dreams by Enkidu, which makes him the speaker even though the dream belongs to the last series. They base their division on the work of Campbell Thompson, The Epic of Gilgamesh (Oxford: Clarendon, 1931), plates 15-16; whereas Heidel's text relies upon the work of A. Schott, ZA 41 (1934): 113-115.

[44] Oppenheim, Interpretation, p. 212.

[45] Wolfram von Soden believes that the function of this messenger is comparable to the function of court prophets like Gad and Nathan. He dismisses the view that perceives this messenger to be a dream interpreter, "Verkündigung des Gotteswillens durch prophetisches Wort in den altbabylonischen Briefen aus Mari," WO 1 (1947-1952): 400-402.

[46] Ibid., p. 398; and Martin Noth, "History and the Word of God in the Old Testament," BJRL 32 (1949-1950): 197.

[47] Lichtenstein, "Dream Theophany," pp. 50-51.

[48] Oppenheim, Interpretation, pp. 225, 232-233, 235-236.

[49] Gaster, Oldest Stories, pp. 154-157.

[50] Oppenheim, Interpretation, pp. 197-199.

[51] Ibid., pp. 199, 226.

[52] ANET, pp. 394-395.

[53] Oppenheim, Interpretation, pp. 199.

[54] ANET, p. 449.

[55] Ibid., pp. 30-32; and Oppenheim, Interpretation, pp. 251-254.

[56] John Wilson, "Egypt," Before Philosophy, pp. 40-51.

[57] Shulman, Dreams, p. 18; and Oppenheim, Interpretation, pp. 195-196.

[58] Ehrlich, Traum, p. 77; and ANET, pp. 29-31, records a text wherein this house is mentioned several times. One is reminded of the late story of Joseph and his dreams, for Egypt is a natural setting for dream interpretation.

[59] ANET, p. 495; and Oppenheim, Interpretation, pp. 244-245.

[60] Encyclopaedia of Religion and Ethics, 1922 ed., s.v. "Dreams and Sleep: Egyptian," by George Foucart, pp. 34-35.

[61] E. A. Wallis-Budge, "The Dream Magic of Ancient Egypt," The World of Dreams: An Anthology, ed. Ralph Woods (New York: Random House, 1947), p. 86.

[62] Hayes, Beginnings, pp. 266-267.

[63] Lichtenstein, "Dream Theophany," pp. 51-52.

[64] Oppenheim, Interpretation, pp. 201, 249.

[65] Ibid., pp. 256-334; Oppenheim gives translation, transliteration, and photographs of the texts. He supplements this material with the later article, "New Fragments," pp. 153-165.

[66] Ibid., pp. 204-205.

[67] Ibid., p. 212.

[68] Ibid., p. 228; and ANET, pp. 412-414.

[69] Ehrlich, Traum, p. 52; and Oppenheim, Interpretation, p. 250.

[70] Heidel, Gilgamesh, p. 103.

[71] Hans Gustav Güterbock, "Die historische Tradition und ihre literarische Gestaltung bei Babylonieren und Hethitern bis 1200," ZA 94 (1938): 56-57.

[72] ANET, p. 451.

[73] Gaster offers both examples in Thespis: Ritual, Myth and Drama in the Ancient Near East (New York: Schuman, 1950), p. 271, but while he believes the former example is a valid observation, he questions whether the latter example is valid, as it was first proposed by Grimme in the ZDMG, Neue Folge, 12 (1934): 194.

[74] John Gray, The KRT Text in the Literature of Ras Shamra: A Social Myth of Ancient Canaan (Leiden: Brill, 1955), p. 7; Godfrey Rolles Driver, Canaanite Myths and Legends, Old Testament Studies, vol. 3 (Edinburgh: Clark, 1956), pp. 28-29; and Harold Ginsberg's translation is provided in ANET, p. 143.

[75] The most extensive work is by Julian Obermann, How Daniel was blessed with a Son: An Incubation Scene in Ugarit, Publications of the American Oriental Society #20 = JAOS Supplement, vol. 116, pt. 2 (1946): 3-9. Other considerations of this text include Cyrus Gordon, UT, AnOr, vol. 28 (Rome: Pontifical Biblical Institute, 1965), p. 247; Driver, Canaanite Myths, pp. 48-49; and Ginsberg's translations appear in ANET, pp. 149-150.

[76] Obermann, How Daniel, pp. 13-18, 28, believes that the word uzr is related to the Hebrew word for Nazirite, a

description that is given of both Samson and Samuel. Both of these men were born to barren mothers after a prayer request. Obermann concludes that the Dan'el and Aqhat stories were the source for this biblical motif, and it was utilized by the Israelite story-tellers as they wove their tales. The long awaited son promised to aged or barren parents is a recurrent theme in the Patriarchal narratives. Ishmael and Isaac both fall into this category, and Obermann thinks that the original longer version of the birth of Jacob and Esau likewise contained this motif. Such an awaited individual who is so born becomes a hero of renown. If this observation is correct, a significant point of contact is revealed between the development of literature in Ugarit and in the Old Testament.

[77] Ehrlich, Traum, pp. 18-19.

[78] Ibid., p. 11. Carl Meier has analyzed Greek incubation dreams with the aid of Freudian principles in Antike Inkubation und moderne Psychotherapie, Studien aus Carl Gustav Jung Institute, vol. 1 (Zurich: n.p., 1949), passim.

[79] Ehrlich, Traum, p. 24.

[80] Ludovicus Deubner, De Incubatione (Leipzig: Teubner, 1900), pp. 5, 56-109.

[81] Ibid., pp. 3-4.

[82] Violet McDermot, The Cult of the Seer in the Ancient Middle East (Berkeley and Los Angeles: University of California Press, 1971), p. 54.

[83] E. R. Dodds, The Greeks and the Irrational (Berkeley: University of California Press, 1951), p. 107.

[84] Alfred Wilkenhauser, "Doppelträume," Bib 29 (1948): 100-111.

[85] Angelo Brelich, "The Place of Dreams in the Religious World Concept of the Greeks," Dream and Human Societies, p. 300.

[86] Oppenheim, Interpretation, pp. 208, 210.

[87] Albrecht Oepke, "Onar," TDNT, 10 vols., ed. Gerhard Kittel and Gerhard Friedrich, trans. Geoffrey Bromiley (Grand Rapids: Eerdmans, 1973), 5:224-225.

[88] Webb, "Dreams," p. 1011.

[89] Brelich, "Place of Dreams," p. 294.

[90] Shulman, Dreams, p. 23.

[91] Meier, "Dream in Ancient Greece," p. 305.

[92] Webb, "Dreams," p. 1011; and Shulman, Dreams, p. 21.

[93] Eric Fromm, The Forgotten Language: An Introduction to the Understanding of Dreams, Fairy Tales, and Myths (New York: Grove Press, 1951), p. 123.

[94] John Priest, "Myth and Dream in Hebrew Scripture," Myths, Dreams, and Religion, ed. Joseph Campbell (New York: Dutton, 1970), p. 59.

[95] MacDermot, p. 241.

[96] E. J. and Ludwig Edelstein, eds., Asclepius: A Collection and Interpretation of the Testimonies, 2 vols. (Baltimore: Johns Hopkins Press, 1945), 1:148-152, 160.

[97] Ambrosius Aurelius Macrobius, Commentary of the Dream of Scipio, trans. William Harris Stahl (New York: Columbia University Press, 1952), p. 9.

[98] Resch, Traum, pp. 9-10. For primary reference to his works the best source is Daldianus Artemidorus, The Interpretation of Dreams: Oneirocritica, trans. Robert White, Noyes Classical Studies (Park Ridge, Illinois: Noyes, 1975), passim; another good selection of some of his interpretative guidelines is found in Arthur Darby Nock, "Sarcophagi and Symbolism," American Journal of Archaeology 50 (1940): 159-161.

[99] White, Oneirocritica, p. 7.

[100] MacDermot, p. 192.

[101] Oepke, TDNT, 5:231-232.

[102] Ibid., pp. 232-233.

[103] Ibid., pp. 233-234.

[104] Fromm, Forgotten Language, p. 129.

[105] Oepke, TDNT, 5:235.

[106] Amos Wilder, "Myth and Dreams in Christian Scriptures," Myths, Dreams, and Religion, p. 71.

[107] Oepke, TDNT, 5:236.

[108] Woods, Worlds of Dreams, pp. 131-133.

[109] Oepke, TDNT, 5:236-237.

[110] Siegfried Raeder, "Die Josephgeschichte im Koran und im Alten Testament," EvT 26 (1966): 178.

[111] Joseph de Somogyi, "Ad-Damīrī's Hayat al-hayawān: An Arabic Zoological Lexicon," Osiris 9 (1950): 41.

[112] Webb, "Dreams," p. 1011.

[113] Laufer, "Inspirational Dreams," p. 214.

56

CHAPTER III

DREAMS IN THE BIBLICAL TRADITION

"The dream in the Old Testament is not so much a psychological phenomenon as it is[1] a traditio-historical and comparative religions phenomenon." The study of dream theophanies in the Old Testament is a demonstration of how the Israelites tried to express their relationship to the divine. Dream reports are literary categories, and any attempt to penetrate behind the report is a subjective and difficult endeavor. In this respect the Israelites parallel their ancient neighbors, who also handled their relationship with the divine by respectfully recording experiences in acceptable literary categories.

The dream was a way in which God could choose to communicate, and the dream report was a form which could be used to describe such an experience. Dream reports are not a testimony to a person's internal or psychological status; they are the literary accounts of an external divine communication, and they differ from theophanies in that the recipient is theoretically asleep prior to the theophany.[2] Israelites believed that they encountered reality in their dreams, whether or not God was the source, for the origin of dreams was external.[3] Only later in the biblical tradition would Sirach and Koheleth posit an internal source for the dream experience.

There are modern scholars who do not recognize this, and they seek to force modern categories upon biblical dream accounts. Pedersen feels that there are real psychological causes behind the biblical dreams.[4] Resch has devoted an entire study to the modern psychoanalytical evaluation of biblical dreams. He tries to apply these categories of evaluation to each dream: 1) the prospective, the function of dreams which awaken possibilities in the dreamer's mind, 2) the telepathic, the actual parapsychological power of dreams to communicate, and 3) the precognitive, the ability of dreams to predict the future by drawing upon the collective unconscious of men.[5] Resch believes that the Old Testament people viewed dreams in the same fashion as modern people. Dreams are human in origin, they reflect the existential condition of the dreamer, but God can work through them, if He so desires.[6]

57

This is evidenced by God's testimony about Moses in Numbers 12:6-8 and the many other references to the futility of everyday dreams that do not come from God (Psalm 73:20, 126:1, Job 20:8, Sirach 34:1-8, 40:5-7, Jeremiah 23:25-32, 27:9-10, 29:8-9, Zechariah 10:2, Isaiah 29:7-8, Koheleth 5:2, 6). Furthermore, this existential value of dreams is demonstrated by the fact that many dreams are meant to be a test (Job 33:14-16, 4:12-16, 7:13-14, Deuteronomy 13:2-6, and Wisdom of Solomon 18:17-19). Dreams in the Old Testament were always a possible means of divine communication, a passive means, for the Israelites never sought actively to induce dreams as did the rest of the ancient Near East. All of Resch's observations lie very heavily upon a presupposition, which he not only admits but affirms. The dreams in the Old Testament are not tales or legends; they are actual historical accounts, and God did indeed work through those reported dreams. This is proven by the fact that the dreams which were experienced later came true; moreover, these dreams can be shown to have psychological explanations. Prophetic dreams are especially precognitive in function; they clearly predict the future. Resch's work stretches the scholarly imagination. Dream reports given in a literary account will naturally come true according to the author, for that is a literary-theological device to verify the divine origin of the dream. One cannot look for objective proof to the very same text or story which contains the original dream account. One can expect subsequent fulfillment to be recorded in some form. This in no way verifies the historicity of a given dream. Resch's psychological analysis is also said to verify the historicity of a given dream. But the poverty of his presuppositions and methodology is reflected in the paucity of his results. As he uses his three categories, he finds himself totally unable to apply these categories to half of the dreams because of a lack of biographical data for the dreamer. In the other half of the examples, his observations are exceedingly brief, frequently trite, usually forced upon the text, and generally the same from dream to dream. His own failure to produce substantial observations reveals the fallacy of his undertaking. The third criticism centers on Resch's own lack of understanding. He fails to perceive the essential nature of Hebrew literature, and the nature of epic, saga, and folk tales. He naively assumes that all this material is historical, and he fails to discern the earmarks of folk literature. He reviews ancient Near Eastern dreams, but he does not really observe their structure or function. Had he done so, he would have perceived the similarities between Israel and the nations in the use of this literary category. He might have perceived that the dream report actually serves literary, theological, and political purposes in all societies; and he might have realized that it is a standardized form, which prevents the reader from fully ascertaining the actual history behind it, if there were any at

all. Finally, Resch uses Jung's categories, but he does not even apply this learning in a valid fashion. He could have discussed the symbols used in the dreams by the folk tales and their significance for the listeners in that day and even our own. He could have addressed himself to a psychological discussion of symbolism and its meaning for revelation, especially as utilized in the dream. However, he failed to do any of that. To conclude, it is impossible to psychoanalyze the dreams of the Old Testament. Even if they were historical, it is a dubious undertaking to psychoanalyze the dreams of a person long dead. This undertaking is rendered even more dubious by the nature of folk tales which use the dream as a literary motif. The stylization in the dream report is theologically acceptable to the narrator, but it makes psychoanalysis impossible.

There are two types of dream accounts in Israel, auditory message dreams and symbolic dreams, the same division found in the ancient Near East. Various scholars have defined these two categories in different fashions. Mendelsohn defines the former as "announcements in plain language," and the latter are dreams "resolved by professional interpreters only."[8] Kaufmann classifies the two categories as symbolic/enigmatic and prophetic. The former category never arose in Israel because it arose with paganism; symbolic dreams only come to foreigners. Dream interpretation was a magic art never accepted in Israel.[9] Hölscher tries to divide the category of message dreams into "dreams" (Genesis 20:3, 6, 28:12, 31:10-11, 24, I Kings 3:5-15) and "night visions" (Genesis 15:1, 46:2, I Samuel 3) because the latter lack the Hebrew word for dream.[10] This author believes that auditory message dreams are found in the Elohist epic, I Samuel 3, and I Kings 3; symbolic dreams are found in Judges 7, the Joseph cycle, and the book of Daniel. Distinctions that try to be more precise run into difficulty.

The meaning of the word $h^a l \hat{o}m$ is debatable. It may mean "to attain puberty," "to be strong," or "to be able to have sexual emission in sleep."[11] These meanings imply that time of life when a youth reaches the age of sexual awareness and fantasy. One then senses that the chief connection of the word must be with sexual fantasies in one's sleep. $h^a l \hat{o}m$ is sometimes connected with $\underline{h}\bar{a}z\hat{o}n$ or $\underline{h}izz\bar{a}y\hat{o}n$, Job 20:8, 33:15, and Isaiah 29:7. The latter is sometimes rendered as "vision;" it occurs less frequently than the former word. Ehrlich believes the difference is that vision implies a more mysterious and numinous phenomenon, but since the prophet may receive both visions and dreams, it is impossible clearly to differentiate between them.[12] Priest feels there is no difference, for Israel did not clearly distinguish between the various forms of perception. Perception is a totality. Dreams are one way of

perceiving the divine message; they are but one of many varied theophanies, and we cannot distinguish between them.[13] However, the basic distribution of these words may indicate some differences. The noun form of ḥᵃlôm is used sixty-six times, thirty-three occurrences are in the Elohist and another twenty-eight separate occurrences are in the Joseph cycle. The verb form occurs twenty-four times, twelve times in the Elohist and another eleven times in the Joseph cycle. The combined total is eighty-eight usages, of which forty-five are in the Elohist and another thirty-nine in the Joseph cycle. Elsewhere the word describes that which is transitory, false, or ephemeral (Isaiah 29:7, Job 20:8, and Psalm 73:20). ḥazôn is found forty-eight times. In that form the word does not occur in the Hexateuch. There are seven references in Isaiah, seven in Ezekiel, thirteen in Daniel, four in Job, three in Chronicles, two in Jeremiah, and individual passages elsewhere. A different form may be found in maḥᵃzeh. It is found in only four texts, three of which show archaic influence (Genesis 15:1, Numbers 24:4, 24:16), and the fourth (Ezekiel 13:7) is used by a prophet who favors such archaisms. These statistics reveal a possible break in usage between the various traditions. ḥᵃlôm is found in epic literature, while ḥazôn is found in later prophetic and apocalyptic material, which may indicate a revival of an earlier archaic work, as the usage of maḥᵃzeh indicates. Only in Joel 3:1 and Isaiah 29:7-8 do forms of both words occur. It seems best to concur with Guillaume on the distinction between the various types of dreams and visions. He feels there was a difference, but he refrains from trying to articulate the demarcation between dreams received in a sleeping state and the visions of semi-consciousness.[14]

The ḥᵃlôm always occurs at night. It involves hearing and occasionally seeing for the reception of a simple message dream, but only seeing for the reception of a symbolic dream. Dialogue is occasionally present. Message dreams come to patriarchs, prophets, and kings; symbolic dreams may come to average individuals, many of whom were foreigners.

The Old Testament writers viewed dreams as a legitimate mode of revelation, and for this reason dreams usually came to be responsible representatives of God. Prophets may have been the recipients of dreams in the early history of Israel, although we have little or no reference to prophets receiving oracles by dreams. The stories of Balaam and Samuel constitute our accounts of such reception. The assimilation of dreams to the prophetic office may have evolved into the wider category of prophetic vision, of which we have several accounts: Isaiah 6:1-13, Jeremiah 1:11-15, Amos 7:1-9, 8:1-3, the night visions of Zechariah, and other accounts.[15]

60

Message dreams occur in the Elohist; clear examples are found in Genesis 20:1-18, 18:10-22, 31:1-54, 46:1-7, and Numbers 22:8-13, 19-21; and outside of the Elohist there are dreams in I Kings 3:5-15 and I Samuel 3. Symbolic dreams are found only in Judges 7:13-15, Daniel, and the Joseph cycle.

Since most of the dreams are in the Elohist, it becomes obvious that dream reports are infrequent in the rest of the Old Testament. The Yahwist did not use the motif even when he had parallel material in the Elohist where dreams occurred: Jacob at Bethel (Genesis 28), endangering the ancestress (Genesis 12; 26), Jacob's sheep tending (Genesis 31), Israel's departure to Egypt (Genesis 46), and elsewhere. The reason might be that for the Yahwist revelation was direct because his deity was anthropomorphic in nature and near to man. He had no need of a distant mode of revelation like dreams. Throughout the rest of the Old Testament one also notes the paucity of references to dreams. "Israel had little interest in the phenomena of dreams as special occurrences to be related to other central phenomena in the Old Testament."[16]

The few dreams which are recorded are integrated into Israel's historical understanding. All of the patriarchal dreams have the affirmation of God's continuing presence with the patriarchs and the nation. They are important for revealing the future covenant promises. Even in the historical romance of the Joseph cycle they are key foreshadowing ingredients for the unfolding plot, which is a plot that indirectly may testify to the abiding presence of God in a silent manner. Thus the dream is a direct revelation of God to a few concerning His involvement in human affairs.[17]

Israel differed from the surrounding nations in attitudes toward dreams. Dreams were not seen to come from the realm of the dead. Magical practices for inducing dreams, common among the Egyptians, are lacking in Israel, for such divination would only yield false dreams. Although Israel was aware of such divination, it never became a science, or at least it was never acceptable to normative Yahwism. The art of interpretation is mentioned only with Joseph and Daniel, and the text goes to some effort to stress that the real ability belongs to God, who then reveals it to His chosen servant. This may have been Israel's polemic against the skilled diviners and interpreters of the nations. For the most part dreams were clear messages, which could be easily understood by the recipient. God was free to give the dream to whomever He wished.

In those cases where there was dream interpretation, as with Joseph and Daniel, there are several words in this process. The common Hebrew word is pātar, and its Aramaic

counterpart is pešer, and in Judges 7:15 the word is šeber. They seem to be related to the Akkadian words, patāru and pašaru, which mean "dissolve, analyze." This is the basic meaning in Hebrew, while šeber also implies "breaking up" the dream, which is like breaking the mystery of the dream's meaning.[18] Early mantics may have interpreted dreams like Arabic seers, utilizing equivalent symbols, word associations, and observing the specific importance of scenes or audible voices of the dream experience.[19] However, we really have no textual evidence for this, nor is there any information about collected dream omina or rules for interpretation. Only a few passages might imply some related form of divination, as in "the sons of the sorceress" in Isaiah 57:3, and "the diviner's oak" in Judges 9:37. The only certain reference to dream divination is Saul's demand for a word from the Lord either by dream, oracle, or prophecy in I Samuel 28:6, and some think the vision conjured by the witch of Endor might have been worked with dream divination. If there was more concrete textual evidence, it may have been excised.

As one surveys the texts in which dreams are reported or discussed, a certain tension is evident. Some texts put a positive evaluation on dreams as revelation, other texts are negative. Dreams receive positive consideration in epic, historical, and apocalyptic literature, but they are viewed critically by the prophets, psalms, and wisdom literature. Mendelsohn believes the difference between these two groups of literature is the difference between authentic dreams and transitory visions, which the two respective literatures are describing.[20] Resch feels the dream is authentic only when God uses it as a vehicle of revelation, otherwise it is a transitory human experience. The historical literature records divinely sent dreams, and the critical texts describe mere human dreams.[21] A better viewpoint would be to admit different theological viewpoints are operative in the respective literatures in regard to the authenticity of dreams. Epic literature uses the dream report as a theological and literary device to foreshadow the unfolding plan of history for God's people. Likewise historical texts, which also contain created dream accounts, have a theological purpose for using this form. Prophetic texts, however, are critical of dreams because dreams infringe upon the exclusiveness of the prophetic reception of the divine Word. Wisdom texts criticize dreams as being ephemeral from the experiential standpoint of the common person. Finally, apocalyptic literature has a renewed fascination with the symbolic, bizarre, and mysterious phenomena, among which dreams are to be included by virtue of their often bizarre and monstrous imagery. This author would also include the possibility of historical development. Not only are the variations observed among the different types of literature valid, but Israel may have developed an increasingly critical attitude

toward dreams in historical experience. With the exception of later apocalyptic, dreams are evaluated positively by the early literature and negatively by the later literature. Since apocalyptic revives earlier material, this would also fit into the pattern. This historical development to a negative attitude may have resulted primarily from the conflict with false prophets who used dream revelation. This schema of historical development, however, can be refuted if certain materials are redated. Late dates for the Elohist and Joseph cycle, both of which have a positive attitude toward dreams, would impair the theory of a later critical attitude developing toward dreams. This author has not come to a resolution concerning the date for the Elohist, but he believes the Joseph material to be late due to its great similarity with the Daniel material. Therefore, the idea of a historical development toward an increasingly negative attitude must be advanced only tentatively.

Epic Literature

The Elohist seems to be the primary source for dream theophanies. Once this is stated, the problem of date immediately arises. Heretofore, the Elohist was thought to be one of the earlier cycles of Israelite literature in either oral or written state.[22] But recently all epic literature has been redated to the exilic period.[23] If the latter opinion is correct, any kind of a development toward a negative attitude toward dreams is vitiated. But for the sake of format this author will consider the Elohist to be early, and thus a certain historical progression will appear.

The Elohist prefers dreams over the Yahwist, and this is due to his theological orientation. Yahweh communicates directly in Yahwist material, but for the Elohist God is more distant. The Elohist has a high view of God, who remains in the heavens and demands fear and obedience for human response. This transcendence demands more indirect forms of revelation than the Yahwist utilizes. Therefore the Elohist has modes of revelation which include fire, the angel of God, the cloud and thunder, dreams and most important, the prophet. This removal of God from the human realm gives greater significance to dreams, says von Rad, for "they are now the spiritual plane on which God's revelation meets men."[24] Even this dream motif is protected, lest it be used to violate the transcendence of God. People cannot interpret dreams and thus encroach upon the deity; they can interpret only "through the power of special inspiration which comes from God."[25] Some scholars see this as an early concept of the prophetic reception of revelation, and thus early prophets received the Word through dreams.[26] Dreams in the Elohist are an important

63

medium for communicating the Word of God, for in them God can speak directly.[27]

Structure of the Dream Report

The dream structure of the Elohist parallels ancient Near Eastern dreams. A setting is given in which the dream reference, recipient, place, time, and conditions under which the dream is received are given. The theophany occurs with the address of the recipient, self-identification of the deity, and the message. The actual message is introduced with the particle hinnēh, it is short and direct, there are either promises or commands, and the message may be interrupted by pious dialogue from the human recipient. A formal termination follows the message, and a report of the subsequent activity by the dreamer may also be mentioned. This pattern is best represented in five Elohist dreams in Genesis 20, 28, 31:10-13, 31:24, and 46:2-6. The usual expression used by the Elohist which compactly embodies most of these components is, "God came to NN in a dream (by night), and he said, 'Behold . . .'"

Genesis 15:1-6

There is debate as to whether this chapter is Yahwist, Elohist, or a mixture.[28] Some scholars think it is primarily Yahwist, others consider it a conflation.[29] However, it may not be valid to identify it with any source, says von Rad, for it has a great deal of cultic language, the oracle of salvation, declaration of righteousness, and the metaphor of God as a shield.[30] Likewise, the ceremony of cutting an animal in half is archaic, for it may represent ancient covenant practices.[31]

Abraham falls into a "deep sleep," just as Adam did in Genesis 2:21. Some scholars deny that this is a dream experience,[32] but most view it as a type of dream.[33] Eichrodt believes it is the ecstatic trance from an Old Bablylonian procedure for mantic divination. The observation of bird flight, which Abraham appears to do, is a divinatory practice in Mesopotamia. For the narrator of this account, however, it has become a half forgotten practice[34] which Abraham performs for purposes of the literary account.

The vision of the "smoking pot" and "flaming lamp" is bizarre and obscure. The "smoking pot" may be an old oven shaped like a hollow clay cylinder tapering toward the top, which would have flat cakes of bread placed on the inner and outer surfaces for baking. It may be a preview of the theophany of Sinai.[35] Resch thinks the dream is a projection

of Abraham's imagination, which portrays God in anthropomophic imagery that Abraham's conscious mind can understand.[36]

The actual dream message comes in 15:13-16, but it may be secondary. The original account may have comprised merely the vision.

The pericope is not easily broken down into component parts. This may be due to the archaic nature of the tradition or because the text was not formed by the Elohist. There is a pattern, however. Abraham falls into a ecstatic sleep, perhaps a form of incubation, he receives the message, which has a divine promise, and he awakens from an apparent dream vision. If the text belongs to the Elohist, it is primitive in structure, for it does not fit the pattern of later dreams.

The ritual process undertaken by Abraham appears to be incubation to some scholars.[37] However, there is no evidence of actual incubation, for there is no real sacrifice, and Abraham is not at a shrine.[38] Only if his cutting the animals constitutes sacrifice, and if the text implies he was at a sacred shrine, can we view this as an incubation.

Genesis 20:1-18

The tradition of Sarah and Abraham at Gerar is a doublet of the Yahwist accounts in Genesis 12 and 26, and as such provides evidence for the independent existence of the Elohist source. The tradition sees Abraham as the prophet who must intercede for Abimelech. Ironically, Abimelech did nothing wrong; it was the duplicity of Abraham which caused the affair to arise. With his usual good taste the Elohist lessens the tone of Abraham's sin, preserves the purity of Sarah, and puts the emphasis upon obedience.

Ehrlich classifies this text with one of the three "dream commands;" the other two are Genesis 31:11-13 and 31:24.[39]

The key components of this dream are found in the terse phrase, "God came to Abimelech in a dream by night and said to him, 'Behold, you . . . ,'" Genesis 20:3: wayyābōʾ ʾᵉlōhîm ʾel-ʾᵃbîmelek baḥᵃlôm hallāyᵉlāh wayyōʾmer lô hinnᵉkā. In this phrase we have: 1) dream reference, 2) name of recipient, 3) time, 4) coming of the deity, 5) statement of auditory address, and 6) introductory formula. The message, including Abimelech's response, occurs in 20:3-5. The formula,

"And God said to him in the dream," wayyō'mer 'ēlā(y)w hā'elōhîm baḥalōm, is repeated in 20:6, and the message follows in 20:6-7. The formal termination occurs in 20:8, "And Abimelech arose in the morning," wayyaškēm 'abimelek baboqer.

Resch seeks to explain the dream as Abimelech's inner psychological struggle. Unconscious guilt assails him for taking another man's wife.[40] This analysis misses the theological point of the text and obscures its lighthearted folkloristic nature.

Genesis 21:16-19

Hagar's experience in the Elohistic account bears similarity to other dream accounts. It may be coincidence, or the Elohist may not have molded this tradition into the tighter dream pattern as he did with other texts. The weeping in 21:6 is like ritual weeping found in incubations, but that may be stretching the text. The angel of the Lord calls forth in auditory fashion, he uses introductory formulas, "fear not," and a question, which are common to dream theophanies. He gives a promise with command, the type of message common to dreams. Finally, there is a reference to the opening of Hagar's eyes in 21:19, as if she were asleep and perceiving this theophany in a dream. These six features may be coincidental, and it is difficult to assert that this is a dream.

Genesis 22:1-2

Although no dream revelation is recorded in the text, there is a suspicion that the report may be a truncated dream account.[41] The Koran records in Sura 37:100 that Abraham received the demand to sacrifice his son in a dream. Evidence that this could be a dream is found in the use of the verb qr', the calling of the recipient's name, and the reply by Abraham, hinnēnî. These motifs are found in Samuel's dream. These motifs are not characteristic of other dreams in the Elohist, so no conclusions can be drawn. Only Genesis 46:2 has these three motifs, and it is an Elohist dream. Perhaps these are part of a truncated dream report format, which is not the pattern used by the Elohist, but remnants of it remained as the Elohist took up these traditions for his epic.

Genesis 26:24

This is another short fragment which has elements of a dream theophany. This Yahwist account of Isaac records, "And

the Lord appeared unto him the same night, and said, 'I am the God of Abraham, your father; do not be afraid, for I am with you; I will bless you, and I will increase your progeny for the sake of Abraham, my servant.'" This theophany has several elements of a dream theophany: 1) time reference, 2) theophany, 3) auditory revelation, 4) self-identification of the deity, 5) introductory formula, which is the second element, "fear not," and 6) the message, a promise by the deity to act on behalf of the recipient. Since the text is not part of the Elohist tradition, it is understandable that it lacks the standardized structure found in the other dreams. It is difficult to call this a dream without debate, but it does share many of the features.

Genesis 28:10-22

Jacob's vision at Bethel is a conflation of Yahwist and Elohist versions. This is evidenced by a change in the divine name, the parallels in verses 16 and 17, 19a and 22a, and the fact that the oath does note fit the context.[42] The dream message is from the Yahwist, which implies either the Elohist had a silent dream vision, or the Elohist's dream message was edited out in favor of the Yahwist message. The source analysis is disputed by scholars who view the text as a unified account. Either way we shall consider the text as a unity, which has been given to us by the redactor or the original author, for it still preserves the dream pattern of the Elohist.

Genesis 28 is often considered to be an incubation dream, though not deliberately intended by Jacob,[43] and it is frequently called an unintentional incubation dream. Some think this incubation was caused by sleeping on[44] a holy stone, of which there were many at this sacred site. Bethel had a shrine as far back as the Middle Bronze Period (2000-1600 B.C.), and the text describes Bethel as a māqôm, often a technical word for a shrine. If so, this sanctuary would be a fitting place for incubation. It might even be possible that the tradition is older than the Jacob cycle. The dream recipient, Jacob, lifts a stone or sacred pillar in 28:18. If this was a stone massebah, such an effort could be performed only by a giant.[45] The original hero in the tale may have a Canaanite hero, the god was El, and the angels were the pantheon of the gods.[46] This tradition was taken up in the Jacob cycle or by the Elohist in order to legitimate the sanctuary.[47] In the original Canaanite setting the story may very well have been about an incubated dream, for we find such accounts at Ugarit. But whether our present account can be called an incubation dream is doubtful. Jacob does not sacrifice or go through rites in order to receive such a dream. The attempt to call it an unintentional incubation dream may also be misdirected. The Israelite

narrator may have masked that aspect of the tradition, and Jacob's surprise at the dream experience is meant to remove any suspicion of deliberate incubation. The lack of intentionality removes this dream from the category of incubation dreams.[48]

What is the ladder observed by Jacob? It may have been suggested by the stones piled upon each other in this old Middle Bronze sanctuary. The word for ladder, sll, is a hapax legomenon, which may mean "to heap up." In Egyptian texts there is a celestial ladder which deceased pharaohs are said to ascend, and the image may reflect strong influence of a solar religion in Egypt, for the rays of the sun suggest such a ladder. When Jacob calls this place the gate to heaven, he may have been using Egyptian terminology.[49] However, there is an Akkadian word, simmiltu, which means "stairway," and it is a cognate of slm, which may mean "step, slab." Sumerian mythology has a gate of heaven in the story of "Nergal and Ereshkigal," where the viziers of the great gods ascend and descend the long stairway of heaven between the realm of the underworld and the gate of Anu, Enlil, and Ea.[50] Unlike the ladder in Egypt upon which men could travel, the Sumerian ladder permitted passage only of gods, which is more comparable to the ladder in Genesis 28, where the celestial messengers of God travel to all the peoples of the earth.[51] It is probable that the motif may have come from Mesopotamia into Canaanite mythology, and from that source it was absorbed by the Jacob cycle in an effort to legitimate the Bethel shrine as an Israelite sanctuary early in the history of the divided kingdom.

The legitimation of the shrine seems to be the point of the text by virtue of other motifs. The narrative is the closest parallel to a covenant in the epic tradition.[52] Jacob promises to build a pillar for the cult of the god upon his return, and this may refer to a pilgrimage that may have linked the two sanctuaries of Shechem and Bethel together during the days of the divided monarchy.[53] The Elohist may have recounted a tradition in order to legitimate a different sanctuary than the one at which calf worship was advocated, for he is reluctant to localize the sanctuary as the Yahwist did in Genesis 12:8.[54]

Resch analyzes the dream as an attempt by Jacob's subconscious to relieve his anxiety about the future. The assurance of blessing given to him by Isaac is not sufficient; he needs divine assurance before he can feel at ease.[55]

The Bethel dream is somewhat abbreviated. Richter observes that in the main body of the dream, there is no message, only a picture. Furthermore, there is no

interpretation of the image; instead, the pericope gives an interpretation to the place, Bethel.[56]

The basic elements are fragmentary in Genesis 28:12-15. These include: 1) dream reference, 28:12, "And he dreamed," wayyaḥᵃlōm, 2) introduction, 28:12, "behold," wᵉhinnēh, 3) theophany, 28:13, "the Lord stood above it," YHWH niṣṣob ᶜālā(y)w, 4) auditory message reference, 28:13, "And he said," wayyōʾmer, 5) self-identification of the deity, 28:13, "I am Yahweh, God of your father Abraham and God of Isaac," ʾᵃnî YHWH ʾᵉlōhê ʾabrāhām ʾābîkā wᵉʾᵉlōhê yiṣḥāq, 6) the message, a promise of blessing, 28:15-16, and 7) formal termination, 28:16, "And Jacob awoke," wayyîqaṣ yaᶜᵃqōb.

The formal structure common to other dreams in the Elohist may have been lost in this pericope during transmission. Perhaps the Elohist received a tradition which he did not choose to alter, or perhaps his format was lost when it was added to Yahwist material by later redaction.

Genesis 31:10-17

This is the first of two dreams found within the chapter, one is experienced by Jacob, the other by Laban. Elohistic material is located in 31:2, 4-18a, 19-24, 26, 28-45, 53-55.[57] The Elohist sanctions the trickery of Jacob by giving it divine origin in a dream. Ehrlich calls this dream a "command dream." Resch believes this dream arises out of Jacob's feelings of guilt, for he needs a divine mandate to justify his theft of sheep.[58]

The important components are: 1) time, 31:10, "And it came to pass at that time," wayᵉhî bᵉᶜēt, 2) visual theophany, 31:10, "I lifted up my eyes and I saw," waʾeśśāʾ ᶜēnāy wāʾēreʾ, 3) dream reference, 31:10, "in a dream," baḥᵃlōm, repeated in 31:11, 4) auditory message, 31:11, "And the angel of God said to me," wayyōʾmer ʾēlay malʾak hāʾᵉlōhîm, 5) recipient, 31:11, "Jacob" (vocative), yaᶜᵃqōb, 6) dialogue/-response, 31:11, "Here am I," hinnēnî, 7) self-identification of the deity, 31:12, "And he said, 'I am the God of Bethel,'" ʾānōkî hāʾēl bêt-ʾēl, and 8) divine message, a command, 31:13.

69

Genesis 31:24

Laban's dream is short and simple; it conforms even more to the Elohist's pattern than does Jacob's. If Laban worshipped a god other than Yahweh, then we would have another Abimelech type dream, where God appears to someone other than one of His chosen people. Ehrlich defines this as a "pure warning dream" in addition to being a command dream, for Laban receives both a warning and a command in this message.[59] This is an Israelite tradition about Laban, the father of the Arameans. The good relations between these two may indicate that the story is prior to the Aramean wars of the Eighth Century; then the entire Elohist epic might be thus dated. The archaic treaty between the two men may have included an appeal to their respective gods, but the reworked text has[60] made it appear as though both men worshipped Yahweh. If Laban worshipped another god, was there a tradition about his reception of a dream from that deity? This is probably not the case, for Laban's dream closely conforms to the Elohist's format, and one suspects it to be a literary format; he could supply a free creation in proper form for his narrative. This reemphasizes the primary literary nature of all these dream reports.

The various components of the dream are: 1) theophany, 31:24, "And God came," wayyābō $^{)}$ $^{)e}$lōhîm, 2) recipient, 31:24, "to Laban, the Aramean," $^{)}$el-lābān hā$^{)a}$rammî, 3) dream reference, 31:24, "in dream," bah^{a}lōm, 4) time, 31:24, "by night," hallāy^{e}lāh, 5) auditory message, 31:24, "And he said to him," wayyō$^{)}$mer, and 6) message, 31:24.

Genesis 46:1-7

This account has evidence of two sources, for in 46:1a the patriarch Israel takes his departure on his own initiative, but in 46:1b it seems that a revelation from God was necessary to encourage the patriarch Jacob to leave Palestine. This revelation comes through a "cult of the God of the fathers," for[61] he sacrificed to the "God of Isaac" at Beersheba's shrine. The elaboration of this account by Josephus makes the[62] experience seem more like an incubation dream, and modern commentators have followed[63] his example by considering it a clear example of incubation. The presence of sacrifice makes it possible that incubation was involved. It may have been the intent of the narrator to suggest that such a dream theophany was deliberately sought by the patriarch.

70

The basic components are: 1) auditory reference, 46:2, "And God spoke," wayyōᵓmer ᵓelōhîm, 2) recipient, 46:2, "to Israel," leyiśrāᵓēl, 3) dream reference, 46:2 "in visions," bemarᵓōt, 4) time, 46:2, "of the night," hallāyelāh, 5) auditory theophany, 46:2 "And he said, 'Jacob, Jacob,'" wayyōᵓmer yacaqōb yacaqōb, 6) dialogue/human response, 46:2, "Here am I," hinnenî, 7) self-identification of the deity, 46:3, "I am God, the God of your father," ᵓānōki hāᵓēl ᵓelōhê ᵓābîkā, and 8) divine message, a command 46:3-4.

The passage is also truncated, for it lacks several of the forms. What is interesting is that it shares the vocative address of the recipient and the response with Genesis 28, I Samuel 3, and Exodus 3. Obviously these cannot be motifs from a call narrative; rather they are items common to different theophanies, and frequently they may be found in dream theophanies as a way of following the dream structure.

Thus there are five particular dreams in Genesis 20, 28, 31, and 46 which constitute the core of the Elohist's auditory message dream pattern. Several other possible dream references seem to share part of this structure. In addition, there are two dream experiences in the Balaam cycle, which may or may not be from the Elohist, which also share this format.

Numbers 22:8-13, 19-21

These two night dreams of Balaam come from old epic traditions; and they may have had a separate existence in a cycle of Balaam stories, or stories about Israel's entrance into the arable land. The entire chapter is a conflation of Yahwist and Elohist according to most scholars for there are several doublets and inconsistencies.[64] Numbers 22:19-21 is inconsistent with 22:22-35, for in the former section the Lord permits Balaam to go, but in the latter the Lord is angry that he went.[65] This becomes a starting point for the division of the material. The dream material is usually considered to be Elohist by the commentators, since dreams are characteristic of that source.[66]

Balaam is a mysterious and unidentified seer, who is a prophet of God according to the narrator. Noth believes he was a seer of a foreign deity from a distant land; where the traditions have been appropriated by both the Yahwist and Elohist, they are testifying to Yahweh's universality.[67]

71

Balaam receives two separate theophanies in regard to the mission of Barak. The dream components in 22:8-13 include: 1) time, 22:8, "this night," hallaylāh, 2) theophany, 22:9, "God came," wayyābōʾ ʾeʹlōhîm, 3) recipient, 22:9, "to Balaam," ʾel-bilʿām, 4) auditory message, 22:9, "And he said," wayyōʾmer, and 22:12, "And God said unto Balaam," wayyōʾmer ʾeʹlōhîm ʾel-bilʿ ām, 5) introductory question, 22:9, 6) human dialogue, 22:10-11, 7) divine message, a command, 22:12-13, and 8) formal termination, 22:13, "And Balaam arose in the morning," wayyāqom bilʿām babōqer. Similar components are found in 22:20-21: 1) time reference, 22:20, "at night," laylāh, 2) theophany, 22:20, "God came," wayyābōʾ ʾeʹlōhîm, 3) recipient, 22:20, "to Balaam, ʾel-bilʿām, 4) auditory message, 22:20, "And he said to him," wayyōʾmer lô, 5) divine message, a command, 22:21, and 6) formal termination, 22:21, "And Balaam arose in the morning," wayyāqom bilʿām babōqer.

The use of formal terms like "the deity came" and the phrase, "the deity came to NN and he said," are very similar to the particular style used by the Elohist in his dream format. Thus critics may be somewhat justified in seeing this material as being related to the Elohist.

Consideration of Numbers 24:4, 16 is appropriate at this point. This reference to ecstatic reception of revelation in the Balaam oracle might have some indirect relation to the dreams in Numbers 22. The text reads, "who saw a vision of the Almighty, (while) falling (into a trance?) with open eyes," ʾaʹšer maḥzēh šadday yeḥzeh nōpēl ûgeʹlûy ʿēnāyim. The meaning of nōpēl is part of the problem. If the word refers to sleeping in bed, it would establish a link with Numbers 22:8-13, 20-21. It may refer to falling down in awe (Ezekiel 1:26, Judges 13:20) or being overpowered by the spirit in ecstasy (Isaiah 8:11, Ezekiel 3:14, I Samuel 19:24). The text does not offer us enough data, so we cannot determine the answer. If the oracle of Balaam is to be closely associated with earlier traditions, the former option is preferable. Some believe that this was an incubation oracle.[68] The phrase "open eyes" may refer to either the fluttering of eyes during the dream experience or to inner sight, the perception of what normal people cannot see. Again, we have too little data to determine the answer. It is

difficult to determine whether Balaam is referring to a dream theophany with this expression.[69] The passage is interesting, but it only raises new questions.

Lichtenstein's Criticism

Murray Lichtenstein has voiced strong criticism against the evaluation of dream theophanies in the Elohist. He believes a false and circular argument has been developed. Dream theophanies are said to be found in the Elohist because all the texts have been classifed as Elohist texts, but the original classification of these texts is often determined by criteria such as the presence of dream reports. According to Lichtenstein there are not two different sources in the Pentateuch, but source criticism has falsely established the existence of the Elohist upon the basis of such circular arguments. The Yahwist is typified by anthropomorphic language in describing God, and the revelation may be described as corporeal, since God often comes physically to the recipient. In the Elohist God is distant and the revelation is auditory, non-corporeal, and more theologically advanced than in the Yahwist. Lichtenstein challenges the view that the use of a dream theophany represents a theological advance over the anthropomorphic imagery of the Yahwist. Furthermore, he claims that the division of revelatory experiences into these two categories is wrong, for ancient Near Eastern dreams have both auditory and corporeal revelation mixed together in the same experience. He believes that throughout the ancient Near East the distinction between dreams and corporeal revelation is a matter of literary convention, not ideological necessity. This mixture of two modes of revelation is found in Ugaritic dreams where El speaks and touches the recipient, Keret. Mari documents also show a mixture of revelatory experience, and even Numbers 12:4-9 is adduced to demonstrate this plurality. Lichtenstein analyzes various passages to show the inconsistency of source critics in evaluating texts. Genesis 26:24 refers to a dream, but it is almost always viewed as Yahwist. Genesis 28 is falsely divided between the Elohist (verses 12, 17-18) and the Yahwist (verses 13-16); it is really one literary unit. This typifies the fallacy of trying to divide the text into two sources. Thus Lichtenstein concludes that the dream theophany is not[70] a stylistic characteristic of the Elohist, for there is no Elohist.

Lichtenstein's arguments have several significant weaknesses. First, he seems to assume that dream experiences are a significant or the single criterion for source criticism. This is false. No one criterion would establish the existence of an epic tradition, but rather, numerous criteria of words, expressions, images, proper names, and theological concepts

constitute a source by their integral relationship. Their concurrent occurrence in certain texts as opposed to other texts with a different set of words, images, and ideas establishes those texts as part of a given source. These criteria are never used in isolation. Dream theophanies occur in texts with many other indications of Elohist narrative formulation. Lichtenstein's observations of ancient Near Eastern material are suspect. As we have noted, ancient Near Eastern dreams do not mix revelational patterns as a rule. The mode of revelation in dream reports is non-physical, auditory, and the deity is passive. Not until later Greek dreams do the deities engage in physical activity. His example of the Keret dream is based on a dubious translation of the Ugaritic text, which has been effectively challenged.[71] His allusion to the Mari examples is vague, and he offers not one specific example to prove his point. One might surmise he is referring to the dream report wherein the recipient is transferred to a shrine in a different city, but no reference is made to the deity's physical contact or physical revelation. Finally, Numbers 12:4-9 does mention several different modes of divine revelation. But this is not a text in which actual revelation occurs; it merely mentions the various types. Individual texts will cast a revelational experience into a given form, and a dream theophany is such a form. The Elohist uses that form, and his dream reports show a peculiar style. Other accounts with possible allusions to dream theophanies, which occur in the Yahwist tradition, lack the stylistic peculiarities of the more complete Elohist dream format. Lichtenstein has failed to perceive this form critical observation about the texts. The texts which we have observed fit a particular pattern. Where that form is best exemplified, (Genesis 20, 31, 46), there is no mention of Yahweh's corporeal revelation. Those same texts in the Yahwist are truncated or do not show the form critical development of the Elohist texts. This use of the dream theophany by the Elohist corresponds to his theological concerns, and thus it is integrated into the Elohist literary structure as a whole.

Elohist Dream Pattern Analyzed

It is necessary to draw all the previously discussed data together in a brief summary in order more clearly to show the legitimacy of this evalution. The most common and basic formula is found in Genesis 20, "And the Lord came to Abimelech in a night dream and said to him, 'Behold you . . . . '" This embodies the basic elements of theophany, recipient, time, dream reference, address and introductory hinnēh. It lacks only the reference to place, but the reader knows from the context of the epic narration that the place is Gerar.

74

Hence, in all of the Elohist's dreams the setting is not part of the formula. This implies that the form critical structure comes with the creation of the epic; it is not a form which exists in the story prior to the creation of the on-going narrative of the epic. Thus this form is a literary form; that is, it is a tool of the narrator of the traditions, whether the source was written or oral. It is not a form that was found in the story before its absorption by the epic cycle. In all biblical dreams only I Kings 3:5 has the setting formula, "in Gibeon." The dream in Genesis 28 adds something not found in Genesis 20: the deity gives self-identification and promise. Dream messages give either promise and assurance or a command. The latter falls into two categories, direction (Genesis 31:11-17, 46:3) or warning (Genesis 20:3, 31:24). The message may include pious dialogue (Genesis 20:4-5, 46:3, Numbers 22:10, Kings 3:6-14). The dream message may include self-identification (Genesis 28:13, 31:13, 46:3). Finally, there is usually a conclusion to the effect that the dreamer awoke. The rest of the epic narrative informs the audience as to the eventual outcome of the dream.

Oppenheim's outline of the ancient Near Eastern message dream contained the following components:

I. Setting

    A. Who
    B. When
    C. Where
    D. Conditions under which the dream came

II. Dream Content

III. End of the dream and reaction

IV. Fulfillment

This author has observed and formulated a similar pattern in the Elohist, which can be outlined as follows:

I. Theophany

II. Recipient

III. Dream reference

IV. Time

V. Auditory address formula

VI. Message

    A. Introductory formula, or particle <u>hinneh</u>
    B. Divine self-identification
    C. Assurance and promise/warnings/commands
    D. Dialogue

VII. Formal termination

A composite analysis of the texts reveals the following pattern in the various dream theophanies (including non-Elohist texts):

Theophany

Gen. 20:3	And God came, <u>wayyābōʾ ʾeˀlōhîm</u>
Gen. 28:13	And the Lord stood above it, <u>YHWH</u> <u>niṣṣob ʿālā(y)w</u>
Gen. 31:11	the angel of God, <u>malʾak-hāʾeˀlōhîm</u>
Gen. 31:24	And God came, <u>wayyābōʾ ʾeˀlōhîm</u>
Gen. 46:2	And God spoke, <u>wayyōʾmer ʾeˀlōhîm</u>
Num. 22:9	And God came, <u>wayyābōʾ ʾeˀlōhîm</u>
Num. 22:20	And God came, <u>wayyābōʾ ʾeˀlōhîm</u>
I Kg. 3:5	the Lord appeared, <u>nirʾāh YHWH</u>

Recipient

Gen. 20:3	to Abimelech, <u>ʾel-ʾaˀbîmelek</u>
Gen. 31:11	to me, <u>ʾēlay</u>
Gen. 31:24	to Laban, the Aramean, <u>ʾel-lābān hāʾaˀrammî</u>
Gen. 46:2	to Israel, <u>leˀyiśrāʾēl</u>
Num. 22:9	to Balaam, <u>ʾel-bilʿām</u>
Num. 22:20	to Balaam, <u>ʾel-bilʿām</u>
I Kg. 3:5	to Solomon, <u>ʾel-sˀeˀlōmōh</u>

Dream Reference

Gen. 20:3	in a night dream, bah^{a}lôm-hallay^{e}lāh
Gen. 20:16	in a dream, bah^{a}lôm
Gen. 28:12	and he dreamed, wayyah^{a}lôm
Gen. 31:10	in a dream, bah^{a}lôm
Gen. 31:11	in a dream, bah^{a}lôm
Gen. 31:24	in a night dream, bah^{a}lōm-hallay^{e}lāh
Gen. 46:2	in visions of the night, b^{e}mar'ōt-hallaylāh
I Kg. 3:5	in a night dream, bah^{a}lôm-hallāy^{e}lāh

Time

Gen. 20:3	in a night dream, bah^{a}lôm-hallāy^{e}lāh
Gen. 31:24	in a night dream, bah^{a}lōm-hallāy^{e}lāh
Gen. 46:2	in visions of the night, b^{e}mar'ōt-hallaylāh
Num. 22:20	at night, laylāh
I Kg. 3:5	in a night dream, bah^{a}lôm-hallāy^{e}lāh

Address Formula

Gen. 20:3	And He said to him, wayyō'mer lô
Gen. 20:3	And God said to him, wayyō'mer 'ēlā(y)w 'e^{e}lōhîm
Gen. 28:13	And He said, wayyō'mer
Gen. 31:11	(angel of God) said to me, wayyō'mer 'ēlay
Gen. 31:12	And He said, wayyō'mer
Gen. 31:24	And He said to him, wayyō'mer lô

Gen. 46:2	And He said,	wayyōʾmer
Num. 22:9	And He said,	wayyōʾmer
Num. 22:20	And He said to him,	wayyōʾmer lô
I Kg. 3:5	And God said,	wayyōʾmer ʾᵉlōhîm

Message

A. Introduction

Gen. 20:3	behold, you,	hinnᵉkā
Gen. 31:11	Jacob (vocative),	yaᶜᵃqōb
Gen. 46:2	Jacob, Jacob (vocative),	yaᶜᵃqōb yaᶜᵃqōb

B. Divine self-identification

Gen. 28:13   I am Yahweh, God of your father Abraham and God of Isaac, ʾᵃnî YHWH ʾᵉlōhē ʾabrāhām ʾābîkā wᵉʾlōhē yiṣḥaq

Gen. 31:13   I am the God of Bethel, ʾānōkî hāʾēl bēt-ʾēl

Gen. 46:3   I am God, the God of your father, ʾānōkî hāʾēl ʾᵉlōhē ʾabîkā

B. Type of Communication

1. Assurance and promise   Gen. 28:13-15
Gen. 46:2-3
I Kg. 3:5-15

2. Directions   Gen. 31:12
Gen. 46:2-3
Num. 22:20

3. Warning   Gen. 20:3
Gen. 31:24

C.   Dialogue

Gen. 20:4-5   response is lengthy
Gen. 31:11   simple response, hinnênî
Gen. 46:2   simple response, hinnênî
Num. 22:10-11   lengthy response to question
I Kg. 3:5-15   lengthy response to question

Conclusion

Gen. 20:8   And Abimelech awoke in the morning,
                 wayyaškēm Ꞌaᵇîmelek bab̄ōqer

Gen. 28:16   And Jacob awoke, wayyîqaṣ yaᶜaq̄ōb

I Kg. 3:15   And Solomon awoke, wayyîqaṣ šᵉlōmōh
                 And behold, it was a dream, wᵉhinnēh haᵃlôm

    Why was the dream format important to the Elohist?   He
had a theological dilemma with his view of a transcendent God
who demanded obedience and inspired fear.   How could this God
make His will known to men from His position of transcendence?
The dream was one of the choices the Elohist used to describe
God's theophanic relationship to people.   For his purposes he
chose the ancient Near Eastern auditory message dream format,
and he developed his own particular formulas in that pattern.
He could omit reference to locale, since context provided that.
He emphasized promise and assurance, shortened the conclusion, and left the fulfillment of the dream to be revealed in the
later epic narrative.

Dreams in Historical Literature

    Outside the patriarchal narratives there are few dreams.
Three alone remain for us in the Deuteronomistic History,
Judges 7:13-15, I Kings 3:5-15, and I Samuel 3.   Only I Kings
3 bears any affinity to the pattern of the Elohist, as we have
shown by including that text in the previous evaluation.   I
Samuel 3 follows the basic auditory message dream pattern, but
it lacks the particular idiom, "and God came to NN in a night
dream and he said, 'Behold, ... '" This is an argument
against those who would include I Samuel 3 in an enlarged
Elohist source simply because it is a dream theophany.   Judges
7:13-15 stands apart from the other two, for it is a symbolic
dream with no spoken message.   It has a pattern which relates
closely to the Joseph dreams.

Wolfgang Richter has evaluated biblical dreams in an effort to determine their structure. His results have given us an excellent format by which to evaluate symbolic dreams. We shall thus use his format in the evaluation of Judges 7:13-15 and the symbolic dreams in the Joseph cycle and Daniel. Richter believes that his pattern fits both the patriarchal dreams and the Joseph dreams, but he fails to note the distinction between ancient message and symbolic dreams, especially as noted by Oppenheim. For this reason his structure is imposed upon the patriarchal dreams. They appear to be very truncated in his dream structure, while the Joseph dreams correspond closely. This author would simply reply that Richter's structure is effective only in evaluating symbolic dreams, while the patriarchal dreams closely correspond to auditory message dreams. The structure of patriarchal dreams is not truncated; they have their own structure, as this work has just demonstrated. Richter's pattern actually uses Judges 7:13-15 as the "basic form." He produced the following structure:

I. Announcement of the Dream

II. Introductory Dream Formula
III. Dream corpus: Image or Expression

> In the development of the Image there is always a Result. The Image is often a nominal sentence, and the Result is composed of clauses. Some dreams have two Results with an additional Result from both Images. This is found in the Joseph dreams in Genesis 41, Pharaoh's dreams.

IV. Meaning of the Dream

> A. Formula of Interpretation
> B. Corpus of Interpretation
> 1. Identification: a nominal sentence
> 1. Meaning: a clause

V. Fulfillment of the Dream[72]

Judges 7:13-15

This little episode is inserted into the cycle of Gideon tales. The dream and its interpretation typify the principles of elementary oneiromancy. Significant words and symbols have a one-to-one correspondence, which, when they are decoded, give the dreamer an interpretation. The tent is a symbol of nomads, the Midianites; the barley cake is a product of settled farmers,

the Israelites. The barley cake topples the tent[73] and that indicates the Israelites will defeat the Midianites. It is a simple literary device used to heighten the suspense of the narrative. However, Resch analyzes the dream as a precognitive experience; it is an expression of anxiety before the impending defeat in battle with the Israelites.[74]

The structure of the dream can be analyzed in Richter's categories in the following manner:

I. Announcement of the dream, 7:13, "behold I dreamed a dream," hinnēh h^{a}lôm ḥālamtî

II. Introductory formula, 7:13, "and behold," hinnēh

III. Dream corpus

    A. Image, 7:13, "a cake of barley fell into the camp of Midian" (nominal sentence)

    B. Result, 7:13, 1. "it came upon a tent" (clauses)
                          2. "it struck it and it fell"
                          3. "it turned it upside down, and the tent fell alongside it"

IV. Dream Interpretation, 7:14

    A. Formula of Interpretation, 7:14, "this is nothing else but," ᵓen zō²t biltî

    B. Interpretation, 7:14

        1. Identification, 7:14, "the sword of Gideon, son of Joash, a man of Israel"

        2. Meaning, 7:14, "for into his hand God has given Midian and all the camp"

I Kings 3:4-15 (II Chronicles 1:6-12)

This dream is the closest example of an incubation dream the Old Testament can offer.[75] Solomon goes to a shrine, offers a great sacrifice, sleeps overnight, and is not surprised

by the dream theophany, which implies he expected it. Resch discounts this as an incubation dream, for he feels there is no connection between the sacrifice in I Kings 3:4 and the actual dream in 3:5-15.[76] However, the present state of the text makes the connection, and it is difficult to deny that. Resch, led by his presupposition that incubation is not compatible with Old Testament theology, denies the presence of incubation in this text. Gaster believes this text merely records a general revelation through a dream, and it is not an incubated dream.[77]

Siegfried Herrmann has noted the great similarity of this passage with dream reports from Egypt. The account parallels the experience of Thutmosis IV, who fell asleep in the shadow of the sphinx, received an auditory message dream, hurried to the royal city, sacrificed, had a feast, and announced his legitimation to the court. Though we lack the texts, such a pattern was apparently recorded for Sesostris III of the Middle Kingdom and Thutmosis III of the New Kingdom. This indicates the presence of a genre which Herrmann believes was used for the legitimation of Solomon.[78] The emphasis in these reports is the legitimacy of succession and how the king was chosen as a little boy. Solomon calls himself a small child in I Kings 3:7, and a similar self description is given by Sesostris III and Thutmosis IV.[79] It is a term of ritual humiliation in Egypt, for Ramses II uses it in this fashion on this PiRamses inscription.[80] I Kings 3 begins Solomon's court history; the Succession Narrative was concluded in I Kings 2. Likewise, Thutmosis IV used his dream report to begin the Karnak inscription, the record of his reign.[81] So it appears that I Kings 3 may have been deliberately formulated along the lines of Egyptian models for royal succession. These Egyptian models are also dreams, which conform to the ancient Near Eastern pattern of dream accounts.

The date for this material is disputed. Herrmann dates it to the time of Solomon, because the similarity with Middle Kingdom and New Kingdom models is so great. He thinks it was a part of a royal ritual in Judah for years after Solomon's reign, and it included material from Psalms 2, 20, 21, 89, and Isaiah 9, 11.[82] Gray connects I Kings 3 with the royal ideology of Isaiah at the time of Hezekiah.[83] Kenik believes the text is a creation by the Deuteronomistic Historian, and this dates the material close to the exilic period. Kenik demonstrates that the text is an artistically created unity with literary inclusios, and the language and concepts found in the pericope betray Deuteronomistic thought blended together with some old traditional elements. It was the Deuteronomist who revived this old royal ritual form, and as with so many other key Deuteronomistically created texts (I Samuel 8, 12), it falls at a significant turning point in the history of God's people.[84] Moshe Weinfeld believes that the passage is a creation of the

Deuteronomist. His belief is conditioned upon the observation that the text is concerned with judicial wisdom. He feels that wisdom material owes its presence in the historical narratives to the Deuteronomic school of reform. He believes that this present text was put there by the Deuteronomist who displaced an old oracle about building the Temple, the act for which Solomon was initially famous. The attribution of wisdom to Solomon was a later development by the Deuteronomist.[85] The date of this material is significant. The dream format of I Kings 3 bears some similarity to the Elohist dream format. It could be that this dream was a prelude to the independent traditions about Solomon's court history. This would explain why the Deuteronomist included a pericope with the story of sacrifice at a shrine outside Jerusalem which has strong overtones of incubation involved in the process. Solomon may be using an old Canaanite shrine.[86] If so, this would be offensive to the Deuteronomist and would explain why the editorial comment in 3:2 takes effort to explain that the Temple had not yet been built, which thus renders the action of Solomon less offensive by Deuteronomistic standards. If the Deuteronomist has received these traditions, he probably has omitted some material, for II Chronicles 1:6 mentions that the sacrifice was performed on the brazen altar of the Lord which was at the Tabernacle of the congregation. The Deuteronomist may also have omitted explicit references to the incubational process of this account, but the present text still leaves the audience with the strong awareness that incubation may have been Solomon's access to divine revelation. However, despite these observations the literary and theological arguments advanced by Kenik are impressive. The present form of the text shows unmistakable Deuternomonistic influence, and the reader finds it difficult not to concur with her view. If the passage is a Deuteronomistic creation, that position would in part validate the view of this thesis, which posits that I Samuel 3 is a late literary creation, though not necessarily Deuteronomistic. To postulate the other dream report in the Deuteronomistic narrative is a late creation would lend support to the observation that Samuel's experience is a late literary creation.

Resch believes Solomon experienced this dream because he needed psychological encouragement after the initial resistance to his reign. As a religious man he sought divine affirmation in the dream experience.[87] Resch fails to perceive the theological purpose of the text; it validates the rule of Solomon. Likewise, he is unaware of corresponding parallels in Egyptian historical annals.

The chief components of the dream are: 1) location, 3:5, "in Gibeon," b^{e}gib^{c}ôn, 2) theophany, 3:5, "the Lord

appeared," nir'ah YHWH, 3) recipient, 3:5, "to Solomon," 'el-s'lomoh, 4) dream reference, 3:5, "in a dream," bah'alom, 5) time, 3:5, "at night," hallay'lah, 6) auditory revelation, 3:5, "And God said," wayyo'mer 'elohim, 7) introductory question, 3:6, 8) human response, 3:6-9, 9) divine message, assurance and promise, 3:10-14, and 10) formal termination, 3:15, "And Solomon awoke, and behold, it was a dream," wayyiqas s'lomoh w'hinneh h'alom.

Various Texts in Samuel

In I Samuel 28:6, 15 there are two references to the fact that the Lord did not answer by dreams, prophets, or the Urim. This text is so brief that we cannot deduce the existence of either a special class of dream oracles, dream interpreters, or dream incubation.[88] But the text does indicate dreams were a respectable form of revelation. This appears to be an old tradition, since it comes from the early Saul source, or pro-monarchical source. The parallel with the expression in Mursilis' Plague Prayer is intriguing, but little may be drawn from the comparison.

A few scholars believe that a reference in I Samuel 21:8 does refer to dream incubation. Doeg was "detained" before the Lord, and some believe he was an incubant at the shrine in Nob, who had come for a dream concerning some illness. This is deduced from comparable parallels in Jeremiah 36:5, "I am shut up in the house of the Lord," Nehemiah 6:10, I Kings 14:10, and several Arabic and Greek parallels.[89] But this appears to be stretching the text.

A dream may be involved in I Samuel 15:10-11 where Samuel cries to the Lord all night after receiving an initial revelation.[90] The text is too fragmentary to make this decision, however.

Conclusion

The attitude of epic and historical literature appears to be quite positive toward dreams as a mode of revelation. The epic narratives utilize the message dream format as a mode of describing the encounter with the divine. The historical sources also use dream accounts as literary formats. This implies that the dream was seen as a positive mode of

84

revelation. If these sources are early, then Israel's initial attitude was positive.

Prophetic Attitude toward Dreams

With the rise of prophetic literature a more critical attitude toward dreams comes to the fore. The early prophets, like Balaam, may have been open to dream experiences, but this decreases with the rise of classical prophecy. Several scholars speculate that early prophets received dreams. They propose that this form of revelation and other forms of divination separate the seer from the prophet.[91] In contrast it appears that the classical prophets did not use dream revelation.[92] Zechariah's night visions may be dreams, but the text does not indicate this. Kaufmann postulates that the dream revelation of the early seers may have evolved into later prophetic visions,[93] like those of Zechariah. If so, they have lost their peculiar nature as dreams. A more critical attitude toward the dream as a medium of revelation may have caused this shift.

Isaiah 29:7-8

In this passage the prophet views dreams as ephemeral, a delusion that fades with the arousal of the sleeper. Like other comparisons (Psalm 73:20, 126:1, Job 20:8) dreams are considered less than real with the object of their comparison. There may have been dream diviners in the cosmopolitan court of Hezekiah, but the court prophet Isaiah seems to view dreams negatively. In this passage the awakening of Jerusalem from the nightmare of siege is like the disillusionment of the Assyrians. Dream and vision are linked in this passage for the first time.[94]

Deuteronomy 13:2-6

This passage belongs to the section on prophetic attitudes because of the close relationship of Deuteronomic reform and the prophetic critique. It is difficult to say how early this proclamation might be. The statement may reflect the reforming stance of the late Seventh Century Deuteronomic school, which sought to return to an exclusive faithfulness to Yahweh and His Word. To this end many former practices were excluded because they carried the danger of apostasy. Dreams as a medium of revelation among the nations had a taint to them, even though they may have been used and accepted by earlier theologians in Israel. The prophetic word had to be safeguarded from the inroads of the false prophet. This had been a problem throughout the ages, as demonstrated by the

affair with Micaiah ben Imlah (I Kings 22). This text is trying to establish a criterion by which false prophets may be condemned.[95]

The text may reflect an early awareness that dreams are unacceptable divination, because they lie outside essential Yahwism.[96] Ehrlich would limit this by saying the passage was directed only against professional diviners from an early period, but prophets could receive dreams.[97] The text speaks of a "dreamer of dreams," who seeks to lead Israel away from the Lord. It is difficult to determine if this deliberate apostasy was hyperbole on the author's part, or if the dreamers did advocate worship of other deities, such as a dream deity. So we cannot be certain if the passage condemned all dream divinators, including prophets of Israel who received dreams, or just a certain professional class, who might be more open to foreign influence and thus more liable to lead Israel to apostasy.

The stress on faithfulness to Yahweh and the discernment of true revelation reflects the turmoil of an era which has struggled with the issue of who is a true prophet. The prophet needs the confirmation of a sign in order to speak, but even false prophets can claim dreams. Therefore, this passage advocates a theological criterion by which to evaluate the prophets. This is ultimately the problem of Jeremiah, for he felt himself to be a faithful prophet to the Lord, and other prophets had supposed signs from the Lord, including dreams.[98] Thus the passage has a negative attitude toward dreams because of their association with false prophecy, be they either from foreign prophets or perverted prophets of Israel. Dreams are not rejected as a possible means of revelation, but one must be very critical of them.[99]

Numbers 12:6-8

This very difficult passage is taken from epic literature, but it is in this section because of its concern for the prophetic role of Moses. The rebellion of Aaron and Miriam against Moses is the foil for the vindication of Moses' prophetic role. With two strands in this account we discern two charges brought against Moses, his marriage to a Cushite woman and his[100] exclusive claim to the divine Word. Both strands culminate with this oracle, which affirms Moses as the intimate confidant of God.

Dreams seem to receive a positive evaluation in this pericope upon initial consideration. They stand as a form of revelation along with visions (mar'ōt). In actuality, the text may view dreams as an inferior form of revelation compared to

86

the authority of the prophetic office exemplified in Moses. Considered inferior to the reception of the prophetic Word, dreams become liable to the criticism of Jeremiah. If Moses is the model for all true prophets, then true prophets function without such a medium as dreams. However, Noth and others feel the text describes Moses as superior to all other prophets, who must then content themselves with lesser forms of revelation such as dreams.[101] In that case dreams are a valid form of revelation. In the final analysis the text is ambiguous, and the information is too limited to make a decision.

Jeremiah 23:25-32, 27:9-10, 29:8-9[102]

Some scholars believe that Jeremiah was not excluding dreams as a possible mode of revelation; only their false usage by lying prophets is condemned. They point to the passage, "The prophet who has a dream, let him faithfully speak my word," as testimony that dreams were positively viewed as a mode of revelation.[103] Dreams can be easily abused; they must be scrutinized carefully, but they should not be rejected altogether. However, most scholars are of the opinion that Jeremiah rejected dreams as a medium of revelation completely.[104] Jeremiah never received a Word of the Lord by a dream. His attitude was that dreams are totally subjective. The call for their verification in 23:28 may be sarcasm, for he knew they could not be substantiated. By their very content the dreams show themselves to be false, and they come from false prophets.[105] Dreamers having such visions stand in opposition to the true Word of the Lord; they concoct such dreams to lead the people into error.[106] Dreams serve only the purpose of building false hopes and meeting the needs of politicians who seek their security.[107] They uplift the false prophets in the eyes of the people. Dream revelations must have made a significant impact upon the people to so arouse Jeremiah's response. But the issue is tied up with a greater conflict in Jeremiah's prophetic ministry: who is a true prophet? Jeremiah had self doubts, and he experienced the failure of his own proclamation. His critique of dreaming prophets was his attempt to defend his own ministry. We shall never penetrate the subjectivity of this debate, for we have only Jeremiah's side of the issue, and we realize that even the entire prophetic movement never came to a conclusive criterion for discerning true and false prophets.[108]

Jeremiah's criticism of dreams was the most severe of all the prophets. It may mark a turn in Israel's understanding of dream revelation, for much of the prophetic material after this is critical. Ehrlich believes the Deuteronomic reform movement is responsible for the demise of dream revelation. Reform which closed local shrines removed places for dream incubation

to occur.[109]   Yet the history compiled by the Deuteronomistic Historian contains two stories, which are not only dream revelations, but have suspicious overtones of incubation.

Isaiah 65:3-4

The Septuagint interprets the concept of keeping vigil in graves as being for the purpose of dream visions, dia enupnia. Many commentators view this as the intent of the Hebrew also.[110]   If so, this is a prophetic polemic again the practice of dream incubation. It is difficult to say if this was a practice coming back into vogue after the exile, or if it was a new custom learned from the Babylonians in exile. Its inclusion with other questionable acts reflects the low esteem in which it was held by Trito-Isaiah.

Zechariah 10:2

Deutero-Zechariah contains another post-exilic criticism of the dream, for it is included with other forms of false revelation. Hanel believes he sees a distinction between false and true dreams in the text. False dreams are to be avoided, but dreams by themselves can be good. But Ehrlich responds that the Hebrew in this text implies dreams are false by their very nature.[111]   The text says nothing positive about dreams, and its inclusion with other forms of false prophecy warrants that conclusion.

Joel 3:1

The last prophetic reference is extremely positive in its view of dreams as revelation. It envisions the day when dream revelation will be the possession of all people. It departs from the usual criticism of prophetic literature, for it belongs to the genre of apocalyptic literature. The affinity with Daniel in its positive assessment demonstrates the high view apocalyptic had of dreams. This passage must be discounted in the overall prophetic critique, for it reflects theological concerns of a later day and age.

Joseph and Daniel Dreams

These two groups of dreams are to be considered together because of their similarity. It appears that the author of Daniel copied the model offered in the Joseph cycle for his dreams. However, the dates for both works are debated.

General consensus places Daniel in its present form in the Second Century B.C. Though some affirm an early prehistory for the first six or seven chapters, most authors date the entire work to the time of the Maccabean Revolt.[112]

The date for the Joseph material is far more problematic. The material was divided between Elohist and Yahwist by many early literary critics. Doublets in Genesis 37, like Midianites and Ishmaelites, the roles of Judah and Reuben, Joseph in a well and sold as a slave, were attestations of two separate sources. In Genesis 39-40 there are several inconsistencies as to whether Joseph was first in Potiphar's house or in prison, and how long he stayed in prison. But the rest of the material in Genesis 39-50 appears to be in an excellent novel, distinguished from the rest of the patriarchal material in the epic literature by virtue of its dramatic unity, a clearly conceived plot, the conflict of character and circumstances, the triumph of moral and personal values, its freedom in handling the material, and the lack of association with shrines.[113] The baby who dreams of future greatness attains royal status, overcomes enemies, and is honored by parents is found in the legends of many cultures.[114] Motifs from ancient Near Eastern sources are also found in the story. Joseph's seduction parallels the Egyptian tales of "Bata and Anubis" and "Tale of Two Brothers." Joseph was the first born of a barren woman, a common motif. The seven year famine motif is found in texts of Pharaoh Djoser of the Third Dynasty, the Gilgamesh Epic, and in Ugarit.[115] This high literary quality of the novel has led some scholars to view the work as a product of the royal court of Solomon, a time of sophistication and enlightenment, while others have deduced that the work must be post-exilic, when other forms of the novel genre arise.

The essential unity of most of the material has led some to believe the novel is not to be divided among sources, at least not in its initial development. Gerhard von Rad advocates that the Joseph cycle was a wisdom creation which originated in the court of Solomon. The novel seeks to represent early wisdom's effort to give an idealized portrait of a state official for young aspiring civil servants in the royal court. The novel reflects the optimism, cosmopolitanism, and enthusiasm of the Solomonic enlightenment. As such it reflects Egyptian wisdom exemplified in the "Wisdom of Amenemope." It is free from the theologizing that is found in much of the Old Testament. This initial wisdom tale was taken over by both the Yahwist and the Elohist, and later a sensitive redactor brought both versions back together.[116] Von Rad's work is indirectly supported by some attempts to evaluate the historical background. Vergote compares the customs exhibited in the Joseph cycle and those of the Nineteenth Dynasty in Egypt.[117]

Recently criticism has arisen against this early date for the Joseph cycle. Ward warns against taking the material too literally. According to a literal interpretation of the text, Joseph was holding many positions at once, Overseer of the Granaries of Upper and Lower Egypt (grain distribution), Royal Seal Bearer (signet ring), the God's Father (Chief advisor to the Pharaoh), Great Steward of the Lord of the Two Lands (over Pharaoh's house), Foremost of the Courtiers (advisor), and Chief of the Entire Land (over all the land). Apparently this elevation of Joseph is a stylized version of Egypt's bureaucratic structure.[118] Whybray sees a flaw in von Rad's logic. For von Rad claims the Joseph cycle is an early wisdom creation, but he then posits the final form to a sensitive redactor. Whybray maintains it can be one or the other, but not both. For if the forms were fixed, the redactor could do little, and if the forms were not fixed, then the later redactor is the true artist and creator.[119] Donald Redford believes that the story is set in ideal times, but there are hints as to which period the story originates, the post-exilic period. He provides a list of fifty-two key post-exilic words and phrases, the reference to the use of money, and other motifs to connect the story to the Saite period of Egypt. This would explain the lack of reference to the earlier epic literature and patriarchal narratives. He analyzes the text to show there is no source division, but rather the doublets occur as a literary device to heighten the effect of the story. If the dreams of the Elohist are eliminated, then the Yahwist has nothing by which to develop the plot. The story is a unity as its literary style indicates. It may have been influenced by later Egyptian tales, for in those tales the generic use of the divine name, "god," is also found. The story may have wisdom motifs, but it is not wisdom in itself.[120] Criticism has been leveled against von Rad's definition of this material as wisdom. Ruppert has noted that Joseph's ability to interpret dreams is a polemic against Egyptian wisdom. Joseph uses no dream book, no native ability, but he relies on God's inspiration, for God alone can interpret dreams, men cannot. Pharaoh is led to perceive the impotence of native wise men, and the famous wisdom of Egypt fails to match that of the Hebrew boy. If the Joseph cycle is from early wisdom, how could this strong polemic be possible, especially since von Rad views wisdom as non-theological? Ruppert maintains that since this criticism results from the prophetic critique, then the Joseph cycle could only represent later wisdom at best.[121] Crenshaw has also lodged a protest against the definition of wisdom for the Joseph cycle. He is critical of any broad definition of wisdom which would seek to include diverse materials in this category merely because of the presence of a few similarities. Von Rad overlooks theological asseverations (Genesis 39:9) and the abundance of non-wisdom themes. He stresses debatable wisdom themes, which in reality may be found in many diverse genres of literature. Von Rad's

category of a wisdom world view is too vague a criterion by which to classify this cycle as wisdom literature.[122]

These criticisms of von Rad's position and the source analysis of the Joseph material render the date of this material tenuous. The novelistic nature of the material tends to affirm the late date proposed by Redford. Thus this author has included the Joseph dreams together with the Daniel material at a later date than epic and prophetic material. The great similarity between the two might suggest a proximity in date.

The symbolic dreams in the Joseph story are "simple, pictorial prefigurations of coming events," which present a silent scene with no divine address and a worldly content.[123] Despite the simplicity of the dreams, Joseph alone is able to understand his dreams and the dreams of the Egyptians. They are not an oracular revelation, but they have "a meaning in themselves which is open to human interpretation."[124] These dreams, simple though they may be, require an interpreter. Joseph is the interpreter, "the master of dreams." One authority views this as referring to a god of the dreams, and against this deity the prophetic movement had to struggle until the name became nothing more than a subordinate appellation, an attribute to Joseph.[125] Some scholars believe that the interpretation of symbolic dreams indicates the presence of wisdom, for the symbolic dream is a type of riddle, which has ciphers which need to be decoded. The interpreter must use mantic wisdom and participate in the symbol in order to perceive the inter-relationship of the component parts and the analogous relationship to reality.[126] However, the definition of wisdom is being stretched here. A symbolic dream may be a riddle, but its interpretation is not necessarily a wisdom function. Rather the mantic diviner, the oneirocritic, interprets the dream. As we have seen in the ancient Near East, the reputation of the oneirocritics was rather low, and their function should not be confused with the scribes or the sage.

Like other symbolic dreams the Joseph dreams are silent and contain no verbal message. The visionary may see himself in his dream, at least as a passive observer, and he will affirm his presence when he recites the dream. This is comparable to epic dreams, in the ancient Near East, like the dreams of Enkidu and Gilgamesh. The text omits any reference to the Lord's coming or His active sending of the dream. The dreams come in pairs, and this establishes their surety. They are interpreted by Joseph, who receives his interpretation from God. They can come to unbelievers as well as believers, but the former do not understand them.

Genesis 37

These two dreams have been exegeted to refer to many diverse things: later tribal relationships, Jeroboam's revolt, or Joseph's later grain policies.[127] Some scholars believe that these two dreams were totally unrelated, for while the first dream of the sheaves is a pastoral scene, the second dream seems alien to the situation, for it reminds the reader of the constellation of the Babylonian Zodiac.[128] However, this is not incongruous if the story is a late literary development. Others maintain the dream is a foreign element in the story, because not only are the symbols pagan; the story does not fit with the context, for Joseph's mother is dead.[129] But without this dream we have only a single dream, and symbolic dreams usually occur in pairs. We should not demand such great precision from the storyteller's symbols; the moon of the second dream might just as well refer to Joseph's other wife. Both dreams have the same interpretation, so it is obvious that one is a variation of the other, and this is the normal function that dreams in pairs perform.[130]

When the brothers try to get rid of Joseph, they may be seeking to free themselves from the power of his dreams. When they call him the dreamer, or the Lord of dreams, they may be attributing to him the power to cast a dream prediction that might threaten them. By destroying the dreamer, they render his prediction null and void, just as killing the prophet would prevent his oracle from attaining fulfillment, as was the experience of Jeremiah.[131]

Resch believes this indirect dream permitted Joseph to present the awareness of his future ascendancy over his parents and brothers tactfully.[132] Resch displays a lack of awareness concerning the difference between symbolic and message dreams, which renders his analysis of all the Joseph dreams inadequate.

Using Richter's structure for dream analysis, we may outline the components of the dream thus:

Sheaves in the Field

I. Announcement of the dream, 37:5-6, "and Joseph dreamed a dream . . . 'hear this dream which I have dreamed.'"

wayyaḥᵃlôm yôsēp ḥᵃlôm . . . šimᶜû-nāʾ haḥᵃlôm hazzeh ʾᵃšer ḥālāmᵉtî

92

II. Introductory dream formula, 37:7, "behold," w^ehinnēh

III. Dream corpus, 37:7

    A. Image, 37:7, "We were binding sheaves in the field"

    B. Result, 37:7, 1. "and behold my sheaf arose"
                          2. "and stood upright"
                          3. "and behold your sheaves stood around"
                          4. "and made obeisance to my sheaf"

IV. Dream interpretation, (none -- dream is self-understood)

V. Fulfillment, (comes later in the novel)

Stars in the Sky

I. Announcement of the dream, 37:9, "And he dreamed another dream . . . And he said, 'Behold, I have dreamed another dream.'"

wayyaḥ^alōm ʿôd ḥ^alôm ʾaḥēr . . . wayyōʾmer hinnēh ḥālamtî ḥ^alôm ʿôd

II. Introductory dream formula, 37:9, "behold," hinnēh

III. Dream Corpus, 37:9

    A. Image, 37:9, "the sun and the moon and the eleven stars made obeisance to me"

    B. Result (none)

IV. Dream interpretation, (none -- dream is self-understood)

V. Fulfillment, (comes later in novel)

Genesis 40:

    Joseph's method of interpretation is simple: a pleasant dream has good results, a bad dream has evil results, and there is a simple one-to-one correspondence. Joseph chides the

men for thinking that professional oneirocritics can interpret their dreams, and then he proceeds to demonstrate how God interprets dreams through him. Some view Joseph as a prophet, and they consider this part of the Elohist source.[133] Joseph selects parts of the dream for interpretation and omits others. He recognizes different meanings in similar dreams, builds them into a deceptive analogy, and then translates them with graceful sophistication.[134]

The issue again arises whether there are two dreams or one. The expressions, "they dreamed a dream both of them," (40:8), and "we dreamed a dream in one night, I and he," (41:11), lead some source critics to believe both men had the same dream; but the two different dreams may come from the Yahwist and the Elohist.[135] But those phrases probably mean to say that each man had his own dream with its respective meaning, thus "each according to the interpretation of his dream," (40:5, 41:1).[136] It is unwise to build evidence for source division out of such an ambiguous phrase.

Resch believes that the dreams of the butler and the baker reflect an unconscious awareness of their ultimate fates. If we knew more about their past actions we would see why they had the particular dreams they had.[137] Resch views the account as a simple history and misses the entire novelistic mood of the account.

The structure of the dreams may be analyzed according to Richter's format:

Butler's Dream

I. Announcement of the dream, 40:9, "in my dream," baḥ^alômî

II. Introductory dream formula, 40:9, "behold," w^ehinnēh

III. Dream corpus

    A. Background imagery, 40:9-10,

        1. Images, 40:9-10,
            a. "a vine was before me"
            b. "and in the vine were three branches"

        2. Result, 40:10, a. "and it was as

though it budded"
b. "and her blossoms
shot forth"
c. "and the cluster
brought forth
ripe grapes"

B. Image, 40:11, "and Pharaoh's cup was in my hand"

C. Result, 40:11, 1. "and I took the grapes"
2. "and pressed them into Pharaoh's cup"
3. "and I gave the cup into Pharaoh's hand"

IV. Dream interpretation

A. Formula of interpretation, 40:12, "this is the interpretation," zeh pitrōnô

B. Interpretation

1. Identification, 40:12, "the three branches are three days"
2. Meaning, 40:13, a. "yet within three days shall Pharaoh lift up your head"
b. "and restore you to the palace"
c. "and you will put Pharaoh's cup into his hand, after the former manner, when you were his butler"

V. Fulfillment of the dream, 40:20-21

Baker's Dream

I. Announcement of the dream, 40:16, "I also was in my dream"

ʾap-ʾᵃnî baḥᵃlōmî

II. Introductory dream formula, 40:16, "behold," wᵉhinnēh

95

III. Dream corpus

    A. Image, 40:16-17, 1. "And there were three baskets on my head"
2. "and in the upper basket there were all kinds of bakery goods for Pharaoh"

    B. Result, 40:17, "and the birds did eat them out of the basket on my head"

IV. Dream interpretation

    A. Formula of interpretation, 40:18, "this is the interpretation" zeh pitrōnô

    B. Interpretation

        1. Identification, 40:19, "and three baskets are three days"
        2. Meaning, 40:19, a. "yet within three days shall Pharaoh lift up your head from off you"
                b. "and shall hang you on a tree"
                c. "and the birds shall eat your flesh off you

    V. Dream fulfillment, 40:22

Genesis 41

Pharaoh has two dreams, or one dream message with two variations for the sake of certitude. The cows are simple images; they are not the goddess Hathor, for in the Greek[138] period the ideogram of a cow represents a year. For the prisoners the periods of time were days, for Pharaoh they are years. Pharaoh is merely a spectator, whereas the servants participated in their dreams. He seeks professional help; the Boharic translation reads "scribes in the house of life," the professional men who helped create later dream omina collections.[139] But they are unable to help, a sad comment upon them. Joseph is also viewed as a professional, but he states the ability is not in him but from God, and thus the narrator makes a significant point.[140] Joseph gives the interpretation not in esoteric mystery but in simple language. He then

proceeds to give simple political suggestions for averting disaster, which more than any dream interpretation creates a positive impression upon Pharaoh. The entire affair was done skillfully by Joseph, and this clever skill in interpretation was highly prized.[141]

Resch admits inability to analyze this dream, for he does not know enough about Pharaoh's personal life. The dream can be described only as a reflection of a ruler's concern with the welfare of his country.[142]

Several components in this dream belong also to the simple message dream patterns. The reference, "and he slept," wayyîšor in 41:5 is the kind of statement that is used to describe a step in the incubation dreams. In 41:7 the formal termination of message dreams is found with "and Pharaoh awoke," wayyîqas par‘ōh, as in Genesis 20:8, 28:15, 31:17, and I Kings 3:15, and "behold it was a dream," wᵉhinnēh hᵃlôm, as in I Kings 3:15. Thus I Kings 3:15 is the closest parallel to this text.

The following analysis may be obtained by using Richter's format:

Dream of Cows

I. Announcement of the dream, 41:1, "and Pharaoh dreamed,"

ûpar‘ōh ḥōlēm

II. Introductory dream formula, 41:1, "behold,"
wᵉhinnēh

III. Dream corpus

    A. Image #1, 41:1-2, 1. "he stood by a river"
                                2. "and there came up out of the river seven well favored and fat cows"

    B. Result #1, 41:3, "and they fed in a meadow"

    C. Image #2, 41:3, "seven other cows came up after them out of the water, ill favored and lean"

D. Result #3, 41:3, "and stood by the other cows at the edge of the river"

E. Result of both, 41:4, "and the ill favored and lean cows ate the seven well favored and fat cows"

IV. Dream interpretation is combined with the next dream.

Dream of the Corn

I. Announcement of the dream, 41:5, "he dreamed a second time"

wayyaḥ^{a}lôm šēnît

II. Introductory dream formula, 41:5, "behold," w^{e}hinnēh

III. Dream corpus

A. Image #1, 41:5, "seven ears of corn came upon one stalk, full and good"

B. Image #2, 41:6, "seven thin ears blasted by the east wind grew up after them"

C. Result of both, 41:7, "and the seven thin ears devoured the seven full and good ears"

Both dreams are retold by Pharaoh with minor variation in 41:17-24 in order to heighten the effect. Then Joseph gives the interpretation.

IV. Dream interpretation

A. Formula of interpretation, 41:25, 26, "the dream of Pharaoh is one," ḥ^{a}lôm par'ōh ʾeḥād hûʾ

B. Interpretation

1. Identification, 41:26-28,
   a. "the seven good cows are seven years"

b. "the seven good ears are good years"

c. "and the seven thin and ill-favored cows that followed are seven years"

d. "and the seven empty ears blasted with the east wind shall be seven years of famine"

2. Meaning, 41:29-31

a. "behold, there shall come seven years of great plenty through the land of Egypt"

b. "and there shall arise seven years of famine after them"

c. "and all the plenty shall be forgotten in the land of Egypt"

d. "and the famine shall consume the land"

e. "and the plenty shall not be known in the land by reason of the famine following"

f. "for it shall be grievous"

V. Dream fulfillment (comes in the following narrative)

Daniel's Dreams

There are a number of similarities between Joseph dreams and the Daniel dreams: 1) The interpreter was a man of God, who decoded the dreams not through his own ability but by the help of God (Daniel 2:21, 30, Genesis 40:8, 41:16); 2) the man of God came to the rescue after professional interpreters failed; 3) the course of history had been set by God (Daniel 2:28, 45, Genesis 41:28); 4) each motif in the dream has an equivalent meaning; 5) the interpretation of the dream is sure; 6) by his interpretation of the dream, the man of God is lifted from the lowly condition into which he fell, and he is given a position of honor (Daniel 2:47, Genesis 41:41); 7) the heathen recognize the true God (Daniel 2:47, Genesis 41:38; 8) court formulas are used: Joseph says, "God shall give Pharaoh an answer of peace," and Daniel says, "My Lord, may the dream be to them

who hate you and the interpretation to your enemies;" and 9) both use the concluding phrase, "it was a dream."

There are some differences. The Joseph dreams have symbols taken from real life, which express their meaning by extraordinary activity, but the Daniel dreams have fantastic[143] symbols, which are the product of a frenetic imagination. Daniel's dream are more elaborate than Joseph's. However, the similarities outweigh the differences. Daniel seems to have been patterned after Joseph to be the servant of God who can decode the symbolic dreams sent by God to a gentile king. Perhaps, the later Maccabean author of Daniel chose the distant setting of Chaldean Babylon because of the fame of Chaldean oneiromancy and the interest of Nabonidus in dreams.

Von Rad believes the similarity of these two stories reflects the actual[144] practice of dream interpretation in the Jerusalem court. Since Daniel is apocalyptic literature, von Rad believes that dream interpretation was the connecting link between wisdom and apocalyptic. Dream interpretation depends upon a predetermined future, and this view of reality is also seen to be[145] a connecting link between wisdom and apocalyptic. Thus apocalyptic grew out of wisdom, and this explains why Daniel was patterned after Joseph. His theory is tenuous. As seen before, the Joseph cycle may not really constitute wisdom. Von Rad defends his position on the common interest in dreams and determinism. He fails to take into account the influence of other movements upon apocalyptic, for the movement seems to have been eclectic drawing upon old mythology, foreign thought, prophetic ideas of justice, and other strains of thought. It is unlikely that apocalyptic grew out of wisdom, even though it might have taken a few conceptions.

Resch sees modern motifs in the dreams which are worthy of analysis. But he is unable to analyze the dream because not enough is known about the life situation of Nebuchadnezzar. Daniel's interpretation is a sound[146] psychological evaluation, and it may be due to telepathy.

The dreams of interest are in chapters 2-4. By chapter 7 the dreams have really become visions, and Daniel receives and interprets them. The dreams of chapters 2-4 are technically described as "visions of my[147] head upon my bed," which may be non-Semitic terminology.

The Daniel dreams may be analyzed as follows:

I. Announcement of the dream, 2:1, "and Nebuchadnezzar dreamed dreams," and 2:3, "I have dreamed a dream," ḥālam n^{e}bukadneṣṣar h^{a}lōmôt . . . h^{a}lôm hālām^{e}tî

II. Introductory dream formula, 2:31, "behold"

III. Dream corpus, 2:31-35

V. Dream interpretation, 2:36-45

    A. Formula of interpretation, 2:36, "we will tell the interpretation," ûpisrēh nē?mar

    B. Interpretation, 2:36-45

The author of the Daniel dreams also added certain stylistic phrases to indicate the certainty of dream fulfillment. These include: 1) 2:45, "the Great God has made known to the king what shall come to pass," and 2) 2:45, "the dream is sure, and the interpretation is to be trusted."

The pattern set by the dreams in chapter 2 again occurs in 3:31-4:34. The wise men fail to interpret the dreams, Daniel is called, he interprets the dreams, and fulfillment comes.

The material in the Joseph cycle and in Daniel has a positive attitude toward dreams. The material seems to be late, and it contrasts with the pejorative view of the prophets. However, if the Joseph material is early, it coincides with the early views of epic literature. There appears to have been a division in the views of post-exilic writers concerning the value of dreams as revelation. Wisdom literature continues the negative polemic, but apocalyptic and the narrative material have a positive attitude.

Allusions in the Psalms

Two clear references to dreams are found in Psalm 73:20 and 126:1, and in both dreams are regarded as ephemeral. They are things which vanish, 73:20, and dreamers are idle people, 126:1. Psalm 73:20 contains the only occurrence of h^{a}lôm in the Psalter, and Psalm 126:1 may contain a variation of the root.[148] It is astounding how little material on dreams there is in the Psalter, a book which reflects the cultic activity of Jerusalem Temple worship, and probably contains the cultic material of many shrines.[149] Either the material was very thoroughly excised, or Israel gave very little emphasis to

101

dreams, revelation by dreams, and incubation. This contrasts with the Akkadian hymns discussed above. There might be allusions to incubation in Psalms 3:6 and 4:9, but the text is too brief to determine that.

Later Syrian apocryphal psalms have clearer references to dreams and incubation. Noth points to Syrian Psalm #3 as an example comparable to the healing incubation dreams of the Greeks.

> I cry to the Lord, and he hears me, and
> he heals the sickness in my heart. I rest
> and sleep, I dream, and already he has
> helped me.[150]

However, Ehrlich doubts whether this actually refers to incubation, for he believes it may merely refer to normal sleeping and dreaming.[151] Thus only with later material do we discover references to dreams.

Wisdom

Wisdom literature is rather critical of dreams. In Job they are fleeting but terrifying experiences. Koheleth sees them as results of bad living habits, and Sirach and the Wisdom of Solomon view them as punishments. In this latter instance wisdom literature uses dreams as part of the greater issue of theodicy and divine retribution, for dreams are an intangible sphere in which the believer can piously affirm divine punishment upon the evil and anticipate no solid refutation from critics. It may also be that wisdom writers have a negative view of dreams because they are reacting against the use of dreams in apocalyptic.

References to dreams are found in Job 4:12-16, 7:13-14, 20:8, and 33:14-16. Job accuses God of tormenting him with dreams in 7:14, Elihu sees them as warning in 33:14-16, Zophar makes an analogy with the elusive nature of dreams compared to human existence in 20:8, and Eliphaz describes a strange dream apparition which brings him a terrifying message in 4:12-16. Some scholars believe that dreams are given credit for being a viable mode of revelation in 4:12-16 and 33:14-16.[152] But their terrifying nature lessens the effectiveness of that[153] communication, and the dreamer has reason to be skeptical. In Job 4:12-16, 7:13-14, and 33:14-16 the terrifying nature of dreams is stressed, and Job views them as God's way of punishing people. His view parallels Sirach 40:5-7, Wisdom of Solomon 18:17-19, and Odyssey 20:83-85. The demonic power of dreams lies in their dread contact with the other realm. Ironically, Job 20:8 contrasts with that view, for here dreams

are ephemeral, as they are seen in Psalm 73:20, 126:1, and Isaiah 29:8. Some scholars believe that Job 4:12-16 and 33:15 imply the possibility of an incubation process.[154] Others reject this because the dreamer is terrified by the experience, and that would not be a willing incubation.[155] Finally, it is interesting to note that 4:12-16 mixes auditory and visual phenomena in the dream.

Koheleth 5:2, 6 contains two questionable readings in reference to dreams. The New English Bible, for instance, reads, "the sensible man has much business on his hands," and "all your achievements will be brought to nothing," instead of reading the reference to dreams. This follows the efforts of earlier critics like Wildeboer, who also repoints the text. Wildeboer reads haḥŏlî, "the sick one," for ḥᵃlôm in 5:2, but he keeps the reference in 5:6.[156] But most scholars read dreams, along with translations like the King James, Revised Standard Version, and Jerusalem Bible.[157] If the text really uses the word dream for the analogies, it may be observed that dreams are seen as ephemeral. In fact, there is an understanding operative here which is similar to our modern view. Dreams are seen as the result of daily concerns and worries, the result of emotion, stress, and fatigue. This is a good observation by an ancient mind. Elsewhere in the ancient world it was perceived that dreams could reflect the health and well-being of an individual, and these types of dreams would be included in what we call the psychological status category, those dreams which reflect a person's mental and physical well-being and cultic purity.

Two aspects of dreams are found in Sirach 34:5-8 and 40:5c-7. The first passage considers dreams to be a possible mode of revelation by God.[158] This is certainly a far more positive evaluation than the other references to dreams in wisdom. But in the same text the author qualifies the statement, the intention is to exhort the reader to ignore dreams, for only a few are sent from God. Thus he sustains the wisdom critique against dreams. He may or may not be criticizing a form of dream divination current in his own day,[159] but he does stress the paramount importance of the Law. Some scholars feel that Sirach gives no positive evaluation of dreams.[160] In Sirach 40:5-7 the author sees dreams as part of the woe which is the lot of everyone.[161] Sirach is deeply concerned with the issue of theodicy, and dreams play a role in that problem for him. They are punishment sent by God upon the sinner, a divine punishment inflicted in the intangible sphere of mental anguish rather than the perceptible realm of political and social endeavor.[162] In this regard, Sirach develops ideas found in Job 7:14 and 33:14-18.

103

Wisdom of Solomon 18:17-18 is a midrash on the captivity of the children of Israel in Egypt. It describes the punishment visited upon the Egyptians for their affliction of the Israelites. As such, it is like Sirach 40:5c-7, for it deals with theodicy and retribution upon evildoers. Again, dreams are a tool to torment sinners.

Thus throughout wisdom literature dreams are either ephemeral or punishments for evil.

<u>Later Literature</u>

The later stages of the biblical tradition begin to develop a positive attitude toward dreams, especially in apocalyptic, narrative material, Philo, and Josephus. This contrasts with wisdom, and it may reflect a breakdown of the wisdom response by the presentation of a new alternative to the issues of theodicy and retribution. Wisdom saw dreams as punishment in order to affirm divine justice in this life, but apocalyptic despaired of justice in this present existence and anticipated the coming of justice in the coming new cosmic order. In this world view dreams foreshadow that anticipated order, and they play a positive role. Dreams function theologically in both wisdom and apocalyptic, negative in the former and positive in the latter. However, there is other literature that lies outside the category of apocalyptic, which also views dreams in a positive fashion. There are also references to dreams as ephemeral, so generalizations are difficult to make. We have too few examples to make decisive judgments. However, positive references outweigh negative references.

II Maccabees 15:11-16 records a dream in which the former high priest Onias and the prophet Jeremiah appear to Judas in a dream in order to give him courage for battle. Onias addresses Judas with words of encouragement, and Jeremiah gives him a sword. The passage comes from the First Century B.C. and shows definite Greek influence upon the old dream pattern. It mixes symbolic and auditory message dream motifs. The reception of a physical object is the most typically Greek motif observable in the dream. Another Greek characteristic is the appearance of human likenesses instead of a deity. Onias and Jeremiah were both martyrs, and as such were exhortations to faithful Jews to resist. The sword was an instrument of destruction Jeremiah threatened that God would send on Israel's enemies in Jeremiah 50:35-37.[163] The dream is basically a simple symbolic message dream, for the presentation of the sword is the real message, a commission to fight boldly. Resch considers the dream a precognitive dream, for although Judas has anxiety concerning the battle, he perceives that the Jews will gain the ultimate victory.[164]

In the Letter of Aristeas, lines 213-216, dreams are mentioned briefly. They are seen to possess no validity, but they are a mirror of the individual dreamer, and no revelation comes from another realm.[165]

In Essene and Pharisaic literature there is a similarity in the methodology for translating textual material and for interpreting dreams. The interpretation of scripture sought to decode the words, transfer the symbols into clear language, discover word plays, and equate the symbols to historical events. Dream interpretation followed the same guidelines. "Symbolic designations are key to (the) pesher of dreams and they also can answer to (the) pesher of scriptures."[166]

Conclusion

The biblical tradition shows a manifold and developing range of opinions about the validity of dreams as a mode of revelation.

Israel's early epic traditions and historical literature could accept dreams as revelation. They used this motif and embodied it in their material. Dream theophanies were cast in a literary model taken from the ancient Near East. The Elohist has a particular stylized version of this form. I Kings 3 can be seen to parallel models from Egypt. Later symbolic dreams have an even more complex form, which may have evolved within the Israelite milieu.

The use of this dream format may reflect the use of dreams as a mode of revelation by early prophets and priests. Of this we can say very little, for the evidence is almost non-existent. Samuel receives a dream as a prophet, according to a later literary version. Balaam has dreams according to an epic tradition. From this we can only speculate.

This situation changed with the rise of classical prophecy. God communicated to these prophets exclusively by His divine Word, and the reception of this revelation is described by the enigmatic phrase, "the Word of the Lord came." With the exclusiveness of these prophets, and because of their conflicts with false prophets, there arose a narrowing of the modes of revelation. Dreams were no longer acceptable as a mode of revelation, not only because this was a medium used by the foreign nations, but it was also a medium of false prophets.

Only after the exile are dreams revived by apocalyptic. The prophetic crisis had passed and new theological problems had arisen. Dreams foreshadow the future in apocalyptic. In a

105

prophet like Zechariah we have visions which may have evolved out of the earlier dreams.

Wisdom exhibits a negative attitude toward dreams; it uses them theologically in the theodicy debate. Dreams are punishment for evildoers. At their best they are ephemeral and fleeting experiences caused by daily worries.

In the later Jewish and Christian traditions dreams again gain respectability. This may be due to the popularity of dreams in the Greek world and in apocalyptic. The dreams serve to foreshadow events in narrative literature by bringing a message from the divine realm.

CHAPTER III

FOOTNOTES

[1] Ehrlich, Traum, p. v.

[2] Ibid., p. vi.

[3] Gustav Hölscher, Die Profeten: Untersuchungen zur Religionsgeschichte Israels (Leipzig: Hinrichs, 1914), p. 54.

[4] Johannes Pedersen, Israel: Its Life and Culture, 2 vols. (London: Oxford, 1926, 1940), 1:136.

[5] Resch, Traum, pp. 26-35.

[6] Ibid., pp. 38-56.

[7] Ibid., p. 137.

[8] Mendelsohn, "Dream," p. 868. A similar distinction is made by Alfred Jepsen, who distinguishes Gottesträume as message dreams and Sachträume as symbolic dreams, Nabi. Soziologische Studien zur alttestamentlichen Literatur und Religionsgeschichte (Munich: Beck, 1934), pp. 46-47.

[9] Yehezkel Kaufmann, The Religion of Israel: From its Beginnings to the Babylonian Exile, trans. Moshe Greenberg (New York: Schocken, 1972), pp. 93-94. However, he cannot explain why a simple message dream comes to Abimelech, nor why Israelites can function as dream interpreters (Joseph and Daniel), when pagans cannot, nor why symbolic dreams are even recorded in Israelite literature, which implies their familiarity with them. It is methodologically simplistic to say that Israel was unfamiliar with symbolic dreams.

[10] Hölscher, Profeten, pp. 84-88, 126.

[11] Francis Brown, Samuel Rolles Driver, and Charles Augustus Briggs, A Hebrew and English Lexicon of the Old Testament (Oxford: Clarendon, 1966), p. 321.

[12] Ehrlich, Traum, pp. 6, 47.

107

[13] Priest, "Myth and Dream," p. 65; and Burke Long, "Prophetic Call Traditions and Reports of Visions," ZAW 84 (1972): 496, observes that all these genres are rooted in a similar theophanic experience (dreams, visions, prophetic call experiences), so the distinction between them is created only by the forms the redactor uses.

[14] Alfred Guillaume, Prophecy and Divination among the Hebrews and other Semites (London: Hodder, 1938), pp. 217-218.

[15] Kaufmann, Religion of Israel, p. 49.

[16] Priest, "Myth and Dream," pp. 61-62.

[17] Ibid., p. 56.

[18] Mendelsohn, "Dream," p. 868.

[19] Hölscher, Profeten, pp. 52-53, 83.

[20] Mendelsohn, "Dream," p. 868.

[21] Resch, Traum, pp. 46-52.

[22] Alan Wilkin Jenks dates the Elohist as early as Jeroboam I, The Elohist and North Israelite Traditions, SBLMS, vol. 22 (Missoula, Montana: Scholars Press, 1977), pp. 101-106, which is taken from his dissertation, "The Elohist and North Israelite Traditions" (Ph.D. dissertation, Harvard University, 1965). Hans Walter Wolff dates it as late as Jeroboam II, "The Elohist Fragments in the Pentateuch," trans. Keith Crim, Int 26 (1972): 170-173.

[23] John Van Seters, Abraham in History and Tradition (New Haven: Yale Press, 1975), passim.

[24] Gerhard von Rad, Genesis, rev. ed., trans. John Marks, OTL (Philadelphia: Westminster, 1972), pp. 26-27.

[25] Ibid., p. 27.

[26] John Marsh and Albert Butzer, "Numbers," IB, 10 vols., ed. George Arthur Buttrick (Nashville: Abingdon, 1952-1956), 2:202.

[27] Wolfgang Richter, "Traum und Traumdeutung im Alten Testament," BZ 7 (1962): 215-219.

[28] John Skinner, A Critical and Exegetical Commentary on Genesis, ICC (New York: Scribners, 1925), p. 277.

[29] Hermann Gunkel, Genesis, HKAT, vol. 1, pt. 1 (Göttingen: Vandenhoeck und Ruprecht, 1901), pp. 177-178; and Ephraim Speiser, Genesis, AB, vol. 1 (Garden City, New York: Doubleday, 1961), p. 110.

[30] Von Rad, Genesis, pp. 182-183.

[31] Martin Noth sees similar practices at Mari, "Old Testament Covenant-Making in the Light of a Text from Mari," The Laws in the Pentateuch and other Studies, trans D. R. Ap-Thomas (Philadelphia: Fortress, 1966), pp. 108-117; and Cuthbert Simpson sees practices derived from the cult of Baal-Berith at Shechem, "Genesis," IB, 1:602.

[32] Such are the views of Duhm and Dhorme as cited by Ehrlich who agrees with them, Traum, pp. 55, 143.

[33] This is the view of most commentators, also Johannes Lindblom, "Theophanies in Holy Places in Hebrew Religion," HUCA 32 (1961): 94.

[34] Walther Eichrodt, Theology of the Old Testament, 2 vols., trans, James A. Baker (Philadelphia: Westminster, 1961), 1:302.

[35] Von Rad, Genesis, p. 188.

[36] Resch, Traum, p. 63.

[37] Julius Wellhausen, Der Text der Bücher Samuelis (Göttingen: Vandenhoeck und Ruprecht, 1871), pp. 21-22; Anton Jirku, "Ein Fall von Inkubation im Alten Testament," ZAW 33 (1913): 153; Dhorme, L'evolution, p. 232; Obermann, How Daniel, p. 28; and Gordon, Ugarit and Minoan Crete (New York: Norton, 1966), p. 25.

[38] Ehrlich, Traum, p. 55.

[39] Ibid., pp. 135-136.

[40] Resch, Traum, p. 20.

[41] Ehrlich, Traum, p. 135.

[42] Von Rad, Genesis, p. 283.

[43] Bernhard Stade, Geschichte Israels, 2 vols. (n.p., 1887), 1:445, 475, and Biblische Theologie des Alten Testaments, 2 vols., Grundriss der Theologischen Wissenschaften, 1st ser., vol. 2, pt. 2 (Tübingen: Mohr, 1905), 1:130; Rudolph Smend, Lehrbuch der Alttestamentlichen

Religionsgeschichte, Sammlung theologischer Lehrbucher: Alttestamentliche Theologie (Leipzig: Mohr, 1893), p. 39; Skinner, Genesis, p. 39; Wilhelm Nowack, Richter, Ruth und Bücher Samuelis übersetzt und erklärt (Göttingen: Vandenhoeck und Ruprecht, 1902), pp. 17-18; Dhorme, L'evolution, p. 232; Aage Bentzen, Introduction to the Old Testament, 2 vols. (Copenhagen: Gads, 1948), 1:186; Gaster, Thespis, p. 271, and "Dreams," p. 208; and Mendelsohn, "Dream," p. 868.

[44] Smend, Lehrbuch, p. 39; Skinner, Genesis, p. 376; and Jastrow, Aspects of Religious Belief and Practice in Babylonia and Assyria, American Lectures on the History of Religions (New York: Putnam, 1911), p. 266.

[45] The massebah is regarded pejoratively by the Yahwist (Exodus 34:14), but the Elohist speaks of it several times (Genesis 31:13, 44, 51, 52, 33:20, 35:14, Exodus 24:4, 34:13). It may have been part of the paraphernalia for a Canaanite sanctuary, Skinner, Genesis, p. 378.

[46] Simpson and Bowie, "Genesis," pp. 689-690; and von Rad, Genesis, p. 285.

[47] Skinner, Genesis, p. 379.

[48] Ehrlich, Traum, p. 32.

[49] Gywn Griffiths, "The Celestial Ladder and the Gate of Heaven (Genesis xxviii. 12 and 17)," ExpTim 76 (1964): 229-230.

[50] A. R. Millard, "The Celestial Ladder and the Gate of Heaven (Genesis xxviii. 12, 17)," ExpTim 78 (1966): 86.

[51] Von Rad, Genesis, p. 284.

[52] Frank Cross, Canaanite Myth and Hebrew Epic: Essays in the History of the Religion of Israel (Cambridge: Harvard, 1973), p. 270.

[53] Noth, A History of Pentateuchal Traditions, trans. Bernhard Anderson (Englewood Cliffs: Prentice Hall, 1972), p. 80.

[54] Simpson and Bowie, "Genesis," p. 695.

[55] Resch, Traum, p. 73.

[56] Richter, "Traum," pp. 210-211.

[57] Von Rad, Genesis, p. 305.

[58] Resch, Traum, p. 76.

[59] Ehrlich, Traum, p. 131.

[60] Simpson and Bowie, "Genesis," p. 716.

[61] Von Rad, Genesis, p. 402.

[62] William Whiston, The Works of Flavius Josephus, 4 vols. (Grand Rapids, Michigan: Baker, 1974), 2:146-147.

[63] Stade, Theologie, 1:130-131; Jirku, "Inkubation," p. 153; Dhorme, L'evolution, p. 232; Mendelsohn, "Dream," p. 868; and Gaster, "Dreams," p. 208.

[64] George Buchanan Gray, A Critical and Exegetical Commentary on Numbers, ICC (New York: Scribners, 1903), p. 309; Marsh, "Numbers," pp. 248-249; Noth, Numbers, trans. James Martin, OTL (Philadelphia: Westminster, 1968), p. 178; and Walter Gross, Bileam: Literar- und formkritische Untersuchung der Prosa in Num 22-24, SANT, vol. 38 (Munich: Kösel, 1974), p. 122.

[65] Gray, Numbers, pp. 310-313, records the opinions of several source critics. Kuenen calls 22:22-35 Yahwist, while the rest is Elohist. Von Gall thinks the material of the two sources is inseparable due to later redaction. Steuernagel believes the two sources are E_1 and E_2, and there is no Yahwist material. Gray outlines 22:5, 8-10, 12-15, 19-21, 36, 40 as Elohist, while the rest is Yahwist.

[66] Abraham Kuenen, Historische-kritische Einleitung in die Bücher des Alten Testaments, vol. 1, pt. 2, trans. Theodore Weber (Leipzig: Fues, 1887), p. 514; Bruno Baentsch, Exodus, Leviticus, und Numeri, HKAT, vol. 1, pt. 2 (Göttingen: Vandenhoeck und Ruprecht, 1903), p. 591; Heinrich Holzinger, Das Buch Numeri, HKAT, vol. 2 (Tübingen: Mohr, 1903), pp. 107-109; Hugo Gressman, Die Schriften des Alten Testaments, vol. 2: Die älteste Geschichtsschreibung und Prophetie Israels (Göttingen: Vandenhoeck und Ruprecht, 1910), p. 59; Simpson, The Early Traditions of Israel (Oxford: Blackwell, 1948), p. 259; Noth, Numbers, p. 178; and most standard commentators. However, a few scholars disagree with this position, Marsh, "Numbers," p. 249. Some scholars deny the existence of the Elohist altogether, and in particular Wilhelm Rudolph gives attention to this passage and in his rejection of the Elohist's existence, Der Elohist von Exodus bis Josua, BZAW, vol. 68 (Berlin: Gruyter, 1938), pp. 97-128.

[67] Noth, Numbers, p. 178.

[68] Stade, Theologie, 1:130; Jirku, "Inkubation," p. 153; and Gaster, Thespis, p. 271.

[69] Theophile Meek, Hebrew Origins, rev. ed. (New York: Harper and Brothers, 1950), p. 153, claims this is not a dream, for his eyes are open; rather, it is a vision of the inner mind.

[70] Murray Lichtenstein, "Dream Theophany," pp. 45-54. He builds upon the work of Paul Volz and Wilhelm Rudolph, Der Elohist als Erzähler: Ein Irrweg der Pentateuchkritik?, BZAW, vol. 68 (Giessen: Töpelmann, 1933), passim; and Rudolph, Elohist von Exodus, passim, who have determined that the Elohist texts are merely a variation of the Yahwist. It must be said that Volz and Rudolph have not really denied the existence of a source; they deny its integral independence.

[71] Dennis Pardee, "An Emendation in the Ugaritic AQHT Text," JNES 36 (1977): 53-56, has shown that in 2 AQHT 1:35 El does not grasp Dan'el's hand. Rather, the text is reconstructed to read, "El takes a cup in one hand," which is a symbolic act meant to accompany the blessing to be conveyed upon Dan'el by the messenger.

[72] Richter, "Traum," pp. 215-216.

[73] Jacob Myers and Phillips Elliott, "Judges," IB, 2:740-741; and James Martin, Book of Judges, CBC (Cambridge, England: Cambridge University Press, 1975), p. 98.

[74] Resch, Traum, p. 110.

[75] Stade, Theologie, 1:130-131; Nowack, Richter, Ruth und Samuelis, pp. 17-18; Jirku, "Inkubation," p. 153; Eichrodt, Theology of the Old Testament, 1:105; Bentzen, Introduction, 1:186; and Ehrlich, Traum, p. 55.

[76] Resch, Traum, pp. 114-115.

[77] Gaster, "Dreams," p. 208.

[78] Siegfried Herrmann, "Die Königsnovelle in Ägypten und in Israel. Ein Beitrag zur Gattungsgeschichte in den Geschichtsbüchern des Alten Testaments," Wissenschaftliche Zeitschrift der Karl-Marx Universität, Leipzig 3 (1953-1954): 51-62; R. A. Carlson, David, the chosen King: A Traditio-Historical Approach to the Second Book of Samuel (Stockholm: Almquist und Wiksell, 1964), p. 220, notes the similarity with Keret's dream.

[79] ANET, p. 446.

[80] John Gray, I and II Kings, 2d ed., OTL (Philadelphia: Westminster Press, 1976), pp. 123-125.

[81] Herrmann, "Königsnovelle," p. 60; and Joseph Robinson, First Book of Kings, CBC (Cambridge, England: Cambridge University Press, 1972), p. 51. II Samuel 7 is also an oracle which begins the court history of David.

[82] Herrmann, "Königsnovelle," p. 60.

[83] Gray, Kings, pp. 121-122.

[84] Helen Ann Kenik, "The Design for Kingship in I Kings 3:4-15: A Study in the Deuteronomistic Narrative Technique and Theology of Kingship" (Ph.D. dissertation, St. Louis University, 1978), pp. 4, 48-49, 64-275.

[85] Moshe Weinfeld, Deuteronomy and the Deuteronomic School (Oxford: Clarendon Press, 1972), pp. 246-250.

[86] Norman Snaith, "Kings," IB, 3:40.

[87] Resch, Traum, pp. 116-117.

[88] Ehrlich, Traum, pp. 139-140, who addresses this opinion against Jirku, "Inkubation," p. 153.

[89] Erwin Preuschen, "Doeg als Incubant," ZAW 23 (1903): 141-146; and Jirku, "Inkubation," p. 153.

[90] Angelus Stellini, Samuel propheta (1 Sam 3,20) et iudex (1 Sam 7,16) in Israel, Pontificium Athenaeum Antonianum Facultas Theologica (Sectio Biblica), Theses ad Lauream, vol. 113 (Rome: Novara, 1957), p. 52.

[91] Jepsen, Nabi, p. 46.

[92] John Bright, Jeremiah, AB, vol. 21 (Garden City, New York: Doubleday, 1965), p. 153.

[93] Kaufmann, Religion of Israel, p. 49.

[94] Otto Kaiser, Isaiah 13-39, trans. R. A. Wilson, OTL (Philadelphia: Westminster Press, 1974), pp. 265-266.

[95] Anthony Phillips, Deuteronomy, CBC (Cambridge, England: Cambridge University Press, 1973), pp. 94-95.

[96] Richter, "Traum," p. 219.

[97] Ehrlich, Traum, p. 162; and Stade concurs, Theologie, 1:130; however, other scholars would maintain that since Israel never had a special class of diviners, this oracle is directed against prophets of Israel who received dreams. This would be comparable to the situation of Jeremiah.

[98] Von Rad, Deuteronomy, trans. Dorothea Barton, OTL (Philadelphia: Westminster, 1966), p. 96.

[99] Ehrlich, Traum, p. 162.

[100] Noth, Numbers, p. 93.

[101] Ibid.

[102] The third passage is considered secondary by Bernhard Duhm, Das Buch Jeremia, KHAT, vol. 11 (Tübingen: Mohr, 1901), pp. 229-230; Sigmund Mowinckel, Zur Komposition des Buches Jeremia, Videnskapsselskapets Skrifter, vol. 2 (Kristiania: Dybwad, 1914), pp. 298-299; Hans Schmidt, Die grossen Propheten übersetzt und erklärt, Die Schriften des Alten Testaments, pt. 2, vol. 2 (Göttingen: Vandenhoeck und Ruprecht, 1915), p. 328; Volz, Der Prophet Jeremia übersetzt und erklärt, KAT, vol. 10 (Leipzig: Scholl, 1922), p. 268; and Rudolph, Jeremia, HAT, vol. 12 (Tübingen: Mohr, 1947), p. 154.

[103] Friedrich Giesebrecht, Jeremia, HKAT, vol. 3, pt. 2 (Göttingen: Vandenhoeck und Ruprecht, 1907), pp. 44-55; Guillaume, Prophecy and Divination, p. 218; Arvin Kapelrud, Joel Studies, UUÅ, vol. 4 (Uppsala: Lundquist, 1948), p. 136; James Philip Hyatt and Stanley Hopper, "Jeremiah," IB, 5:993; and Bright, Jeremiah, p. 153.

[104] Carl Heinrich Cornill, Das Buch Jeremia (Leipzig: Tauchnitz, 1905), pp. 272-274; Johannes Hänel, Das Erkennen Gottes bei den Schriftpropheten (n.p., 1923), pp. 136-138 as cited by Ehrlich, Traum, p. 156; Norman Habel, Jeremiah, Lamentations, Concordia Commentary (St. Louis: Concordia, 1968), p. 190; and Ernest Nicholson, Jeremiah 1-25, CBC (Cambridge, England: Cambridge University Press, 1973), p. 200.

[105] Ehrlich, Traum, p. 157.

[106] Ibid., p. 158; and Duhm, Jeremia, pp. 229-230.

[107] Ehrlich, Traum, p. 159.

[108] James L. Crenshaw, Prophetic Conflict: Its Effect Upon Israelite Religion, BZAW, vol. 124 (Berlin: Gruyter, 1971), pp. 90-106.

[109] Ehrlich, Traum, pp. 18-19.

[110] Ehrlich, Traum, pp. 53-54; James Muilenburg and Henry Sloane Coffin, "Isaiah 40-66," IB, 5:747; and Claus Westermann, Isaiah 40-66, trans. D. M. G. Stalker, OTL (Philadelphia: Westminster Press, 1966), p. 401.

[111] Hänel, Erkennen, pp. 139-140, as cited and criticized by Ehrlich, Traum, p. 163.

[112] Harold Henry Rowley, "The Unity of the Book of Daniel," The Servant of the Lord and other Essays on the Old Testament (London: Lutterworth, 1952), pp. 235-268; Arthur Jeffrey and Gerald Kennedy, "Daniel," IB, 6:349-350; and Norman Porteous, Daniel, OTL (Philadelphia: Westminster Press, 1956), p. 18.

[113] Skinner, Genesis, p. 440.

[114] Aniti Amatus Aarne, The Types of the Folktale: A Classification and Bibliography, trans. Stith Thompson (Bloomington: University of Indiana Press, 1964), p. 250.

[115] Orval Wintermute, "Joseph, Son of Jacob," IDB, 2:984.

[116] Von Rad, Die Josephgeschichte: Ein Vortrag, BibS(N), vol. 5 (Neukirchen: Erziehungsvereins, 1956), passim; and "The Joseph Narrative and Ancient Wisdom," Problems of the Hexateuch and other Essays, trans. E. W. Trueman Dicken (New York: McGraw-Hill, 1966), pp. 292-300.

[117] Josef Vergote, Joseph en Égypte: Genese chap. 37-50. A la lumière des études égyptologiques récentes (Louvain: Publications Universitaires, 1959), pp. 208-213 et passim.

[118] W. A. Ward, "The Egyptian Office of Joseph," JSS 5 (1960): 144-150.

[119] Roger Whybray, "The Joseph Story and Pentateuchal Criticism," VT 18 (1968): 522-528.

[120] Donald Redford, A Study of the Biblical Story of Joseph, (Genesis 37-50), VTSup, vol. 20 (Leiden: Brill, 1970), pp. 65, 106-186, 234-243, et passim.

121 Lothar Ruppert, Die Josepherzählung: Ein Beitrag zur Theologie der Pentateuchquellen, (Munich: Kösel, 1965), pp. 78-81.

122 Crenshaw, "Method in Determining Wisdom Influence upon 'Historical' Literature," JBL 88 (1969): 135-137, and "Prolegomenon," Studies in Ancient Israelite Wisdom, ed. James Crenshaw, The Library of Biblical Studies (New York: KTAV, 1976), p. 11.

123 Von Rad, Genesis, p. 351.

124 Skinner, Genesis, p. 445; and Thompson and Irwin, "Moses and Joseph," p. 189.

125 Wintermute, "Joseph," p. 983.

126 Hans Peter Müller, "Der Begriff 'Rätsel' in Alten Testament," VT 20 (1970): 476-477.

127 Von Rad, Genesis, p. 352; and Ehrlich, Traum, p. 59, both discuss and reject these options.

128 Gressmann, "Ursprung und Entwicklung der Josephsage," Eucharisterion: Studien zur Religion und Literatur des Alten und Neuen Testaments: Hermann Gunkel zum 60. Geburtstag, dem 23, Mai 1922 dargebracht von seinen Schülern und Freunden, ed. Hans Schmidt, FRLANT, vol. 36 (Göttingen: Vandenhoeck und Ruprecht, 1923), p. 123.

129 Gunkel, Genesis, p. 405; Alfred Jeremias, Das Alte Testament im Lichte des Alten Orients (Leipzig: Mohr, 1916), p. 330; Ehrlich, Traum, p. 61; von Rad, Genesis, p. 308; and Ruppert, Josepherzählung, p. 33.

130 Wikenhauser, "Doppelträume," pp. 100-111.

131 Von Rad, Genesis, pp. 352-353.

132 Resch, Traum, p. 82.

133 Gunkel, Genesis, p. 429.

134 Oppenheim, Interpretation, p. 210.

135 Simpson and Bowie, "Genesis," p. 770.

136 Skinner, Genesis, p. 461.

137 Resch, Traum, pp. 94-96.

[138] Oepke, TDNT, 5:229.

[139] Ibid., p. 226.

[140] Gunkel, Genesis, p. 435.

[141] Oppenheim, Interpretation, p. 210.

[142] Resch, Traum, p. 106.

[143] Jeffrey and Kennedy, "Daniel," p. 372.

[144] Von Rad, Wisdom in Israel, trans. James Martin (Nashville: Abingdon, 1972), p. 280.

[145] Von Rad, Old Testament Theology, 2 vols., trans. D. M. G. Stalker (New York: Harper and Row, 196), 2:307; and this same view is espoused by Robert Gordis, Poets, Prophets, and Sages: Essays in Biblical Interpretation (Bloomington: University of Indiana Press, 1971), p. 282.

[146] Resch, Traum, p. 123.

[147] Jeffrey and Kennedy, "Daniel," p. 409.

[148] However, Mitchel Dahood maintains the text refers not to dreams, but to "sands of the sea," Psalms, 3 vols., AB, vols. 16-17a (Garden City, New York: Doubleday, 1970), 2:218-219.

[149] Mowinckel, Psalmenstudien, 6 vols. (Amsterdam: Schippers, 1961), 1:145-146, 156.

[150] Noth, "Die fünf syrisch überlieferten apokryphen Psalmen," ZAW 48 (1930): 10.

[151] Ehrlich, Traum, pp. 52-53.

[152] Georg Fohrer, Das Buch Hiob, KAT, vol. 16 (Gütersloh: Mohn, 1963), p. 458.

[153] Marvin Pope, Job, AB, vol. 15 (Garden City, New York: Doubleday, 1965), pp. 36, 249-250; Ehrlich, Traum, p. 148; and Habel, The Book of Job, CBC (Cambridge, England: Cambridge University Press, 1975), pp. 28, 178. Habel notes that it is unusual for a wisdom source to have Eliphaz speak of dreams as a possible mode of revelation; therefore, this text is the exception not the rule in wisdom literature, Job, p. 28.

[154] Obermann, How Daniel, p. 28; and Bentzen, Introduction, 1:186, calls 4:12-21 a parody on incubation.

[155] Karl Budde, Das Buch Hiob, HKAT, vol. 2, pt. 1 (Göttingen: Vandenhoeck und Ruprecht, 1896), p. 19; and Ehrlich, Traum, p. 145.

[156] G. Wildeboer, "Der Prediger," Die Fünf Megillot, KHAT, vol. 17 (Freiburg: Mohr, 1898), p. 139.

[157] Ehrlich, Traum, p. 164; Oliver Rankin and Gaius Atkins, "Ecclesiastes," IB, 5:57; R. B. Y. Scott, Proverbs, Ecclesiastes, AB, vol. 18 (Garden City, New York: Doubleday, 1965), pp. 226-227; and Gordis, Koheleth -- The Man and His World: A Study of Ecclesiastes, 3d. ed. (New York: Schocken, 1968), p. 250.

[158] Ernest Lussier, The Book of Proverbs and the Book of Sirach, OTRG, vol. 24 (Collegeville: Liturgical Press, 1965), p. 100; and John Snaith, Ecclesiasticus or the Wisdom of Jesus son of Sirach, CBC (Cambridge, England: Cambridge University Press, 1974), p. 165.

[159] Snaith, Ecclesiasticus, p. 166.

[160] Ehrlich, Traum, p. 167, feels that this is an exaggeration by Sirach, for Sirach really does not believe that God communicates through dreams anymore, because the Law is complete and needs not further revelations.

[161] Von Rad, Wisdom, pp. 256-257; and Snaith, Ecclesiasticus, p. 197.

[162] Crenshaw, "The Problem of Theodicy in Sirach: On Human Bondage," JBL 94 (1975): 57.

[163] John Bartlett, The First and Second Book of the Maccabees, CBC (Cambridge, England: Cambridge University Press, 1973), p. 339.

[164] Resch, Traum, p. 128.

[165] Ehrlich, Traum, p. 168.

[166] Asher Finkel, "The Pesher of Dreams and Scriptures," RevQ 4 (1963-1964): 364.

CHAPTER IV

ANALYSIS OF I SAMUEL 3

I Samuel 3 appears to be a well-defined narrative unit. Consideration of the form and content of the text will seek to determine the structure and intent of the passage. The author will maintain the retention of the Massoretic Text in most instances where other scholars have proposed emendations, and that the form of the narrative is not a call narrative, as commonly assumed, but a simple auditory message dream in conformity with the ancient Near Eastern pattern. The narrative is a late literary creation which seeks to proclaim a word of judgment. The significance of the passage in its literary and theological context will be considered in a later chapter.

Text Criticism

The text of I Samuel 3, like much of the book, is corrupt and subject to extensive emendation. Since the work of Thenius (1842) the Septuagint has been used to correct the readings of the Massoretic Text. He reacted against Frankel, who asserted that the Septuagint was merely a translation of an Aramaic targum.[1] Despite Thenius' fear of a poor reception, his work was favorably received. Wellhausen disputed his method but still preferred the Septuagint over the Massoretic text (1871). Klostermann (1887), Ehrlich (1910), Schulz (1919-1920), Tiktin (1922), Caspari (1926), and others followed Wellhausen in this attitude. Driver (1913) was even less hesitant about using the Septaugint. Only Budde (1902) displayed reluctance about such emendation when he claimed that the Septuagint may have used a poor version of the Massoretic Text.

In the last generation a greater respect arose for the Massoretic Text with the scholarship of Nyberg.[2] Pieter de Boer built upon Nyberg's work and applied it to the text of I Samuel. Upon evaluating the translations of the Targums, Peshitto, and Septuagint, he concluded that the Septuagint, unlike the Peshitto, was a free rendering of the Hebrew, a

119

translation whose text had never received finishing touches.
He concluded,

> . . . this part of G can be considered of
> little value for the determination of the
> 'original' Hebrew text. The divergences
> give important material for the deter-
> mination of the intrinsic value of the
> translation and point out the difficulties
> which M. has not smoothed out, but they
> cannot emend the Hebrew text.[3]

De Boer discovered that the text of I Samuel 1-16 in the
Septuagint did not have literal translations in regard to place
names, names for God, and other proper names. It was
consistent with certain idiosyncratic translations and omitted
certain Hebrew words in some places and added certain Greek
words in other places.[4] This makes any attempt to reconstruct
an original Hebrew text impossible. The critics should
determine the recension and interpret the text, but emendation
should be postponed.[5] Kittel had previously demonstrated this
kind of caution in Biblia Hebraica 3, for he used the Septuagint
sparingly. More recently Hans Joachim Stoebe (1973) preserves
the Massoretic Text as often as possible, even though this
occasionally produces garbled Hebrew. He views the Septuagint
as an alternate attempt to interpret the same garbled Hebrew.

The discovery of material at Qumran adds a new
dimension to the debate. Fragments of 4QSam[a] and 4QSam[b] (I
Samuel 16:1-11, 19:10-17, 21:3-7, 8-10, 23:9-17) indicate the
presence of a textual tradition at slight variance with the
Massoretic Text. Initial observations by Frank Cross affirmed
the existence of a separate Hebrew recension behind the
Septuagint. If so, this boosts the credibility of the Septuagint
in emending the Hebrew text. Cross maintains there were three
recensions of the Hebrew text, Babylonian, Palestinian, and
Egyptian. The Massoretic Text arises out of the first, the
Septuagint may arise out of the latter, and the Qumran texts
show affinity to the latter two. The Qumran texts are
therefore based on a better textual tradition than the "inferior
textual recension" underlying the Massoretic text. Qumranic
texts can be used in conjunction with the Septuagint to correct
the inferior readings in the Hebrew text. 1QSam[a] stands in
close relationship with the Lucianic version of the Septuagint
and in particular, Lucianic minuscules boc_2e_2 in regard to II
Samuel 11:2-24:25, while Codex Vaticanus is related to I Samuel
1:1 - II Samuel 11:1.[6] These texts have subsequently been
utilized by other scholars in their reconstruction of the text.[7]

This approach has not gained complete consensus.
Orlinsky praises the older methodological approach of Wellhausen

120

and Driver, and with them he affirms the need to use a more balanced approach in weighing the Massoretic Text against the Septuagint. He exhibits a position of moderation between Cross and some of his critics. Initial enthusiasm for a renewed use of the Septuagint waned with the realization that many Qumran readings lie between both the Massoretic Text and the Septuagint.[8] Eybers is very critical, for after a careful consideration of all the variant readings, he finds that 4QSam[a] and 4QSam[b] concur more with the Septuagint only because of the preponderance of 4QSam[a]. 1QSam[b] is not as close to the Septuagint as Cross initially maintained, and he has gone too far in declaring the Massoretic Text to be inferior. In fact, the Massoretic Text may contain a more nearly original text than 4QSam.[9] Thus the work of Stoebe, which predominantly retains the Hebrew text, is a very viable option.

The author will follow the presuppositions of Stoebe and retain the Massoretic text when it seems logical. The Septuagint may rely on a better Hebrew text, but as de Boer has shown, it still is a translation with all the attendant idiosyncrasies of a translator. The Qumran material is good for comparison, but whether it affirms the superiority of the Septuagint for textual emendation of the Massoretic Text remains questionable until more data is forthcoming. An eclectic approach which weighs each reading on its own merit is the most balanced procedure to follow. We shall pursue that option while maintaining a preference for the received Hebrew of the Massoretic Text over the translation of the Septuagint.

Translation of I Samuel 3

1. [a] So the young boy, Samuel, ministered to the Lord under Eli.[a] The Word of the Lord was rare in those days; no vision was received.[b]

2. [e] On that day Eli slept in his place,[c] and his eyes[d] were dim;[e] he was not able[f] to see.

3. Before the lamp of God went out,[g] Samuel was asleep in the temple of the Lord,[h] where the ark was located.

4. The Lord called to Samuel,[ij] and he said, "Here am I!"

5. He ran[k] to Eli and said, "Here am I!"[k] For you called me." But he said, "I did not call you! Go back to bed! Lie down!" So he went and lay down.

6. The Lord again[m] called to Samuel. Samuel arose,[l] went to Eli,[m] and said, "Here am I! You called me!" But he said, "I did not call you, my son!"[m] Go back to bed! Lie down!"

121

7.   Samuel had not yet experienced[n] the Lord, and the Word[o] of the Lord was not yet revealed to him.

8.   The Lord called again to Samuel[p] a third time. He arose, went to Eli, and said, "Behold, here I am! For you called me." Then Eli understood that the Lord was calling[p] the boy.

9.   Eli said to Samuel, "Go, lie down![q] If he calls you, you will   say,   'Speak,   Lord,[r]   for   your   servant   is   listening!'" Samuel went and lay down in his bed.

10.   The Lord came and stood, and He called as the other times,[s]   "Samuel, Samuel!"[s]   Samuel said, "Speak, for your servant is listening!"

11.   The Lord said to Samuel, "I am planning to do something in Israel which[t] will ring[u] in the ears of all who hear it.

12.   In that day[v] I will raise up against[w] Eli everything I said about his family from beginning to end.[x]

13.   I have told him[y] that I am judging his family forever for the sin which he knew:[z]   that his sons cursed God,[z] and he did not rebuke[aa] them.

14.   Therefore,[bb] I have sworn to the family of Eli that the sin of the family of Eli can never be atoned[cc] with sacrifice and offerings forever."

15.   Samuel lay until morning and he arose in the morning.[dd] He opened the doors of the house of the Lord. But Samuel was afraid to tell Eli[ee] the vision.

16.   Eli called to[ff] Samuel and said, "Samuel, my son." He replied, "Here am I."

17.   He said, "What is the Word which He said to you?[gg] Do not hide it from me. May God so do to you, if you try to hide from me any part of the message He spoke to you."

18.   Samuel told him all the words, and he hid nothing from him.[hh] He responded,[ii] "May the Lord[jj] do what is good in His eyes."[kk]

19.   Samuel grew and the Lord was with him, so that none of his words[ll] fell to the ground.

20.   All Israel knew from Dan to Beersheba that Samuel was a prophet[mm] faithful to the Lord.[mm]

122

21.   The Lord again appeared in Shiloh, for the Lord revealed to Samuel in Shiloh the Word of the Lord.[nn]

4:1a. The Word of Samuel was declared for all Israel.[nn]

Translation Notes

a.   The Septuagint adds ho hiereus after Eli's name.

b.   The Septuagint reads diastellousa for nipraṣ as though the text had originally read pōrēṣ, a qal active participle. If so, this form is also found in II Chronicles 31:5. The initial nun arose by dittography from the previous word.[10] The meaning then would be "open," and the text would read, "there was no open vision." A second option is the passive form pāruṣ or pārūṣ, which would avoid the "violence" of the first option.[11] More recently a third alternative has gained consensus; scholars preserve the text as it stands. Driver maintains there are two meanings for the root prṣ, "break through," and "command." I Samuel 3:1 is the latter of the two options, and it should be translated as "ordained" rather than "open," which is a forced derivation of the first root.[12] Vaccari has shown the form of the verb in II Chronicles 31:5 to be from a different root.[13] This author concurs with those who read the text as is.[14]

c.   Caspari maintains that bamāqôm should be read at the end of the first line, for the final letter, waw, came from the following word.[15]

d.   Most scholars concur with the Qere reading wᶜyênîw for the Kethib wᶜēnāw.

e.   The real debate centers on the phrase hēhēllû kēhôt. Wellhausen pointed out the difficulty of viewing kēhôt as an infinitive without the lᵉ in his debate with Bottcher. For Wellhausen it was either an adjective or a participle.[16] Since then scholars have debated whether it is an adjective or an infinitive. Klostermann reads the qal infinitive likēhôt and emends the line to read waᶜēyynô hēhēllah likhôt. Thenius prefers the qal infinitive kᵉhôt, Schulz reads kᵉhôt because of the Greek barunesthai, Smith reads kᵃhôt, Budde elects to read kᵉhôt, which led subsequent scholars to do likewise.[17] More recently commentators have read it as an adjective. Driver maintains that verses 2-3 are circumstantial clauses describing conditions prior to verse 4, which then make kēhôt a feminine plural adjective of kēhah, accusative form which describes the aspect of Eli's eye; hence, "(they) began as dim ones," or

"(they) began to be dim."[18] Other scholars preserve the text and read it as an adjective.[19]

f.   The peculiar form lo³ yûkal is explained by Driver as the way to express the continued disability of Eli more clearly than lo³ yākōl would.[20]

g.   Some have seen yikbeh as an imperfect, since ṭerem usually takes the imperfect, and the Septuagint translates the verb with episkeusthēnai. However, this may be simply a loose translation.[21]

h.   Since Codex Vaticanus omits YHWH, so also do many scholars. Stoebe retains the text because it is also found in 1:9.[22]

i.   The Septuagint text proposes alternate readings in this verse. It reads a double vocative, "Samuel, Samuel," which Wellhausen believes the verb demands.[23] Others view ³ el as the remnant of the fuller šᵉmûʾēl.[24] Tiktin reconstructs the text to read: "and the Lord called to Samuel saying, 'Samuel, Samuel,' and he answered, "Here am I,'"[25] Some maintain the integrity of the text by viewing the double vocative as a corruption due to its presence in verse 10.[26]

j.   The Lagardiana Codex of the Septuagint inserts kai katestē kai ekalese kurios to parallel verse 10. Smith thinks this reflects the original wᵉyityaṣēb, which was omitted due to its anthropomorphism. Caspari thinks the text read wayyāqom, which corrupted into wayyiqrāʾ.[27] It seems more likely the text expanded due to the influence of verse 10.

k.   The Codex Alexandrinus offers minor changes: it omits the first verb and reads hinnēnî for hinnî.

l.   The Septuagint again gives rise to textual issues. The omission of wayyāqom by Codices Vaticanus and Lagardiana has led scholars to reconstruct a similar Hebrew text. "By its omission we lose nothing, and the second call is made uniform with the first."[28] Pfeiffer calls it a useless type of late midrash, which repeats the text and ruins style.[29] The presence of this verb in verse 8 after the same wayyōsep caused it to creep in here.[30] Others have defended the integrity of the text by maintaining the Septuagint created the double vocative by omitting the verb.[31]

m.   The Septuagint has some poor renderings in this verse. Most scholars consider the to deuteron of the Septuagint to be superfluous, although Schulz seeks the original šᵉnît.[32] The

vocative b^{e}nî is blurred in the Greek translation as se, and the ᶜôd remains untranslated.[33]

n.   ṭerem usually takes the imperfect, but the text has a perfect tense. Therefore, many read the imperfect yēdaᶜ to bring the first verb into agreement with the following verb.[34] Codex Lagardiana tried to interpret this phrase by incorrectly translating edouleue prin ē.[35]   Genesis 24:15 has ṭerem with the perfect tense, so the construction is not impossible.   To change the tense would ruin the meaning, for it would imply that Samuel knew nothing of God prior to this experience. Rather, the perfect is used to show that Samuel has not yet received a revelation.[36]   Stoebe's syntactical argument is sound, but his theological argument seems forced.

o.   Some feel that dābar should be omitted, because it cannot appear physically, whereas the Lord can. The word was inserted to avoid anthropomorphism.[37]   However, if retained, the word balances the phrase yādaᶜ ꜣet-YHWH.[38]

p.   Because Codex Alexandrinus has epi Samouēl, Schulz reads lišᵉmûꜣēl.[39]   For qōrēꜣ in the last line the Septuagint reads keklēken, which could be taken to imply an original qārāꜣ in the text.[40]   Both examples illustrate the fallacy of converting a free Greek translation back into Hebrew.

q.   The presence of teknon in Greek encourages the reconstruction of lak šᵉkab b^{e}nî in the first line, but this is probably an addition in Greek.[41]

r.   Codex Vaticanus omits YHWH and has only the verb lalei, and some scholars accordingly alter the Hebrew.[42]

s.   Codex Vaticanus omits the double vocative in the Hebrew and reads ekalesen auton. The double vocative also appears unnecessary with the presence of kᵉpaᶜam bᵉpaᶜam in the Hebrew.[43]   Some would rather omit the kᵉpaᶜam bᵉpaᶜam and retain the double vocative.[44]   A third option is to retain the text and accuse the Septuagint of a misunderstanding such as haplography.[45]   Driver explains the text by reference to I Samuel 20:25, Judges 16:20, 20:30-31, Numbers 18:10, 24:1, II Kings 17:4; for he translates the expression as "one time like another," "generally," or "as at other times."[46]   A fifth possibility is to relate these two words to the verb and not the subject, so they would indicate the finality of the third call.[47]

t.   Septuagintal versions differ over the inclusion of the

relative. Codex Vaticanus lost the ᵃšer due to the influence of 2:27-36, whereas Codex Alexandrinus uses hōste.[48]

u.   tᵉšillenāh is problematic. It has been repointed as tᵉssullenāh[49] and as tiṣṣalnāh from ṣll.[50]

v.   Caspari omits bayôm hahûᵓ and ᵓel-bētô and reads hēqîm for ᵓāqîm.[51]

w.   For the first ᵓel the Septuagint reads epi instead of the expected eis, the Peshitto and Targums read ʿal, and the Vulgate reads adversum. Thus ʿal is proposed in the original text.[52] But others maintain that ᵓel should be read in the text with the meaning of ʿal.[53]

x.   hāhēl wᵉkallēh causes some problems. It has been seen as an idiom and translated either "beginning and ending" or "completely."[54] It has also been reconstructed as an infinitive absolute dependent upon ᵓāqîm.[55]

y.   Several scholars emend the first word to wᵉhiggadtā, "you shall tell him," instead of "I have told him," or "I will tell him."[56] The form was corrupted to the first person by the first person form, "I will do," in verse 12,[57] or because pious Massoretes wished to absolve Samuel from the deed of conveying the divine curse to Eli.[58] Recent scholars retain the text; since the message in 3:11-14 differs from 2:27-36,[59] this reference points back to the message in 2:27-36. Kittel suggests lak instead of lô, so the text reads, "I have told you," and the reference is to the message just spoken to Samuel.[60] Caspari emends lô to read ʿali and renders "I have already told Eli."[61]

z.   The second line of the verse is rendered thus by the Septuagint: en adikias huiōn autou hoti kakologountes theon hoi huioi autou. This particular interpretation of the text has given rise to several questions.

baʿaôn is considered by many to be improper. One emendation proposes yaʿan on the assumption that ba came from bāna(y)w.[62] Others omit it entirely, for it is superfluous with ᵓašer.[63] However, the Septuagint presupposes bāna(y)w and baʿaôn as a unit. Some critics omit ᵓašer yādaʿ, for it does not fit with wᵉlôᵓ kihāh bām.[64] Others declare the Septuagint in error and retain ᵓašer yādaʿ.[65] Tiktin calls baʿaôn bāna(y)w a facilitation of the text, and baʿaôn is a

126

degeneration of ᶜqb.[66]   Klostermann proposes the text was baᶜᵃônô, "Eli's sin," the Septuagint read a text with baᶜᵃônôt, "(their) sins," and the text corrupted to read baᶜᵃôn.[67] Stoebe refrains from altering the text, for the present form can be read sensibly.[68]

mᵉqallîm is reconstructed variously as mᵉqallîm (with dagesh forte),[69] as a pual passive mᵉqᵉllaîm following the Peshiṭto,[70] and as a hiphil passive participle mᵉqillîm,[71] which are attempts to correlate the verb with kihah. But this debate is part of the debate on the whole phrase, mᵉqallîm lāhem. The phrase has been compared to a later tiqqunê ha-sopherîm, for the text may have originally read mᵉqallîm ᵓlōhîm, but the combination of qll with a divine name was so blasphemous that pious scribes modified the form.[72] The use of špṭ anticipates reference to a specific sin, the blasphemy of the sons. The qal meaning, "to curse God," is more common than the piel meaning, "to curse oneself."[73] The verb qll can take an accusative like "God," but it cannot take a dative or a reflexive "themselves."[74] Only a few scholars, like Caspari, diverge from this consensus by viewing lāhem a dittography of the ending on mᵉqallîm, which renders "the sons are accursed."[75] De Boer views the two words as an addition to the Massoretic Text, and the Septuagint misread lāhem to get theon.[76]

aa. The piel kihāh in the last line has been variously emended to hōkiᵃh, a short form of hōkiᵃᵃh, the hiphil of wkh;[77] kihāh, a transliteration of the Septuagint's enouthetai;[78] hikāh;[79] māhāh;[80] and lōᵓ-kēn or lākēn.[81]

bb. The Septuagint renders the first word as kai oudᵓ houtōs, as though the first word were a contracted form of lōᵓ -kēn.[82] The Septuagint may have read gam wᵉlākēn or wᵉgam lākēn, and the original text was lōᵓ-kēn.[83] Stoebe believes the Septuagint had a text with lōᵓ-kēn, which was a corruption of lōᵓ kōᵓāh in verse 13, so he retains the text.[84]

cc. The hithpael verb yitkapēr is translated by the Septuagint as exilasthēsetai. Therefore, some prefer to read yikpēr,[85] but others prefer to retain the text.[86]

dd. The Septuagint reads kai orthrisen to prōi, which leads scholars to insert wayyaškēm babōqer. This was theoretically lost by haplography or homoioteleuton as a result of the repetition of bqr.[87] Ehrlich diverges by reading wayyaškēm

127

$\check{s}^e$mû'ēl baḇōqer.[88] Only a few call this an addition by the Septuagint.[89]

ee.   Caspari believes the ending was originally l^{ec}ēlî, and the 'et was due to dittography.[90]

ff.   The Septuagint reads pros for 'et, which leads some to insert 'el in its place as do fifty manuscripts.[91]

gg.   The Septuagint translates en tois ōsin sou, which implies the insertion of b^e'oznekā after 'ēlekā in the first line.   This would accord well with passages where the same construction appears, Genesis 20:8, 44:18, I Samuel 18:23, and II Samuel 3:19.[92]   The text is retained by de Boer who claims the Greek is exaggerated, and Stoebe who feels the Septuagint used a poor Hebrew Text.[93]

hh.   The Septuagint encourages the addition of dābar, because Codex Lagardiana has hrēma.

ii.   The Septuagint puts Eli's name after wayyō'mar.

jj.   On the basis of the Ethiopic translation Caspari proposes to omit hû' as a dittography of YHWH.[94]

kk.   Qere reading, b^{ec}ēnā(y)w, corrects the Kethib, b^{ec}ēnāw.

ll.   The Septuagint may have read nāpal for hipîl,[95] but some believe napal was the original form.[96]   If so, the translation of the Targums and Vulgate are justified.   Stoebe concurs, for this same form occurs in other classic Deuteronomistic passages: Joshua 21:45, 23:14, I Kings 8:56, and II Kings 10:10.[97]

mm.   Klostermann declares the preposition l^e belongs on the divine name to indicate its dependent relationship to the entire sentence rather than just l^{e}nābî'.[98]   Others feel the preposition l^e on both final words is a double dittography from the final letter of $\check{s}^e$mû'ēl.[99]   If they belong, the first might indicate an accusative of mode as in Deuteronomy 31:21, and the latter may show possession in relation to l^{e}nābî', "the prophet who belongs to the Lord."[100]

nn.   The Septuagint omits the last three words of verse 21 and all of 4:1a, and in its place reads: kai episteuthē Samouēl tou prophētēs genesthai tō kuriō eis panta Israēl ap akrōn tēs gēs kai heōs akrōn kai Hēli presbytēs sphodra, kai hoi huioi autou poreumenoi eporeuonto kai ponēra hē hodos autōn enōpion kuriou.   The similarity of this material with verse 20 has been

noted frequently. The chief text-critical option is to view this Greek material as a paraphrase. kai episteuthē Samouēl prophetēs genesthai tō kuriou is a paraphrase of the Hebrew in verse 20b, which reads: kî neʾemān sᵉmûʾēl lᵉnābîʾ lᵉYHWH, and the Greek phrase, eis panta Israēl ap akrōn tēs gēs kai heōs akrōn, is a paraphrase of the Hebrew in verse 20a, kol-yisraʾēl midōn wᵉʿad bᵉʾēr-šebaʿ.[101] The remaining material may reflect an original Hebrew text, which scholars reconstruct from the Septuagint and Latin Codex Legionensis to read: wᵉʿēlî zāqān mᵉʾod ûbānā(y)w holkû hālôk wᵉhareʿac darkam lipnē YHWH.[102] This Elide material would complement the material in I Samuel 2:11, 12, 21, 22, and it would contrast with the positive material in 3:21 about Samuel. The method of contrasting the Elides with Samuel is a literary device in chapter 2, for 2:11, 21 describe Samuel's obedience, while 2:12, 22 describe Elide disobedience.[103]

For those who wish to preserve the Elide reference in the text, the question of where to place it arises. Some place it after both 3:21 and 4:1a believing it was lost[104] due to haplography and the finality of the word dābar. Budde places the phrase after 3:21 and 4:1a, but he omits the last three words of 3:21 and reconstructs the text to read, [19]"Samuel grew and the Lord was with him and none of his words fell to the ground, [21]The Lord again came to Samuel at Shiloh, for the Lord revealed himself to Samuel. [20]Israel from Dan to Beersheba knew that Samuel was a prophet faithful to the Lord. [21(LXX)] Eli was very old and his sons continued to walk in evil before the Lord."[105] Smith places all of verse 21 after 4:1a. He emends YHWH to yisraʾēl following wayyōsep, and he considers lᵉheraʾoh an infinitive construct rather than a niphal infinitive absolute. He obtains the translation: "And Israel again appeared in Shiloh, because Yahweh revealed himself to Samuel."[106]

Several scholars believe the Elide reference is not original to the text. The hypothetical construction of holkû hālôk and wᵉhareʿac on the basis of the Greek is considered grammatically incorrect in Hebrew.[107] The phrase was an insertion in the Greek for the sake of continuing the parallel between Samuel and the Elides in preparation for the Elide downfall in chapter 4.[108]

A greater number of scholars are critical of translating the Greek material back into Hebrew. Some go even further and excise some of the Hebrew due to its absence from the Septuagint. bidbar YHWH is often omitted because it is redundant with niglāh YHWH, and it seems to serve the

function of connecting 3:21 to 4:1a artificially.[109] Many scholars omit the last three words of the verse and alter the sentence structure.[110] Others keep the text but reconstruct it. Klostermann begins the verse with a parenthetical particle kî, and he obtains the translation, "and Yahweh was again sought in Shiloh, because Yahweh had revealed himself to Samuel in Shiloh for the sake of his Word." l^{e}hērā$^{\circ}$ōh is seen as a passive form of r$^{\circ}$h and not a niphal infinitive construct attached to ysp.[111] Caspari reads l^{e}har$^{\circ}$ōtô, omits b^{e}šilô and $^{\circ}$el-š^{e}mû$^{\circ}$ēl in accord with the Peshiṭto, and reads bidbirô instead of bidbar YHWH.[112]

Recent scholarship has been more conservative with the text. The text is maintained with only one alteration; bidbar YHWH is read at the end of 4:1a, so the translation becomes; "thus the Word of Samuel was as the Word of the Lord to all Israel."[113] Stoebe reads the Massoretic text as it now stands and resists the insertions of the Septuagint.[114] His treatment is a cautious attempt to deal with the text coupled with a recognition of the impossibility of reconstructing the original text. This may be the best way to approach the text, so this author concurs with Stoebe.

Form Criticism

In its present form I Samuel 3 appears as a unified narrative. Some believe it was a unity from its origin.[115] However, there may be seams where material might once have been separate. I Samuel 3:11-14 is a word of judgment, which might have had independent existence prior to the present narrative. I Samuel 3:19-4:1a appears to be a summary, which may have been meant to serve as conclusion for all of chapters 1-3. Because it is an oracle, 3:11-14 may be studied as a specific form whether or not it had an independent existence. Another form is the imprecation formula in 3:17, "may God so do to you," a formula used for pronouncing an oath. Similar formulas are found in I Samuel 14:44, 20:13, 25:22, II Samuel 3:9, 3:35, 19:14, I Kings 2:23, II Kings 6:31, and Ruth 6:31. The only reference in the Pentateuch may be the oath God takes upon Himself before Abraham in Genesis 15, but the full formula is lacking. The formula may be connected to that part of the ceremony in which an animal is slain and the curse is laid upon the participant; and should he break the oath, he would receive the same treatment as the animal.[116]

Major consideration should be given to 3:11-14 because of a similar word of judgment in 2:27-36, and the relation between these two oracles immediately raises questions of their integrity

130

and origin. Since 2:27-36 is considered to be a late addition by some scholars, there are manifold possibilities for explanation. Various positions have been articulated:

1. If the text of 3:21 is repointed to read, "you will tell him," the problem is gone, for 3:11-14 is seen to be a separate oracle unrelated to 2:27-36. It is the uncomfortable "I have told him," which connects these two oracles so closely.[117] This emendation escapes the problem rather than solving it, for the content of both oracles is still closely related.

2. Both 2:27-36 and 3:11-14 were inserted into the text at the same time. They might be considered Deuteronomistic editing in the earlier narrative material, whether that material be seen as Elohistic or independent stories.[118]

3. Both were inserted secondarily, but 2:27-36 was inserted prior to 3:11-14, which was a shortened reference to the former.[119]

4. Only 3:12 is the addition, the rest of 3:11, 13-14 is integral to chapter 3. Material in 2:27-36 and 3:12 was added at the same time.[120]

5. 3:11-14 was an old anti-Elide element that had an existence prior to the rest of chapter 3. In the oral stage it was related to other anti-Elide elements like 2:27-36. When the author created chapters 1-3, these elements were woven into text. The reference to previous judgment already existed in the oral setting.[121]

6. The text has been mutilated, and our present text in 3:11-14 has displaced previous material.[122] A longer passage of similar content to the present text might have been here, for Jeremiah 19:3 appears to quote it when he says, "Behold, I will bring evil upon this place, that which whoever hears, his ears will tingle." The same passage may appear in paraphrased form in Jeremiah 7:2-15 in the Temple oracle.[123] Perhaps the text of 3:11-14 was altered, shortened, or modified when 2:27-36 was added.[124] There was a modified version of 3:11-14 in the text, because such a word of judgment is commonly found in most prophetic legends, and it is usually directed against the king or leader, as here.[125]

7. The oracle in 3:11-14 does not refer to 2:27-36 at all, since the latter was a late insertion. Rather, 2:27-36 was put in to foreshadow 3:11-14.[126] This ignores the reference in 3:12, however.

8. The oracle in 3:11-14 is integral to the text; it builds upon a different tradition than 2:27-36. Though it represents

a different interest than the rest of chapter 3, the judgment in 3:11-14 was woven into the text when the entire chapter was created. It shows no awareness of 2:27-36, because Samuel's reluctance to tell the oracle implies he is unaware of the curse in 2:27-36.[127] Stoebe's view is similar to Dus, who also believes there were various anti-Elide traditions in existence, but Dus believes they were all used by the creator of the unit, chapters 1-3, whereas Stoebe believes chapter 3 was created at a different stage than 1-2.

9. When chapter 3 was composed, chapters 1-2 already existed.[128] This is why 3:12-14 is so brief, and 3:12 refers to 2:27-36.

10. Both oracles are independent of each other, for 2:27-36 refers to the punishment upon the house of Eli, while 3:11-14 is directed at the Elides and all of Israel. Both oracles are fulfilled by the same misfortune in chapter 4.[129]

11. All of 2:27-4:1a was created at the same time, and 3:11-14 refers back to 2:27-36 in this unified account.[130]

This author is convinced that 3:12 does refer to 2:27-36. Both words of judgment in 2:27-36 and 3:11-14 may have come from an oral setting prior to the creation of chapter 3. But 3:11-14 was not inserted into an already existing text, as the earlier literary critics envisioned. It was woven into chapter 3 when that chapter was created. The word of judgment is integral to the text, even though the particular tradition used may have had a prior history. The oracle in 3:12 refers to 2:27-36, and since 3:12 seems to be integral to the text, it implies the presence of 2:27-36 at the creation of chapter 3. Though 3:12 may refer in some vague way to anti-Elide oracles in general, this author thinks it is more probable that 2:27-36 is the material the creator really had in mind with the reference in 3:12 when the composition arose. Stoebe's view is possible; chapter 3 may be independent, and 3:12 may merely refer to anti-Elide oracles that floated in the cycles of tradition. But given the present state of the debate, the best position seems to be a theory like that of Dus which views the material arising as a literary unit that utilizes earlier traditions.

The present form of the text under consideration will exclude 2:27-36, even though it may have arisen as a traditio-historical unity with chapter 3. It is a different narrative account, and it contains a continuous narrative of its own. So far we have investigated the forms found within chapter 3, but we must now justify consideration of 3:1-4:1a as a separate unity by identifying its form as a whole, or its peculiar genre. When we find what kind of structure underlies this section, we

132

shall perceive not only the rationale for its delimitation, but also the message it conveys.

It may well be that the unit under consideration is to be defined as 3:1-18. Most scholars concur that 3:19-4:1a may form a conclusion to chapter 3, and perhaps to all of chapters 1-3. An observation that would label these few verses as a later insertion is mitigated by the fact that 2:27-4:1a was a conclusion that arose with the original creation of the greater unit. Because it arose with that material, and because it does play an important role in concluding chapter 3, it will be considered with the narrative in 3:1-18 as a form critical unit. The oracle in 2:27-36 has been excluded from consideration, even though 3:12 refers to it, because it does not share in the formal structure of chapter 3. However, 3:19-4:1a does share, if only partially, in that structure. Only Press would maintain that 3:19-4:1a was totally unrelated to 3:1-18 at first. He believes it was a conclusion to a narrative account which terminated with 2:27-36. The account in 3:1-18 was a later insertion, and this account of Samuel's oracle was a variation on the account about the nameless man of God, for Samuel was that man of God.[131]

Thus we have determined 3:1-18 (3:1-4:1a) is a prophetic legend with a word of judgment, and it related to many of the[132] other stories in the books of Samuel and Kings. But this vague category must be further delimited by a closer consideration of the text.

<u>Genre Criticism</u>

A chief concern is the definition of this pericope. Scholars usually concur that it functions as a call narrative of Samuel.[133] Samuel receives a prophetic Word from the Lord at a time when such a Word is rare. This verifies Samuel as the true prophet while condemning the Elides both by the content of the message and by Eli's own failure to receive such a Word himself. Since this is Samuel's first reception of the Word of the Lord, it is logical to assume that the narrative functions equally as a call narrative. It is the only experience of the Samuel traditions which can be considered as such.[134] Since Samuel is a prophet, and since prophets are called, therefore Samuel was called, and this must be the call narrative. This is the spurious kind of logic which has been used to ascertain the text's genre.

This author disclaims this logical deduction and sides with those who refuse to define the pericope as a call narrative. The text lacks the formal characteristics of a call narrative,

and the motifs found in this text are actually common to other theophanic experiences.

This text may have displaced a prior account of Samuel's call in the development of the traditions. Budde believes the text once contained the call of Samuel, but it has been modified to become a message of misfortune against the Elides by the insertion of 3:11-14.[135] Richter, however, feels this explanation is unnecessary, for there is no reason why a word of judgment would displace a call narrative. He feels there never was a call narrative of Samuel.[136] The text is primarily concerned with the condemnation of the Elides, not the prophetic call of Samuel.

This text makes the separate existence of a call narrative for Samuel difficult. The Word of the Lord comes to a young novice unprepared for such an encounter. This precludes a prior encounter on his part, which might function as the call. The inexperience of Samuel is stressed for literary effect, for he contrasts vividly with the experienced Eli, who is too blind to see. Because of this literary stress it becomes impossible to have a prior call experience after the initial reception of the Word of the Lord by Samuel. Therefore, this experience becomes the likely candidate. Yet for his purposes the narrator did not see fit to use a call narrative structure for the creation of this account, but he chose instead the ancient Near Eastern message dream.

Prophetic Call Narrative Structure

The call narrative structure has received excellent scholarly attention in recent years. The development of such a call narrative form was necessitated by the actual prophetic experience. Prophets realized that they were compelled by the spirit of the Lord in a manner set apart from the usual ecstatic or hallucinogenic experience; therefore this category developed in order to give full expression to their personal experience and a legitimacy to their prophetic ministry.[137]

Georg Fohrer and Klaus Baltzer believe the idea of being called to perform an action is common in prophetic accounts. It serves a role in the created literary structure of prophetic symbolic action; Fohrer outlines this structure as call to action, performance of action, and interpretation of action.[138] Evolving out of this structure a more specific call may have arisen: the call to a prophetic ministry. Ernst Kutsch isolates the components of this type of call with a man who was not a prophet but a deliverer, Gideon. The specific components found in Judges 6:11-24 are: 1) appearance of God, 2) commission, "I send you," 3) human protestation, "I am not the

134

right man," 4) divine affirmation, "I will be with you," and 5) the sign of testimony. Similar patterns may be found in the call experiences of Moses, Exodus 3:10-12; Jeremiah, Jeremiah 1:5-10; and Saul in I Samuel 10:1-7, 9:21.[139] Johannes Fichtner outlines a similar pattern: 1) divine speech, 2) human protest, 3) confirmation of commission, and 4) sign. He likewise perceives the pattern in Exodus 3:1-20, 6:1-7:7, Jeremiah 1:4-19, and Judges 6:11-24.[140] Wolfgang Richter has carefully studied various forms of call narratives, and he distinguishes between the mosi'a formulate for delivers (I Kings 6, I Samuel 9:1-10:16) and the prophetic formula (Exodus 3). The two forms are sometimes difficult to distinguish, but the latter usually contains a command to proclaim the Word of the Lord and reports a vision received by the messenger of the Lord.[141] The most thorough evaluation has been undertaken by Norman Habel. After analyzing the calls of Moses and Gideon, he discerns six formal elements. He believes that these two accounts became normative for later prophetic call experiences.[142] These elements include:

Divine Confrontation: The Lord comes in a vision and appears before the recipient. Judges 6:11b-12 reads, "Gideon was beating out wheat in the wine press and the angel of Yahweh appeared to him." Exodus 3:1-3, 4a has, "Moses was tending the flock . . . a messenger of Yahweh appeared." Isaiah perceived a vision in Isaiah 6:1, "I saw the Lord, sitting on a throne, seraphim standing above Him, whom shall I send, one called to another and said, 'Here am I, send me.'" Isaiah's vision format has been influenced by I Kings 22:19, which reads, "I saw Yahweh sitting on this throne and all the host of heaven on His right hand. 'Who will entice?' One said one thing, 'I will entice!'" Ezekiel has a confrontation in Ezekiel 1:1-28.

Introductory Word: The Lord calls on the individual, uses his name frequently, and identifies himself. In Exodus 3:4b-9 the Lord calls, "Moses, Moses," identifies himself as the god of the patriarchs, and laments the misery of this people in Egypt. Judges 6:12b-13 reads, "Yahweh is with you, mighty man of valor." Jeremiah is called from before his birth according to his account of the encounter. Ezekiel 1:29-2:2 is the word for that prophet.

Commission: The Lord tells the individual what his mission entails. Judges 6:14 reports, "and Yahweh turned and said to him, 'Go in this might of yours and deliver Israel from the hand of Midian; do I not send you?'" Exodus 3:10 has, "I will send you to Pharaoh and you may bring forth my people, the children of Israel out of Egypt." Ezekiel is commissioned in 2:3-5, and Jeremiah is ordained a prophet to the nations in Jeremiah 1:5.

135

Objection: Out of humility the prophet declares his unworthiness, and thus indicates that the prophetic call is truly the will of God and not the individual prophet's own desire. Judges 6:15 says, "and he said to him 'Pray Lord, how can I deliver Israel? Behold, my clan is the weakest in Manasseh, and I am the least in my family.'" Exodus 3:11 reads, "Who am I that I should go unto Pharaoh, and that I should bring forth the children of Israel out of Egypt?" Isaiah objects in Isaiah 6:11 saying, "How long, O Lord," Jeremiah 1:6 has the prophet declare, "I cannot speak, for I am a child," and Ezekiel's objection is registered in Ezekiel 2:6, 8.

Reassurance: The prophet's objection is met by divine assurance of presence. Judges 6:16 reads, "And Yahweh said to him, 'I am indeed with you! And you shall smite the Midianites as one man.'" Exodus 3:12a has, "But I will be with you." Jeremiah is forbidden to call himself a child and is ordered to go wherever and say whatever God commands him in Jeremiah 1:17. Isaiah's objection is answered in Isaiah 6:11, and Ezekiel is reassured in Ezekiel 2:6-7.

Sign: A physical demonstration gives testimony of the reality of the revelation. Judges 6:17 has Gideon demand a sign; "he said to him, 'If I have found favor with you, show me a sign.'" The subsequent narration describes this sign. The burning bush may be the sign for Moses. Jeremiah is touched on the tongue in Jeremiah 1:9, and Ezekiel eats the scroll in 2:8-3:11. Habel concludes that the call narratives are "open proclamations of the prophet's claim to be Yahweh's agent at work in Israel."[143]

Since Habel's work Richter has adopted a similar structure for the prophetic call account: 1) demonstration of need,[144] 2) commission, 3) objection, 4) promise, and 5) sign. Any consideration of I Samuel 3 has to take these observations into account.

Prophetic Call Narrative Structure and I Samuel 3

Only a few scholars have directly addressed themselves to the evaluation of I Samuel 3 as a call narrative, with only two of them having undertaken to utilize the call narrative categories just delineated.

Murray Newman feels that the prophetic calls of Moses, Elijah, and Samuel are preserved in order to establish the succession by northern, prophetic, and Elohistic circles of tradition. The three constitutive elements for Newman are the reception of the call at a holy site where God "sits" or is "enthroned," the auditory nature of the call, and the

commission to do the will of the Lord. This typical Elohistic prophetic call comes to Moses in Exodus 3, Elijah at Horeb in I Kings 19, and Samuel at Shiloh in I Samuel 3. The ark in I Samuel 3 functions as a minature Horeb. God is not seen, He is only heard.[145] Both Samuel and Moses have their names called twice according to Exodus 3:4 and the Septuagint reading of I Samuel 3:4, 10.[146] The prophets are then summoned to carry out the mission of the Lord in order to save Israel.[147] Unfortunately, Newman's analysis is too superficial. His isolation of only these three motifs pales in comparison to the previous analysis of the call narrative structure. The reception of a revelation is incidental to a number of divine theopanies, not just call narratives. The double vocative is lacking with Elijah, and it may be an insertion with Samuel. Furthermore, Jacob is called by a double vocative, in an auditory revelation, at a holy site in Genesis 46:2. Yet no one advocates that this is a call narrative. Newman does not satisfactorily demonstrate that Samuel's experience is exclusively auditory. The commission is the best sign of a prophetic call, and with Samuel this commission to deliver Israel is totally lacking, for he receives only the word of judgment. Newman's most valid criterion, the prophetic commission, is lacking in Samuel's experience.

Although he does not advocate the influence of the call narrative pattern on Samuel's experience, Alan Jenks has isolated three formal elements in the calls of Moses and Samuel. In both instances there is the use of the word $qr^{\jmath}$, the recipient is called by name, and the recipient responds, "Here am I."[148]

Moses: wayyiqrā$^{\jmath}$ $^{\jmath}$elā(y)w . . . wayyō$^{\jmath}$mer mōšeh mōšeh

wayyō$^{\jmath}$mer hinnēnî

Samuel: wayyiqrā$^{\jmath}$ YHWH $^{\jmath}$el-š^{e}mû$^{\jmath}$ēl

wayyō$^{\jmath}$mer hinnēnî

In both instances there is stress upon the auditory, although there is implication of visual phenomenon with ḥāzôn in 3:1 and hammor$^{\jmath}$āh in 3:15. These three formal similarities appear to fulfill the requirements of Habel's second category, Introductory Word. Jenks also finds other similarities between Moses and Samuel; both were seers who received visions, they led the people in holy war, delivered the people from oppression, mediated for the people, and they became paradigms in Israel for years. These similarities, he believes, are due to the formulation of both cycles of tradition in northern, prophetic, and Elohistic circles, where revelations generally came in

137

auditory night visions.[149] Thus the formal similarity between Exodus 3 and I Samuel 3 is due to the influence of Moses and Samuel traditions upon each other, and it is not necessarily due to the influence of a prophetic call narrative structure.

Scholars have utilized the categories of Habel in evaluating[150] Samuel 3 to perceive the call narrative structure. However, a reconstruction is necessary.

Confrontation: This is said to occur in 3:1-4 with phrases that describe the prior setting and circumstances surrounding the call experience. These include: 1) infrequency of the divine Word, 2) Eli's poor eyesight, 3) Samuel's ministry before the Lord, 4) the reference to Samuel's sleep, and most important, 5) the presence of the ark, the physical representation of the Lord. Unfortunately, none of these really constitutes the key ingredient of the confrontation, which is the sudden appearance of the deity. The ark itself does not constitute a special confrontation, unless the Lord visibly appears with it, for the ark is a permanent fixture. Therefore, the only possible phrase that might constitute a confrontation is found in 3:10, "the Lord came and stood." But this formulation is present in the text for a different reason; it is part of a different form critical structure, and it is unrelated to a call narrative.

Introductory Word: I Samuel 3:5-14 begins with the same language as does the call of Moses. The Lord "calls" to Samuel, and he replies, "Here am I." This is a good observation, but it remains only a truncated form of the category described by Habel. Furthermore, Samuel's response, "Here am I," is given to Eli; he speaks to the Lord the message given him by Eli, "Speak, your servant is listening." Other elements are lacking. The Lord gives no self-identification nor historically conditioned statement. However, Eli has already identified the deity for Samuel. But the lack of a direct introductory statement by the Lord is significant. The similarities that do exist may be in the text because of a confluence of traditions, or the author's desire to use well-known words. The Lord "calls" to Abraham in Genesis 22:1, and he responds "Here I am," and in Genesis 46:1 the Lord "calls" to Jacob with a double vocative and Jacob replies, "Here am I." These formulas appear to be common to several types of theophanic experience. The Jacob experience, in particular, is a dream theophany, as is I Samuel 3.

Divine Commission: This category is completely lacking, as all will admit. Ritterspach explains this by deducing that Samuel is not a prophet in the later classical sense, nor is he completely like Moses. He is the beginning of the prophetic movement, but he is not a full-fledged prophet; therefore, he lacks the commission. He is only called a prophet twice in all

the Samuel traditions (I Samuel 3:10, 9:9) and he utters the prophetic formula, "Thus says the Lord," only twice (I Samuel 10:18, 15:2).[151] This may well be true, but the divine commission is still lacking for Samuel, and that constitutes the heart of a prophetic call narrative.

Prophetic Objection: I Samuel 3:15 records that "Samuel feared to tell Eli the vision." This fear is different than the fear of Moses, but both scholars believe there is enough similarity to use this phrase to fulfill the requirement of the category. But the prophetic objection is to be directed to the commissioner, the Lord, not another human agent. This makes the rest of the structure disjointed, for the Lord would not be able to respond with reassurance nor give a sign, unless the objection had been voiced before Him during the call experience itself. Samuel's activity the next morning is temporarily removed from the so-called call experience of the previous night. The prophetic call is an experience between God and the prophet; there can be no involvement with another human being. The self-doubt voiced in the prophetic objection is to demonstrate that the call is from God, not the prophet's own desire. To express this objection before another human being runs counter to the whole idea behind the motif in the call narrative.

Reassurance: Eli is said to be the instrument for reassurance to Samuel in I Samuel 3:16-18. The arguments of the previous section apply here. Reassurance is given by God to verify the divine origin of the prophetic call. To receive assurance from a human agent undermines that divine authority. The scene is enacted the next day and it is totally removed from the experience between God and Samuel of the previous night. The call experience has been terminated by the ensuing morning. Stretching the categories into the next day loses the intention and effect of the call experience.

Sign: In I Samuel 3:19-4:1a the sign is said to be composed of Samuel's verification as prophet, the validity of his words, and the recognition of his prophetic authority. This is no sign. This is the concomitant result that should come ideally with every true prophet's ministry. Unlike Exodus 3:12 which refers to the future worship of God at the mountain as the sign; this text does not call the categories in I Samuel 3:19-4:1a a sign; that has been the deduction of scholars. The verses mention nothing which is physical, a demonstration of divine presence. Nor can it be said that there is a sign which gives the prophet courage and assurance to go forth and proclaim the initial Word of the Lord. The text merely refers to the outcome of Samuel's ministry, an outcome about which he was not informed during the divine experience.

This author concludes that the text may not be construed as a call narrative, for it lacks the important characteristics of a call narrative. Richter takes a similar critical view of this text, for he also finds the call narrative structure lacking in the account. He responds to a number of other scholars who term this a call. Hylander believes the presence of the call is verified in the impending crisis of chapter 4, but Richter replies there is then no formal call, for the defeat follows the experience in chapter 3, and it is difficult to perceive a call in that. Hylander and Hertzberg both maintain that the theophany makes this a call experience, but theophanies are found in many experiences other than call narratives. Richter criticizes Newman for being vague and failing to produce any concrete evidence of a call experience. Newman's double vocative is insufficient for defining the text as a call narrative, for it is simply an address. Therefore, he also concludes that Samuel's experience[152] is merely a prophetic oracle, the first which he received.

The form of this pericope is not a prophetic call narrative. It is a type of prophetic oracle, as we determined earlier, but we must now seek to discover the specific structure into which this text has been cast.

I Samuel as an Auditory Message Dream

Since the prophetic call narrative has been eliminated as an option, the possibility of a dream structure, as we observed in the ancient Near East, should be considered. A comparison of the ancient Near Eastern dream structure and the various expressions found in ancient dreams with the structure and content of I Samuel 3 will produce evidence that Samuel's experience has been molded by this comparative material.

There has always been a debate as to whether Samuel's experience could be defined as an authentic dream. Several scholars firmly declare that this text is not a dream, and they offer several reasons. Samuel appears to be awake when he receives the message, he runs back and forth to Eli before receiving the message, and it appears he is conscious throughout the experience. Since these scholars use the modern definition of dream, they believe this experience[153] cannot be called a dream, because Samuel is not sleeping. But ancient Near Eastern dreams often have the recipient in a semi-conscious or even conscious condition for the reception of the message. A second criticism is that Samuel responds audibly in his experience, and he[154] cannot be asleep and dreaming if he is awake and talking. But audible response on the part of the recipient occurs in ancient Near Eastern dreams. Some scholars point out that the word $h^a l \hat{o} m$ does not

140

appear in the text. But if the experience has all the earmarks of a dream, the actual use of the word is not necessary. In the Elohist epic the use of the word in dream theophanies is a fixed formula, but I Samuel 3 lies outside that epic narrative, and it does not need to use that fixed formula.[155] A fourth criticism is that this is not a dream, for a vision is lacking, only a voice is heard. It is unlike Jacob's dream at Bethel. There are two responses to this argument. As we have seen in the auditory message dream of the ancient Near East, a dream report can be auditory with little or no reference to the visual aspects. So it is also with this dream. Then, too, we cannot quickly discount the possibility of an accompanying vision. Some scholars feel that Samuel did not see Yahweh, because no clear statement is given to that effect.[156] But the phrase, "the Lord came and stood," indicates that there may have been some form of visual appearance.[157] Like so many ancient Near Eastern dreams there is at least a passing reference to the physical presence of the deity, but the emphasis upon the visual phenomenon fades in importance before the auditory phenomena.

A final criticism against calling I Samuel 3 a message dream could be offered by denying the essential difference between the genre of prophetic call narrative and dream theophany. Long maintains that both forms are rooted in a common visionary epiphany formula, and there is little difference between dream reports and call narratives. He observes the elements of several ancient Near Eastern dream reports and biblical call narratives in order to find the common structure. This structure was used by the biblical authors and slight variations in the text provide us the apparent differences between prophetic call narratives and dream reports. Ultimately he is correct, for the religious experience between such reports is probably very similar. But the religious experience is also indescribable, or so say the mystics who have them. What is reported is a literary form designed to communicate the experience in human terms. What we observe are those literary forms. The authors of the biblical text chose different ways of describing religious experience, and two of those ways are dream reports and prophetic call narratives. Long is correct; there is a common experience and a common way of expressing visionary theophanic experiences which has influenced all of our theophanic accounts. But our present biblical text uses different literary forms to report those experiences. The prophetic call narrative and the dream theophany are two variations of Long's visionary epiphany formula. Hopefully, the separate integrity of both forms has been established by the previous discussion, as well as by the work of other scholars.[158]

141

Some scholars concur that this experience is a dream experience, or an experience with dream-like elements.[159] It carries the implication of being an early morning experience, a time when dreams are most frequent, for the lamp is nearly burned out according to I Samuel 3:3.[160] The reference to Samuel's lying in bed implies a return to the state of sleep or semi-consciousness in I Samuel 3:9.[161] It was the vividness of the dream call that awoke Samuel, but he returned to sleep. Finally, the fact that Samuel slept until morning indicates that this was probably a dream.

Fashioned carefully by the narrator, the text of I Samuel 3 betrays the auditory dream message pattern of the ancient Near East. One can observe similarities in regard to both the setting of the dream experience and the actual theophany of the deity. A closer comparison of the various component parts of the Samuel experience with various ancient Near Eastern dreams is necessary to demonstrate this observation.

1. Setting of the Dream Theophany

Dream revelations were frequently received in sanctuaries or at sacred sites. This was often taken for granted, and thus the accounts often omit reference to a specific place. Yet the texts often indicate that a shrine or sacred place was the locale of the theophany. I Samuel 3:2 records that, "Samuel slept in the temple of the Lord where the Ark of God was." Keret and Dan'el in their two Ugaritic dreams both have special places to receive their respective theophanies, because they both undergo an incubation process which entails being in a private chamber. The dream of the šabrû priest in Ashurbanipal's day was received in a shrine. Thutmosis IV was "in the shadow of the great god," that is, the sphinx.[162] Solomon goes to Gibeon in order to receive his revelation. With the mention of extensive sacrifice in I Kings 3:4-5, the reader might assume the presence of a shrine. Jacob receives his dream at the well-known holy place, Beersheba, in Genesis 46:1. Other texts may be added, but they are somewhat ambiguous. Dreams of Bekhten in Egypt, Ashurbanipal in Assyria, Nabonidus in Babylon, and presumably Hattushilis of the Hittites come to their recipients in the royal palace. Whether such a locale constitutes a sacred site or special location is difficult to decide.

Before the theophany occurs, it is customary to indicate that the recipient is asleep. Mesopotamian dreams of royalty usually state, "thereupon his majesty rested." Assyrian dreams also include the word utullu, "to be in bed," for emphasis. Prince Bekhten of Egypt, "was sleeping in his bed," when he received his dream.[163] Thutmosis IV "rested in the shadow of the great god, sleep took hold of him."[164] Nabonidus received

142

his dream from Sin in that part of the night meant for sleep.[165]
Ugaritic dreams render it thus:[166]

KRT A:I, 31-34:

31. bm bkyh wyšn   with his weeping he sleeps

32. bdm^ch nhmmt   in his tears, slumber

33. šnt tluan   sleep overcomes him

34. wyškb nhmmt   he lies down, slumber

2 AQHT: I, 15-16:

15. y^cl wyškb   he goes up and lies down

16. (   ) mizrt pyln   (?) the garment and passes the
                             night (or sleeps)

I Samuel 3:3 likewise takes care to mention that Samuel was
asleep, "While Samuel slept in the Temple of the Lord." Other
biblical dreams do not stress that the recipient was asleep.
Only Jacob "lay down to sleep" before his dream vision in
Genesis 28:11-12. Genesis 15:12 describes Abraham's condition
as a tardemah, a deep sleep, in which his visionary experience
occurs. The more general phrase, "to spend the night,"
appears in other texts, which imply that the recipient was
asleep.

A reference to time is sometimes mentioned. The
precision of Greek dreams in this regard is lacking in the
ancient Near East. Early morning hours predominate as the
favorite time for Greek deities to appear in dream theophanies.
The Akkadian word for dream, munattu, implies sleep in the
early morning hours. Likewise, Ludlul-bēl-nēmeqi mentions
dreams in the early morning hours.[167] Nabonidus receives his
dream in the night,[168] but it is the part of the night when men
are fast asleep. Though I Samuel 3:3 is vague, it gives
some indication of the time when it states, "before the lamp of
God went out." Despite our inability to determine the precise
meaning of this phrase, many feel that the reference is to a
time just before dawn when the oil was almost consumed in the
lamp. If so, Samuel's dream occurs at the same time as
Assyrian and Greek dreams. The one exception to this
particular time is the experience of Thutmosis IV, for "sleep
took hold of him, slumbering at the time when the sun was at
its peak."[169] Biblical dreams consistently record the reception
of dreams at night, but the specific time is not given. Genesis
15:11 reports the dream to be "after the sun went down,"
perhaps early in the night. Otherwise dreams are said to come

143

to the recipient by night (Genesis 20:3, 31:24, Numbers 22:22), or the theophanies are specified as night visions (I Kings 3:5, Genesis 46:2), or the text indicates that the recipient is spending the night somewhere when the theophany comes (Genesis 28:11, Numbers 22:8).

Samuel's experience bears close similarity with ancient Near Eastern dreams in regard to the setting in a sanctuary, reference to his being asleep, and allusion to the time of night.

2.   The Dream Theophany

With the consideration of the actual theophanic experience the correspondence between Samuel's dream and other ancient Near Eastern dreams becomes increasingly evident.

The actual encounter between man and deity contrasts the activity of the god with the passivity of man. The simplicity of "the Lord called to Samuel," in I Samuel 3:4a demonstrates that clearly. The Sphinx Stela uses the term "to find," implying the sudden encounter between Thutmosis IV and Atum-Re. The Memphis Stela of Amenhotep II states how Amon came before the king in his dream.[170] Keret's dream indicates that El took the initiative in the encounter.[171]

KRT A:I, 35-37

35. wbḥlmh   . . . and in his dream

36. il yrd bdhrth!   El comes down in a vision

37, ab adm wyqrb   the Father of Man draws near

Nabonidus describes how the god Sin appeared in his glory before him and spoke.[172] In all ancient Near Eastern message dreams the deity initiates the theophany and addresses the human recipient. Biblical dreams frequently use the technical phrase, "the Lord came to NN in a dream by night," (Genesis 20:3, 31:24, Numbers 22:20, I Kings 3:5). In Genesis 15:1 the formula involves the "Word of the Lord," which comes. In these cases the emphasis is upon the active speaking of the Lord, who has an important message to deliver. In Genesis 31:11 it is only a slight variation when it reads, "the angel of God said to me in my dream." In these instances the text records of the Lord that "he said," (Genesis 20:3, 31:11, 31:24, 46:2, 15:1, Numbers 22:9, 22:20, and I Kings 3:5). Only in Genesis 28:13 is there the implication of an accompanying vision when it states, "the Lord was standing beside him." These dream theophanies of the ancient Near East and the Bible stress the active communication of the deity in a verbal fashion, which then overshadows the visual aspects of

144

the theophany. Samuel's dream likewise is a verbal theophany and the visual aspects, if they are present, are secondary.

One of the initial components of the message dream theophany is the awakening of the recipient in order for him to hear the message. Since it has been noted in the format that the recipient is asleep, it becomes necessary to awaken him. In I Samuel 3:4-10 the calls come to Samuel three times presumably to arouse him and obtain his undivided attention. Unfortunately, in the first two instances Samuel misunderstands and runs to Eli. This threefold call is probably due to the literary artistry of the narrator, for it heightens the suspense and entertains the audience. But it clearly functions as a prelude to the divine message by ensuring that the recipient is awake and ready to listen. The priest of Ishtar was aroused, negeltû,[173] and "when he awoke Ishtar showed him a night vision." Keret is awakened in his dream: KRT A:I, line 35: wyqms wbhlmh, "and he is startled, and in his dream."[174] The Egyptian word for dream, rswt, is related to the verb, "to awaken," and is written with the symbol of an open eye. In the more developed Greek format the deity often cries, "Are you asleep, NN?"[175] Is the dreamer awake, semi-conscious, or asleep and yet dreaming that he is conscious? This is unanswerable, but we cannot exclude these experiences from the category of dream because the recipients seem awake, as some commentators do with the Samuel experience. The ancients included the aspect of being awake in order to receive the message, and we have no right to impose our[176] modern definition of dream upon the ancient literary category.

After the deity has obtained the attention of the recipient, the deity utters an introductory word, usually an exclamation, imperative, or a rhetorical question. In Samuel's case it was merely the word of address, "Samuel, Samuel," which was also the awakening formula.[177] Ishtar addresses Ashurbanipal by saying, "Be not afraid."[178] To Hattushilis this same goddess declares, "Shall I abandon you to a hostile deity? Be not afraid!"[179] El asks a question of Keret:

KRT: A:I, 38-40:

38. bšal krt mn!   in order to ask Keret, "What ails

39. krt kybky   Keret, that he weeps

40. ydm^c n!^cmn ǵlm   the good servant, he cries"

Biblical dreams frequently begin the divine message with the particle hinnēh, "behold," (Genesis 20:3), or the vocative (Genesis 31:11, 46:2, I Samuel 3:10). Abraham is addressed

145

like Ashurbanipal, "Be not afraid," (Genesis 15:1). In Genesis 28:13 the introductory word is the self-identification of the deity. Another form of introduction is the question. Balaam is asked, "Who are these men with you?" (Numbers 22:9). Solomon is asked, "What shall I give you? Tell me!" (I Kings 3:5).

With the word of introduction frequently comes divine self-identification. Thutmosis IV hears, "I am your father Harmakhis-Khepri-Re-Atum," And Djoser hears, "I am Khnum, your fashioner."[180] Patriarchal dreams in the Old Testatment have similar introductions, especially for Jacob. In Genesis 28:13 he hears, "I am the Lord, the God of your father Abraham, and the God of Isaac," in Genesis 31:12 it is merely, "I am God of Bethel," and finally in Genesis 46:3 the formula is "I am God, the God of your Father." This element is lacking in Samuel's dream experience. However, it also is wanting in many ancient Near Eastern dreams, especially where the deity also appears visually. Does this imply that Samuel could see the Lord, and thus the need for self-identification is eliminated? It may, but not necessarily. Eli has already identified the deity for Samuel, and subsequently Samuel calls the deity by name, "Speak, Lord, your servant hears you." Divine self-identification would be superfluous.

This leads us to another component of the dream experience, allusion to the visual appearance of the deity. Since the message dream is primarily an auditory experience, the visual phenomena would be mentioned initially and subsequently left undeveloped in the rest of the report. To us the ancient deities might seem to be talking mannequins; in reality, the literary convention chose not to dwell on visual phenomena in simple message dreams. Visual phenomena were more important in symbolic and mantic dreams. I Samuel 3:10 mentions that the "Lord came and stood." Commentators are left to debate whether this implies a visual appearance. The text is ambiguous. But so are other similar reports. Genesis 28:13 also indicates that the Lord came and stood beside Jacob in the Yahwist account. Ishtar's message for Ashurbanipal may have a visual aspect if the corrupt text is properly reconstructed when it reads, "Be not afraid that you see me!"[181] Several ancient dreams, however, clearly report the visual apparition of the deity as the message is delivered. Eannatum's Vulture Stela records a visual dream experience in VI:25-27: na.a.ra...sag.gamu.na.gub, "he (deity) took his stand at the head of the sleeper." Ludlul-bêl-nêmeqi states, i-ru-ba-am-ma i-taz-zi-iz, "he (deity) entered and took his stand." Here and elsewhere the Akkadian word for the god's activity is zazu, "to take one's stand," a very physical activity. The šabrû priest of Ashurbanipal describes the god's activity by saying, erēbu, "he entered," and asû "he left."

146

Nabonidus had a dream in which he saw "Marduk, the Great Lord, and Sin, the luminary of heaven and earth, stood there both." In another dream he described how the deity as "a man stood suddenly beside me."[182] In a third dream he stated how Sin appeared in all his divine glory.[183] On the Hunger Stela Djoser records, "I found the God standing over against me."[184] Merneptah records, "then his majesty saw in a dream as if it were the image of Ptah standing in the presence of Pharaoh."[185] Keret's dream may imply a visual appearance.[187]

KRT A:I, 35-37:

35.	wbḥlmh	. . . and in his dream
36.	il yrd bdhrth!	El comes down in a vision
37.	ab adm wyqrb	the Father of man approaches

Driver's interpretation of the Dan'el dream account has El begin his address with a physical gesture: 2 AQHT II, 35: (bkm) yiḥd il ᶜbdh, "Forthwith El took hold of his servant."[188] In Homer the phrase epistanai kata, "to stand over the head," occurs twice in dream experiences: Iliad 24:683, Hermes and Priamos, and Odyssey 20:32, Athena and Odysseus.[189] Throughout the ancient world the sources use the term "to stand" as a description of the deity's action. The deity stands before the dreamer in a way as to be seen. For this reason it is possible that the references in Genesis 28:13 and I Samuel 3:10 describe the Lord as standing by the recipient.

It is difficult to reduce all the divine messages to a basic pattern, for some are so brief as to defy an evaluation. Yet there appear to be two common types of messages. In one the deity declares something that he or she is about undertake on the listener's behalf or for the people among whom the listener is found. Thus in I Samuel 3:11 the Lord says, "Soon I shall do something in Israel which will ring in the ears of all who hear it." The other type of message is the imperative, whereby the deity gives instructions or a command to the recipient.[190]

The former type of message is more common to ancient Near Eastern dreams. Ishtar boldly declares to Ashurbanipal's entire army, "I shall go in front of Ashurbanipal, the king whom I have created myself." In a dream to Ashurbanipal himself she declares, "Be not afraid (that you see me), I have already had mercy upon you on account of the prayer you performed and because your eyes were full of tears." In a dream to the šabrû priest she orders the king to remain where he is, because she is going out to fight his enemies for him. Here, both command and promise are combined. The god Sin

147

also declares that he will destroy Ashurbanipal's enemies.[191] Thutmosis IV is told that he will be made pharaoh. In a rather vague text Sennacherib receives the promises that he will conquer Egypt.[192] The wife of Hattushilis hears Ishtar promise her, "I shall assist your husband . . . I will exalt him."[193] In Ugarit Dan'el receives the promise of a son.[194]

Biblical dreams also reveal a God who promises to do things for the recipient. Abraham receives the promise of children in Genesis 15:1-5 and is told how God would bring about the sojourn and exodus in 15:13-16. In Genesis 20:3 Abimelech is told, "you shall die because of this woman whom you have taken." Jacob is promised land, descendents, blessing, and divine accompaniment in Genesis 28:13-15. Solomon receives the promise of wisdom, honor, and wealth in I Kings 3:11. A number of biblical dreams vary from this kind of message; they are the imperative message dreams listed previously. Thus the image of a deity promising or commanding in a dream might be part of the pattern.

Despite the passivity of the human recipient, occasional dialogue occurs between dreamer and deity. It might be said that Samuel's remark, "Speak, for your servant hears you," in I Samuel 3:10, could be considered dialogue even though it really initiates the divine theophany. After this statement Samuel is silent, his lines in the scene are short. But this is typical of other dreams. Nabonidus argues with Marduk and Sin about rebuilding the temple in Haran because it is held by the enemy, "The Umman-manda are laying siege to the very temple which you have ordered me to rebuild and their armed might is very great."[195] Merneptah responds briefly to Ptah.[196] Hattushilis responds twice to lady Danu-Hepa, "I have already before made a golden zaḫum-ewer for the Weather-god!," and, "Why did you not give the ḫuḫupal-instruments and the lapis-lazuli stones which you have promised to him, to the Weather-god?"[197] Biblical message dreams have far more dialogue than these. The most significant example is in I Kings 3:5-15, where Solomon manages to respond at length to God. Abraham responds to God in his first vision, Genesis 15:1-5. In Genesis 20:4 Abimelech protests his innocence after the initial divine threat. Jacob responds, "Here am I" in Genesis 31:11 and 46:2. Balaam has no choice but to respond to the question asked by the Lord in Numbers 22:10-11.

Most message dream reports have a formal termination which implies the continued sleep of the recipient, or sudden arousal, or continued sleep until morning. This particular form indicates that the recipient truly was asleep and that the dream is valid. Ancient Near Eastern dreams emphasize the sudden-ness of the arousal and the conviction of the dreamer after the theophany terminates. The Akkadian word is negeltû, "to

148

awaken with a start." The second dream of Gudea terminates with: i.ḫa.luḫ ma.mu.dam, "he woke up with a start, it was but a dream."[198] His startledness demonstrates the importance of the dream. Tanutamon's report declares, "his majesty awoke and found them not (the snakes)." A priest of Queen Taimhotep had a dream and "on this he awoke and kissed the earth."[199] Djoser says, "then I awoke refreshed."[200] Thutmosis IV terminates his account, "and the king's son (himself) awoke when he heard this . . . he recognized the words of this god."[201] Keret's dream report ends thus:[202]

KRT A:I, 154-155:

154. krt yḫṭ wḫlm   Keret awoke and it was a dream

155. ᶜbd il whḏrt   the servant of El and it was a fantasy

This startledness is also found in Greek dreams, for in Odyssey 4:839 it states, "But Icarus' daughter waking with a start."[203] Biblical dreams are more stylized in this respect: "And NN arose in the morning" is a formula common to Genesis 20:8 and Numbers 22:13, 22:21. In Genesis 41:10 and I Kings 3:15 the formula is, "and NN awoke and it was a dream." The only variations are, "Jacob awoke from his sleep" (Genesis 28:16), and "Jacob arose" (Genesis 31:17). Samuel's formula for termination is unique, but it is similar to the examples in Genesis 20:8 and Numbers 22:13, 22:21. I Samuel 3:15 reads, "and Samuel lay until morning." Though unique in its wording, it is the same as the others in regard to content and function.

Upon observing these particular parallels it seems logical to conclude that the author of I Samuel 3 has used a common literary genre in order to describe the Samuel experience. The various parts of the auditory message dream found in the ancient Near East are well represented in this text. Samuel's experience is truly an auditory message dream.

3.   Samuel's Experience and Incubation

Does the text of I Samuel 3 indicate that Samuel was undergoing an incubation process? I Samuel 3:1 describes how the Word of the Lord was rare in those days, and 3:2 parenthetically adds information about the poor status of Eli's eyesight, which implies his failure to see a vision or hear a Word from the Lord. Given this background one might infer that the boy Samuel was placed in the shrine in order to receive long-expected dream theophanies. But one might also infer that since the Word of the Lord was rare, no one expected Samuel to receive a vision. Furthermore, no preparation for incubation is mentioned in the text. But then,

it need not have been mentioned, if it were self-understood that Samuel was in the shrine for that very reason. Finally, the implication of I Samuel 3:20-4:1a is that such revelations continued at Shiloh, and the boy Samuel had further dream visions. However, the text does not say how the Word of the Lord came to Samuel. These final verses might be a general reference to Samuel's entire prophetic ministry and in no way imply further dream theophanies induced by incubation at Shiloh.

A number of scholars have felt[204] that incubation really did occur in the Samuel experience. Eli tells the boy to go lie down, and this may reflect Eli's awareness of the incubation procedure.[205] Samuel slept by the ark, an object which symbolized the presence of the deity. It is by the Ark that God would appear, so Samuel awaits the theophany there.[206] However, there are really little or no concrete data in the text to imply incubation. There are a number of scholars who consider this experience to be a dream but reject the idea that it might have been incubated. Though they might view other passages as incubation dreams, they are reluctant to see it in this passage due to the absence of preparatory incubation rites.[207] Samuel appears to be surprised by the whole affair, for he runs to Eli twice, and even Eli does not perceive what is happening at first. This makes the idea of a deliberate dream incubation improbable. The lamp indicates the time of the dream, but it in no way can be associated with any known ancient Near Eastern incubation, despite the debate among commentators over this issue. Samuel's presence in a shrine, and particularly his presence beside the ark, does not imply an incubation, either. He may have slept by the ark for a different reason; perhaps he was guarding the ark as did Joshua in Exodus 33:11.[208] It may symbolize Samuel's replacement of Eli, for Samuel can perform the watchman's role, which the almost blind Eli can no longer do.[209]

In the face of the arguments both for and against the idea of incubation in this text one is struck by the absence of any reference to incubation, sacrifice, and preparatory rites. All the evidence is implied. The best possible example of incubation is I Kings 3, where sacrifice is performed and a dream is experienced at a sacred site. Jacob's journey to Beersheba and performance of sacrifice in Genesis 46:2 also tempts the reader to think of this text as incubation. But the Samuel text lacks these motifs. Samuel is at a shrine, but he works and lives there. There is no allusion to sacrifice. One might respond that since Shiloh was a shrine such sacrifice normally occurred and need not have been mentioned After all, the ancient Near Eastern dream reports did not always record the full incubation process. That is true, but we cannot hypothesize what the writer did not tell us. If incubation were

150

part of the account, we should find some allusion to some special sacrifice or rite of preparation. The question of whether such a rite might really have occurred is irrelevant, since the chapter is probably is literary creation. The lack of such reference implies that the narrator did not see fit to mention incubation, therefore he did not wish to give his readers the impression that incubation occurred. In fact, the surprise of Samuel seems to be the narrator's way of indicating that there was no incubation for a dream. Since the narrator used the ancient Near Eastern model for dream reports and has no allusions to incubation, we are unjustified in calling this an incubation dream.

There still remains the subtle possibility of calling this experience an "unintentional dream incubation."[210] We may have such examples in the ancient Near East with the dream of the šabrû priest in the reign of Ashurbanipal and the dream of Thutmosis IV in the shadow of the Great Sphinx.[211] It is difficult to say how many other dreams might also be unintentional. A good example might be Genesis 28:10-19, where Jacob is surprised by his dream at Bethel. If I Samuel 3 is seen as an unintentional incubation dream, this might be the purpose of indicating the infrequency of the Word of the Lord. It would mean that Samuel slept continually in the shrine where dreams might come, but it was never really expected on any given night; hence, incubation rites were not performed with any regularity. It might mean that the reception of such a dream was not expected, nor really induced at the shrine, but a theophany or prophetic word of some kind was ultimately anticipated. By virtue of the fact that the dream came to its recipient who was sleeping in a shrine, this dream can be termed at least an unintentional incubation dream.

This author is critical of the endeavor to call this or any experience an unintentional incubation dream, as though that were a formal category in itself. The label is our creation, which is placed on experiences which do not explicitly mention an incubation process. The phrase is a contradiction in terms, for incubation implies purpose, unintentional incubation is accidental; therefore unintentional incubation is the same as no incubation at all. Theophanies often come at holy sites whether the recipient desired them or not. To say that they were accidentally desired is absurd. The logical implication of an unintentional incubation dream is to posit a magical cause and effect relationship. By the mere physical presence at a shrine the recipient brings about a theophany, as though his mere presence forces the deity to appear like a genie out of a bottle. Such is definitely not the intention of the author of Genesis 28 or I Samuel 3. God appears of His own will, and He chooses to make this appearance at a shrine. Samuel's surprise at the theophany demonstrates this. To introduce the category of

unintentional incubation dream confuses the narrative with semantic and theological difficulty.

In conclusion, it has been shown that the narrator of I Samuel 3 utilized the ancient Near Eastern auditory message dream structure for the basis of his narrative. He did not choose to utilize any aspect of ancient Near Eastern incubation rituals. This lack of reference may indicate late theological priorities of the Deuteronomist, which affirm the centrality of Jerusalem and would abhor a process of incubation at a local shrine like Shiloh. Incubation would also imply the human ability to manipulate God, an even more abhorrent thought for the Deuteronomist. Without the incubation, I Samuel 3 still stands as a model of ancient Near Eastern message dreams. It is the literary form by which the narrator tells the story. But the structure removes the experience from historical scrutiny, for the standardization of the genre of message dream[212] obscures the historical experience, if there ever was any.

Content Analysis

Further observations need to be made concerning the content of this passage in order to make an adequate assessment of the theology, intent, and date of the passage, and in order to lay groundwork for later discussion of the relationship of this passage to its context.

Verse 1: "In those days" is an expression which betrays the late literary origin[213] of this chapter. It looks back to a period long since past. Some, however, believe the phrase refers back to I Samuel 2:27-36, so that the narrator is saying the events of the oracle given by the anonymous man of God and Samuel's experience happened at the same time. Ralbag or Rabbi Levi ben Gershon (1288-1344 A.D.) felt that the phrase meant "on the same day."[214] The former option is more viable considering the presence of anachronisms in the text.[215]

"The Word of the Lord was rare" sets the stage for Samuel's remarkable reception of the Word of the Lord, an act which elevates him above the corruption of the Elides. It prepares us for the failure of both Eli[216] and Samuel initially to perceive the coming Word of the Lord.

Verse 2: "And his (Eli) eyes were dim, he was not able to see." Was Eli actually blind, so that he could not stand watch over the ark, or was he spiritually blind and unable to receive a vision or Word from the Lord? Many scholars prefer the latter option, for physical blindness would mean little if he were merely sleeping by the ark at night. But blindness to an inner reception of the Word would be more meaningful in this context,

152

for it describes his inability "to see" while asleep.[217] If so, it implies that Samuel's role of sleeping by the ark has the intent of perceiving a revelation. But the apparent surprise of Samuel in receiving the Word strongly mitigates against this whole idea. On the surface level it would be better to assume that Samuel is guarding the ark because he has better physical eyesight than Eli.[218] But beneath the surface the narrator may really have a theological pun. Eli is both physically and spiritually blind. The author of chapter 3 may have drawn the idea for Eli's blindness from I Samuel 4:15 and used it to create a double contrast. Not only can Samuel see to guard the ark; he can "see" a dream from the Lord, neither of which Eli is capable of doing.[219] Thus our present text does not seem to indicate that Samuel was sleeping by the ark deliberately to perceive a vision.[220]

Verse 3: "Samuel was sleeping in the temple of the Lord, where the Ark of God was." Where did Samuel sleep? Some believe that Samuel slept near the ark, but others believe he was actually in it.[221] The discussion is rendered complex by the anachronisms in the text. The later imagery of the Temple in Jerusalem may have been imposed upon the text.[222] I Samuel 1:9 uses the word hēkal, while 1:7 uses the word bēt to describe the abode of the ark. Here the former word is used, and with 1:9 it may be the sign of a late theological perspective. Words like "temple" and "doors" in 3:15 describe the shrine as a fixed building, not a portable tent shrine, in which we assume the ark was housed. II Samuel 7:5-7 testifies that the ark was never lodged in a permanent shrine, while these verses in I Samuel 1-3 give the impression that Shiloh was a fixed shrine. No archaeological evidence has been adduced as proof of a fixed sanctuary at the site, but that may not mean anything, for our excavation might have missed it, or the shrine might have been separate from the city. However, some scholars dismiss the statement in II Samuel 7:5-7 as a later Deuteronomistic insertion,[223] which tries to lessen the importance of earlier shrines. Hence, Shiloh was a fixed sanctuary. The "temple" may refer to the buildings around the ark, as Ralbag says, and this would remove the contradiction, for then the ark never really was in a permanent building.[224] Considering the other data it seems more probable to choose the former option and consider these features as anachronistic touches.

Verse 4: "Before the lamp of God went out," implies a lamp that does indeed go out, which is then not to be equated with the lamp that never goes out in Exodus 27:20 and Leviticus 24:2.[225] The reference to the lamp serves to indicate the time of the theophany; it has nothing to do with incubation. Merrill believes that the reference is a veiled allusion to the king, for David is referred to as the "lamp of Israel" in II Samuel 21:17.

153

Merrill concludes that sleeping by the ark was a royal prerogative undertaken on New Year's Day for the purpose of receiving divine revelation.[226]

Verses 4-10: The three-fold call contained in these verses is a literary characteristic unique to this dream theophany. Its primary purpose is to heighten suspense for the audience, but it also serves to demonstrate that Samuel did not expect the revelation. His innocence contrasts with the old Eli, who should have known what the revelation was, and who should have received such a revelation himself. The repeated approach of a deity in comparative literature demonstrates the veracity of the revelation, as is the case with repeated symbolic dreams in the ancient Near East. Ernst Ehrlich adduces a number of examples from comparative literatures. 1. In the Mohammedan story about the life of Ibn Ishak an angel comes to get his attention three times in the tower of the temple. After the third attempt he finally awakens him in order to deliver the message. 2. Another Arabian tale tells about an angel who comes to a sleeping king in order to tell him that his seventy year old wife will have a child named David. The angel repeats the message three times. 3. An African tale tells how a woman heard a voice three times in her sleep declaring that she would have a baby. 4. A Celtic tale tells how Laisrin fell asleep in a church and was awakened on a third attempt. He was then taken into heaven. 5. The Celtic Thorstein was visited three times by three women who prophesied his death. 6. A Bohemian tale recounts how a young man was visited by a figure three times on successive nights. Later a man came during the day and claimed to have been the dream messenger.[227] Thus the three-fold call is common as a literary device in other literatures.[228]

Verses 11-14: As previously observed this section constitutes a word of judgment against the Elides. It is somehow related to I Samuel 2:27-36 by virtue of 3:12. However, if the text is repointed to "you will tell him," instead of "I have told him," the strong connection between the two is removed. The reluctance of Samuel is due to the fearful burden of telling this message of doom to Eli for the first time. But one cannot push the argument too far, because Samuel could be fearful to repeat an already received oracle of doom. The word of judgment in this text differs from 2:27-36, for the curse is definitive and there is now no longer the hope of repentance. So this text moves beyond the oracle received in 2:27-36; it removes the possibility for repentance the first oracle offered.[229] If this is so, then the two oracles fit into the context comfortably, but this accommodation of the text may have been accomplished by the final editor of I Samuel 1-3. The language of the message has Deuteronomistic affinities. Veijola points out several parallels: 1) "all they that hear, their ears will ring" is

154

comparable to statements in II Kings 21:12, Jeremiah 19:3, 2) "I will fulfill all that I have said" is in I Kings 2:4, and 3) words like bēt and cōlām are typical Deuteronomistic words.[230] The message refers to the defeat in I Samuel 4 and perhaps the later bloodbath at Nob. In both instances the message serves to connect this passage with later accounts. Chapters 1-3 are tied to 4-6, and this is one of the links. One might conclude that the message or all of the chapter is a late creation by the editor who brought much of the Samuel material together.

Verses 15-18: Eli's acceptance of the judgment indicates his desire to put his will in accord with the divine will, a response quite typical of Semitic piety.[231] It can be seen as a model of acceptance that would lead readers or listeners to accept divine judgment for the fall of Jerusalem.[232]

Verses 3:19-4:1a: This section concludes the chapter with an inclusio. In verse 1 the Word of the Lord was rare, but in these verses it comes as a conclusion to all of chapters 1-3 by interpreting all of Samuel's actions at Shiloh as part of his prophetic ministry. If so, this reflection belongs to a later period. The text may be telescoping the activities of Samuel's life throughout I Samuel 1:1-16:13, 19:18-24.[233] It implies that the events of chapter 4 have already transpired, for they are the immediate fulfillment of the word of judgment in 3:11-14. It may also imply the fulfillment of later prophecies.[234] Such would be the case in order to verify Samuel as the true prophet by the criteria of Deuteronomy 18:22.[235] The fulfillment of the one prophecy would be inadequate for such prophetic verification, especially since Eli was the only confidant of the oracle.[236] If one takes this material to be a historical reflection, certain problems arise. Where did Samuel receive these other prophecies, if Shiloh was destroyed or disgraced by the loss of the ark? Why are these oracles not recorded? Noth believes Shiloh continued to be important even after the fall, as witnessed by the prophetic ministry of Ahijah at a later date. The Samuel traditions were kept at Shiloh by prophetic circles which witnessed to his activity there.[237] But this does not explain why Samuel never again appears associated with Shiloh in the traditions of I Samuel 7:2-16:13. That absence leads this author to conclude that chapters 1-3 are a late literary creation. The conclusion in 3:19-4:1a is artificial, and there are no further prophecies of Samuel at Shiloh. The narrator is not worried about the anomalies he may have created by the inclusion of 3:19-4:1a. He is giving testimony to the greatness of Samuel. By his day Samuel is known as the great prophet, and further stories need not be adduced to verify his status. Historically Samuel was probably never connected to Shiloh. The writer of chapter 3 and all of chapters 1-3 seeks to condemn the Elides of Shiloh by placing the great prophet

Samuel in their midst as a small boy. He then redeems the shrine from the sins of the Elides by having further prophecies come to Samuel at Shiloh, even though he records none. Thus the legitimacy of Shiloh is preserved. The Elides are condemned, and this justifies the transfer of authority to Jerusalem in the ensuing historical development; Shiloh's integrity is redeemed, and this permits authentic religious leadership to pass from Shiloh to Jerusalem in the connected cycles of tradition of the Deuteronomistic History. I Samuel 3:19-4:1a is the grand conclusion for chapters 1-3, and it is also the summation of Samuel's entire ministry. It has been telescoped into this short passage by the editor of a later age.[238] The passage is determined by theological priorities.

Theological Meaning of I Samuel 3

The most direct purpose of this chapter is to criticize the Elides for their abuse in Shiloh. This criticism is assured by the finality of the judgment in I Samuel 3:11-14.[239] This judgment is rendered even more effective by the contrast of the pious boy Samuel with Eli. Samuel receives the message, Eli does not; and Eli does not even understand what is happening at first.[240]

Though the text is not a call narrative, it does elevate the boy Samuel to a role of importance. Kraus thinks this account indicates that Samuel has received charisma and thus has become the "authorized mediator," the one who fulfills the covenantal roles for Israel.[241] Newman goes further and declares that Samuel now succeeds Eli as prophet, priest, and mediator of the covenant amphictyony. Like Moses Samuel fulfills the demands of Deuteronomy 18:15-22, for he speaks of the Lord, preaches to the peoples, recalls the mighty deeds of the Lord, and proclaims His righteousness. The presence of the ark in Shiloh implies this was the center of the amphictyony, and the leader there is covenant mediator for all Israel. Samuel was the transition from cultic covenant mediator to prophetic covenant mediator. As such he performed his function more than once a year, as Eli had done in the role of cultic mediator at the annual festival. Samuel performed the role several times in various places, such as Gilgal, Bethel, Mizpah, and Ramah. Samuel could interpret the law, not just proclaim it. He became instrumental in the development of the office of charismatic prophet and ultimately the later classical prophet. Whether chapter 3 is historical is irrelevant, for it preserves the memory that Samuel arose as a charismatic prophet and covenant mediator in a time of crisis. Even though he is only called a prophet twice (I Samuel 3:20, 9:9), he is the father of the prophetic movement, founder of ecstatic prophecy. However, he is not a prophet in the later classical

156

sense.[242] Both Kraus and Newman offer intriguing and comprehensive theological evaluations of the text, but they may put a lot more into the text than is really there.

Less sweeping evaluations of Samuel's role in this chapter[243] see him uniting the role of prophet and priest. Eli was a priest of a hereditary line. As long as the line of priests was faithful to the Lord, the Word of the Lord would come to the people. When the line degenerated, as with Eli's sons, a crisis was reached. Against this situation there arose the prophetic figure of Samuel, who brought the Word of the Lord back to Israel. It would be logical to see in Samuel both roles, prophet and priest, for this would solve the old dilemma of institutional authority and charismatic renewal. But there is no warrant in the text for that conclusion. Samuel may have been a trainee at Shiloh under Eli, but according to the story he never assumed Eli's post. If he continued to function at Shiloh after the defeat, he did so without the ark, in which case he was exercising a prophetic function, but not a priestly function. Samuel's critique through the word of judgment is a paradigm for the later criticism of the prophetic movement against the hereditary priesthood.[244] In actuality, since the text is late, it embodies a prophetic criticism which had been voiced for several generations, and this criticism is another indication of the lateness of the account.

Greater caution should be exhibited in the evaluation of this account. The story indicates that Samuel succeeds Eli in function, but not in office.[245] The ark is gone, and the priestly office of Eli is lost. Newman and Kraus rely heavily upon presuppositions concerning the historicity of the account. Stoebe criticizes both of them for this. If the text is a literary creation, then Newman has gone too far in projecting so much into Israel's early history. It is an assumption to associate the ark in Shiloh with the entire covenantal process. Both Ritterspach and Newman build upon this assumption. The ark's presence in chapter 3 may be nothing more than a literary device meant to connect chapter 3 with the accounts of the ark in chapter 4-6. The story is literary and theological in its orientation, and appears to have been a creation placed between material in chapters 1-2, 4-6. It is tenuous to derive theories of Samuel's role from this chapter.[246]

Conclusion

We have determined that the structure upon which I Samuel 3 is constructed is not a prophetic call narrative, but rather it is an auditory message dream, a common format throughout the ancient Near East. Scholars have too often assumed that this is a prophetic call and therewith made far-

reaching conclusions. Presupposing historicity in an account which seems to be a late literary and theological creation, they have comprehensively created an early history for Israel. The text appears to have been brought together at a late date, either with 2:27-4:1a or 1:1-4:1a as a unity. But this is the subject of ensuing study.

CHAPTER IV

FOOTNOTES

[1] Z. Frankel, Vorstudien zu der Septuagint (Leipzig: Vogel, 1841), passim.

[2] Henrik Samuel Nyberg, "Das textkritische Problem des Alten Testaments am Hoseabuche demonstriert," ZAW 52 (1934): 241-254; and Studien zum Hoseabuche: Zugleich ein Beitrag zur Klärung des Problems der alttestamentlichen Textkritik, UUÅ, vol. 6 (Uppsala: Almquist und Wiksell, 1935), passim.

[3] Pieter Aric Henrik de Boer, Research into the Text of I Samuel 1-16: A Contribution to the Study of the Books of Samuel (Amsterdam: Paris, 1938), p. 69 et passim.

[4] gam (I Samuel 1:28), kol (1:4, 2:22, 4:13, 6:4, 7:47, 11:2), and other words were consistently omitted in the Greek translation, p. 51.

[5] Here he builds upon the work of Paul Kahle, Massoreten des Ostens, die ältesten punktierten Handschriften des Alten Testaments und der Targume, BWAT, vol. 15 (Leipzig: Hinrichs, 1913), passim; and Massoreten des Westens, 2 vols., BWAT, Neue Folge, vols. 8 and 14 (Stuttgart: Kohlhammer, 1927 and 1930), passim.

[6] Cross, "A New Qumran Biblical Fragment related to the Original Hebrew underlying the Septuagint," BASOR 132 (1953): 15-26; "The Oldest Manuscripts from Qumran," JBL 74 (1955): 147-172; The Ancient Library of Qumran and Modern Biblical Studies, 2d ed. (Garden City, New York: Doubleday, 1958), p. 135; and "The History of the Biblical Text in the Light of Discoveries in the Judean Desert," HTR 57 (1964): 292-293.

[7] Kyle McCarter, I Samuel, AB, vol. 8 (Garden City, New York: Doubleday, 1980), pp. 49-444, offers the most effective use of Qumran material in text-critical evaluations of Samuel.

[8] Harry Orlinsky, "The Textual Criticism of the Old Testament," The Bible and the Ancient Near East: Essays in

159

Honor of William Foxwell Albright, ed. George Ernest Wright (Garden City, New York: Doubleday, 1961), pp. 145-148, 151.

[9] I. H. Eybers, "Notes on the Texts of Samuel found in Qumran Cave 4," Studies on the Books of Samuel: Die Ou Testamentiese Werkgemeenskap in Suid-Afrika, Papers read at the 3rd Meeting held at Stellenbosch 26-28 January, 1960 (Potschefstroom: Pro-Rege-Pers-Beperk, 1960), pp. 15-16 et passim.

[10] Wellhausen, Samuelis, p. 51; Karl Budde, Die Bücher Samuel, KHAT, vol. 8 (Tübingen and Leipzig: Mohr, 1902), p. 26; Nowack, Richter, Ruth, und Samuelis, p. 17; Wilhelm Caspari, Die Samuelbücher, KAT, vol. 7 (Leipzig: Scholl, 1926), p. 53; and McCarter, Samuel, p. 95.

[11] Arnold Ehrlich, Randglossen zur Hebräischen Bibel: Textkritisches, Sprachliches und Sachliches, 7 vols. (Leipzig: Hinrichs, 1910; reprint ed., Hildesheim: Olms, 1968), 3:178; Henry Preserved Smith, A Critical and Exegetical Commentary on the Books of Samuel, ICC (New York: Scribners, 1899), p. 27; and McCarter, Samuel, pp. 95, 97.

[12] G. Driver, "Studies in the Vocabulary of the Old Testament," JTS 32 (1931): 365.

[13] Vaccari, "Le radici tws̩ e pr̩s̩ nell' Ebraico Biblico," Bib 19 (1938): 308-315.

[14] De Boer, Text of I Samuel, p. 57; and Hans Joachim Stoebe, Das Erste Buch Samuelis, KAT, vol. 8, pt. 1 (Gütersloh: Mohn, 1973), p. 121.

[15] Caspari, Samuelbücher, p. 53.

[16] Wellhausen, Samuelis, p. 52.

[17] August Klostermann, Die Bücher Samuelis und der Könige, Kurzgefasster Kommentar zu den heiligen Schriften Alten und Neuen Testament, vol. 3 (Nördlingen: Back, 1887), p. 11; Otto Thenius, Die Buch Samuelis, 2d ed., Kurzgefasstes exegetisches Handbuch zum Alten Testament, vol. 4 (Leipzig: Hirzel, 1864), p. 16; Alfons Schulz, Die Bücher Samuel: Übersetzt und erklärt, 2 vols., EHAT, vol. 8 (Münster: Aschendorff, 1919-1920), 1:58; Smith, Samuel, p. 27; Budde, Samuel, KHAT, p. 26; and Caspari, Samuelbücher, p. 53.

[18] S. Driver, Notes on the Hebrew Text and the Topography of the Books of Samuel, 2d ed. (Oxford: Clarendon, 1913), p. 42.

[19] Dhorme, Les livres de Samuel, Études Bibliques, vol. 9 (Paris: Gabalda, 1910), p. 42; and Stoebe, Samuelis, p. 121.

[20] S. Driver, Hebrew Text, p. 42.

[21] Thenius, Samuelis, p. 16; Smith, Samuel, p. 27; and de Boer, Text of I Samuel, p. 62.

[22] Budde, Samuel, KHAT, p. 27; Dhorme, Samuel, p. 43; Caspari, Samuelbücher, p. 54; Stoebe, Samuelis, p. 122; and McCarter, Samuel, p. 95.

[23] Wellhausen, Samuelis, p. 52; and McCarter, Samuel, p. 95.

[24] Klostermann, Samuelis, p. 11; Budde, Samuel, KHAT, p. 27; Nowack, Richter, Ruth und Samuelis, p. 18; Dhorme, Samuel, p. 43; S. Driver, Hebrew Text, p. 42; and Schulz, Samuel, 1:60.

[25] Hariton Tiktin, Kritische Untersuchungen zu den Büchern Samuelis, FRLANT, vol. 16 (Göttingen: Vandenhoeck und Ruprecht, 1922), p. 9.

[26] Thenius, Samuelis, p. 16; A. Ehrlich, Randglossen, 3:179; de Boer, Text of I Samuel, p. 52; and Stoebe, Samuelis, p. 181.

[27] Smith, Samuel, p. 27; and Caspari, Samuelbücher, p. 54.

[28] Wellhausen, Samuelis, p. 52; Klostermann, Samuelis, p. 11; and Smith, Samuel, p. 27.

[29] Robert Henry Pfeiffer, "Midrash in the Books of Samuel," Quantulacumque: Studies presented to Kirsopp Lake, ed. Robert Casey and others (London: Christophers, 1937), p. 315.

[30] Budde, Samuel, KHAT, p. 27; and Dhorme, Samuel, p. 43.

[31] A. Ehrlich, Randglossen, 3:179; Tiktin, Samuel, p. 9; de Boer, Text of I Samuel, p. 53; and Stoebe, Samuelis, p. 122.

[32] Schulz, Samuel, 1:60.

[33] Caspari, Samuelbücher, p. 26; and de Boer, Text of I Samuel, p. 53.

[34] Rudolf Kittel, ed., BHK, 3d ed. (Stuttgart: Württembergische Bibelanstalt, 1937), p. 409, reflects the consensus of Wellhausen, Samuelis, p. 52; Klostermann, Samuelis, p. 11; Smith, Samuel, p. 27; Budde, Samuel, KHAT, p. 27; Nowack, Richter, Ruth und Samuelis, p. 18; Dhorme, Samuel, p. 43; S. Driver, Hebrew Text, p. 42; Schulz, Samuel, 1:60; Caspari, Samuelbücher, p. 54; and McCarter, Samuel, p. 95; only Thenius, Samuelis, p. 16, maintains the text.

[35] Smith, Samuel, p. 27.

[36] Stoebe, Samuelis, p. 122.

[37] A. Ehrlich, Randglossen, 3:179; and Caspari, Samuelbücher, p. 54, calls it a targumic usage.

[38] Stoebe, Samuelis, p. 122.

[39] Schulz, Samuel, 1:61.

[40] Klostermann, Samuelis, p. 11.

[41] Schulz, Samuel, 1:61; and de Boer, Text of I Samuel, p. 58.

[42] Smith, Samuel, p. 27; Dhorme, Samuel, p. 43; Caspari, Samuelbücher, p. 54; and McCarter, Samuel, p. 95.

[43] Klostermann, Samuelis, p. 11; Budde, Samuel, KHAT, p. 27; Caspari, Samuelbücher, p. 54; and McCarter, Samuel, p. 96.

[44] Caspari, Samuelbücher, p. 54.

[45] Dhorme, Samuel, pp. 43-44.

[46] S. Driver, Hebrew Text, p. 43.

[47] A. Ehrlich, Randglossen, 3:179; and Stoebe, Samuelis, p. 122.

[48] Stoebe, Samuelis, p. 122.

[49] Dhorme, Samuel, p. 44.

[50] S. Driver, Hebrew Text, p. 43.

[51] Caspari, Samuelbücher, p. 55.

[52] Thenius, Samuelis, p. 17; and Smith, Samuel, p. 28.

[53] Dhorme, Samuel, p. 43; and S. Driver, Hebrew Text, p. 43.

[54] S. Driver, Hebrew Text, p. 43; and Thenius, Samuelis, p. 17.

[55] Klostermann, Samuel, p. 11.

[56] Ibid.; Budde, Samuel, KHAT, p. 28; Nivard Schlögl, Die Bücher Samuelis oder erstes und zweites Buch der Könige übersetzt und erklärt, Kurzgefasster Wissenschaftlicher Commentar zu den Heiligen Schrift des Alten Testaments, vol. 3 (Vienna: Mayer, 1904), p. 22; Smith, Samuel, p. 29; Dhorme, Samuel, p. 43; A. Ehrlich, Randglossen, 3:179; S. Driver, Hebrew Text, p. 43; Schulz, Samuel, 1:63; Caspari, Samuelbücher, p. 55; and Peter Ackroyd, The First Book of Samuel, CBC (Cambridge, England: University Press, 1971), p. 44.

[57] Schulz, Samuel, 1:63.

[58] Klostermann, Samuelis, p. 11.

[59] Hans Wilhelm Hertzberg, I and II Samuel, trans. John Bowden, OTL (Philadelphia: Westminster, 1964), p. 40; and Stoebe, Samuelis, p. 122.

[60] Kittel, BHK, p. 409.

[61] Caspari, Samuelbücher, p. 55.

[62] A. Ehrlich, Randglossen, 3:180; Schulz, Samuel, 1:62; Caspari, Samuelbücher, p. 55; Kittel, BHK, p. 409; and Hertzberg, Samuel, p. 40.

[63] Wellhausen, Samuelis, p. 53; Budde, Samuel, KHAT, p. 28; Dhorme, Samuel, p. 44; and S. Driver, Hebrew Text, p. 43.

[64] Smith, Samuel, p. 27.

[65] Wellhausen, Samuelis, p. 53; and Budde, Samuel, KHAT, p. 28.

[66] Tiktin, Samuel, p. 9.

[67] Klostermann, Samuelis, p. 12.

[68] Stoebe, Samuelis, p. 122.

[69] Hertzberg, Samuel, p. 40.

[70] Caspari, Samuelbücher, p. 54.

[71] Budde, Samuel, KHAT, p. 28.

[72] Thenius, Samuelis, p. 17; Wellhausen, Samuelis, p. 53; Klostermann, Samuel, p. 12; Smith, Samuel, p. 29; Budde, Samuel, KHAT, p. 28; Nowack, Richter, Ruth und Samuelis, p. 19; Dhorme, Samuel, p. 44; S. Driver, Hebrew Text, p. 44; Schulz, Samuel, 1:63; Stoebe, Samuelis, p. 122; and McCarter, Samuel, p. 95. However, some scholars would challenge the use of tiqqunê ha-sopherîm as a category to describe this textual phenomenon, Bleddyn Jones Roberts, The Old Testament Text and Versions (Cardiff: University of Wales Press, 1951), pp. 34-35.

[73] Thenius, Samuelis, p. 17.

[74] S. Driver, Hebrew Text, p. 44.

[75] Caspari, Samuelbücher, p. 55.

[76] De Boer, Text of I Samuel, pp. 62, 82.

[77] Klostermann, Samuelis, p. 12; and Dhorme, Samuel, p. 44.

[78] Schulz, Samuel, 1:63.

[79] A. Ehrlich, Randglossen, 3:180.

[80] Stoebe, Samuelis, p. 122.

[81] Caspari, Samuelbücher, p. 55, reads this in verse 14.

[82] Wellhausen, Samuelis, p. 53; and S. Driver, Hebrew Text, p. 44.

[83] Klostermann, Samuelis, p. 12.

[84] Stoebe, Samuelis, p. 122.

[85] Budde, Samuel, KHAT, p. 28; and Caspari, Samuelbücher, p. 55.

[86] Stoebe, Samuelis, p. 122.

[87] Thenius, Samuelis, p. 17; Wellhausen, Samuelis, p. 53; Klostermann, Samuelis, p. 12; Smith, Samuel, p. 29; Budde, Samuel, KHAT, p. 28; Nowack, Richter, Ruth und Samuelis, p. 19; S. Driver, Hebrew Text, pp. 44; Schulz, Samuel, 1:29; Caspari, Samuelbücher, p. 55; Kittel, BHK, p. 409; Dhorme, ed., La Bible: Ancien Testament, 2 vols. (Paris: Gallimard, 1956), 1:821-822; and McCarter, Samuel, p. 96.

[88] A. Ehrlich, Randglossen, 3:180.

[89] De Boer, Text of I Samuel, p. 58; and Stoebe, Samuelis, p. 122.

[90] Caspari, Samuelbücher, p. 55.

[91] Klostermann, Samuelis, p. 12; and S. Driver, Hebrew Text, p. 44.

[92] Thenius, Samuelis, p. 17; Wellhausen, Samuelis, p. 52; Klostermann, Samuelis, p. 12; Schulz, Samuel, 1:65; and McCarter, Samuel, p. 96.

[93] De Boer, Text of I Samuel, p. 58; and Stoebe, Samuelis, p. 122.

[94] Caspari, Samuelbücher, p. 56.

[95] Smith, Samuel, p. 30.

[96] Thenius, Samuelis, p. 17-18; and Schulz, Samuel, 1:66.

[97] Stoebe, Samuelis, p. 122.

[98] Klostermann, Samuelis, p. 12.

[99] Caspari, Samuelbücher, p. 56.

[100] A. Ehrlich, Randglossen, 3:181.

[101] Wellhausen, Samuelis, p. 54; Klostermann, Samuelis, p. 12; Norbertus Peters, Beiträge zur Text- und Literarkritik, sowie zur Erklärung der Bücher Samuel (Freiburg: Herder, 1899), pp. 104-105; Thenius, Samuelis, p. 18; Dhorme, Samuel, p. 45; and McCarter, Samuel, p. 97.

[102] Kittel, BHK, p. 409; Dhorme, La Bible, 1:822, and Samuel, p. 45.

[103] Klostermann, Samuelis, p. 13.

[104] Thenius, Samuelis, p. 18; Smith, Samuel, p. 30; Budde, Samuel, KHAT, p. 28; and Dhorme, La Bible, 1:822.

[105] Budde, Samuel, KHAT, p. 55.

[106] Smith, Samuel, p. 30.

[107] A. Ehrlich, Randglossen, 3:181; S. Driver, Hebrew Text, p. 44; and Stoebe, Samuelis, p. 123.

[108] Nowack, Richter, Ruth und Samuelis, p. 20; and Schulz, Samuel, 1:66-68.

[109] Peters, Samuel, pp. 104-105; A. Ehrlich, Randglossen, 3:181; Dhorme, Samuel, p. 45; and de Boer, Text of I Samuel, p. 82.

[110] Wellhausen, Samuelis, p. 54; Smith, Samuel, p. 30; Budde, Samuel, KHAT, p. 28; Nowack, Richter, Ruth und Samuelis, p. 20, who considers 4:1a a continuation of the same gloss and omits it; and Schulz, Samuel, 1:66-68.

[111] Klostermann, Samuelis, p. 12.

[112] Caspari, Samuelbücher, p. 56.

[113] S. Driver, Hebrew Text, p. 45; Kittel BHK, p. 409; and Hertzberg, Samuel, p. 40, also adds the Septuagint's version of verse 21 after this Hebrew version of verses 21 and 4:1a.

[114] Stoebe, Samuelis, p. 123.

[115] George Caird, "First and Second Books of Samuel," IB, 2:894; and Smith, Samuel, p. 25.

[116] Smith, Samuel, p. 29.

[117] Klostermann, Samuelis, p. 11; Thenius, Samuelis, p. 24; Budde, Samuel, KHAT, p. 28; S. Driver, Hebrew Text, p. 43; Archibald Robert Sterling Kennedy, Samuel: Introduction, Revised Version with notes, index and maps, The Century Bible (Edinburgh: Jack, 1905), p. 54; and Patrick Miller and J. J. M. Roberts, The Hand of the Lord: A Reassessment of the "Ark Narrative" of I Samuel, The Johns Hopkins Near Eastern Studies (Baltimore: The Johns Hopkins University Press, 1977), p. 21.

[118] Wellhausen, Samuelis, p. 53; Kuenen, Einleitung, p. 53; Budde, Samuel, KHAT, p. 25; Gressmann, Geschichtsschreibung, p. 4; Nowack, Richter, Ruth und Samuelis, p. 19; Joseph Schäfers, "I Sam. 1-15 literarkritisch untersucht," BZ 5 (1907): 11; Hertzberg, Samuel, p. 42; Hölscher, Geschichtsschreibung in Israel, Acta Regulata Societatis Humaniorum Litterarum Lundensis, vol. 50 (Lund: Gleerup, 1951), p. 364; E. C. B. MacLaurin, The Hebrew Theocracy in the Tenth to the Sixth Centuries B.C. (London: Angus and Robertson, 1959), p. 123; and Arthur Lewis Merrill, "I Samuel 1-12: A Traditio-Historical Study" (Ph.D. dissertation, University of Chicago, 1962), pp. 13-14.

[119] Timo Veijola, Die Ewige Dynastie: David und die Entstehung seiner Dynastie nach der deuteronomistischen Darstellung, Suomalaisen Tiedeakatemian Toimituksia, Annales academiae scientiarum Fennicae, ser. B, vol. 193 (Helsinki: Suomalainen Tiedeakatemia, 1975), pp. 35-41, calls 2:27-36 an insertion by DtrG, and 3:11-14 is a later insertion by DtrP, which displaced the original prophetic call oracle, for one editor would not put in both oracles.

[120] Roland de Vaux, Les livres de Samuel, La Sainte Bible (Paris: Cerf, 1953), p. 32; and Eugene Maly, The First Book of Samuel, OTRG, vol. 6a (Collegeville, Minnesota: Liturgical Press, 1970), p. 20.

[121] Jan Dus, "Die Geburtslegende Samuels I Sam. 1: Eine traditionsgeschichtliche Untersuchung zu I Sam. 1-3," RSO 43 (1960): 188.

[122] Veijola, Dynastie, p. 38, believes 3:11-14 displaced an earlier call narrative.

[123] Cornill, Introduction to the Canonical Books of the Old Testament, trans C. H. Box, Theological Translation Library, vol. 23 (New York: Putnam, 1907), p. 186.

[124] Otto Plöger, "Die Prophetengeschichten der Samuel- und Königsbücher" (Ph.D. dissertation, Greifswald, 1937), p. 47.

[125] Ibid., p. 65.

[126] Caird, "Samuel," p. 894.

[127] Stoebe, Samuelis, p. 125.

[128] M. H. Segal, "Studies in the Books of Samuel," JQR 6

(1915-1916): 563; and Noth, "Samuel und Silo," VT 13 (1963): 392-393.

[129] Schulz, Samuel, 1:62.

[130] Arthur Zannoni, "An Investigation of the Call and Dedication of the Prophet Samuel: I Samuel 1:1-4:1a" (Ph.D. dissertation, Marquette University, 1975), p. 183.

[131] Richard Press, "Der Prophet Samuel. Eine traditions-geschichtliche Untersuchung," ZAW 56 (1938): 179.

[132] Plöger, "Prophetengeschichten," p. 65.

[133] Gressmann, Geschichtsschreibung, p. 7; Jepsen, Nabi, p. 53; von Rad, Old Testament Theology, 2:55; Caird, "Samuel," p. 894; MacLaurin, Theocracy, p. 41; Murray Newman, "The Prophetic Call of Samuel," Israel's Prophetic Heritage: Essays in honor of James Muilenburg, ed. Bernhard Anderson and Walter Harrelson (New York: Harper and Brothers, 1962), pp. 86-97; Austin Ritterspach, "The Samuel Traditions: An Analysis of the Anti-Monarchical Source in I Samuel 1-15" (Ph.D. dissertation, Graduate Theological Union and San Francisco Theological Seminary, 1967), pp. 263-281; Ackroyd, Samuel, pp. 42-44; Stoebe, Samuelis, p. 125; Jenks, Elohist, p. 89; and Benjamin Hubbard, "Commissioning Stories in Luke-Acts: A Study of their Antecedents, Form and Content," Semeia, vol. 8, ed. Robert Funk (Missoula, Montana: Scholars Press, 1977), p. 107, all maintain that this is a clear example of a prophetic call narrative, a model for later prophetic call narratives, and for this reason Samuel can be seen as the forerunner of the prophetic movement. But a number of scholars exhibit caution and admit that the structure is truncated and lacks the full form of the prophetic call narrative; E. Ehrlich, Traum, p. 417; Johannes Fichtner, "Berufung, II. Im Alten Testament," RGG, 3d. ed., edited by Kurt Galling (Tübingen: Mohr, 1957), p. 1085; Georg Christian Macholz, "Untersuchungen zur Geschichte der Samuel-Überlieferungen" (Th.D. dissertation, Heidelberg, 1966), pp. 91-92, considers this pericope to function as a call narrative, but 3:1-18 by itself is not a call narrative, for it lacks a prophetic commission, and it is only with the addition of 3:19-21 that the pericope is transformed into one by the editor; Hans Bardtke, "Samuel und Saul. Gedanken zur Entstehung des Königtums in Israel," BO 25 (1968): 255, 294. The criticism of Long, "Prophetic Call," pp. 494-500 will be considered later.

[134] Caird, "Samuel," p. 894.

[135] Budde, Samuel, KHAT, p. 25; and Veijola, Dynastie, p. 38.

[136] Wolfgang Richter, Die sogenannten vorprophetischen Berufungsberichte: Eine literaturwissenschaftliche Studie zu I Sam 9,1-10,16, Ex 3f. und Ri 6,11b-17, FRLANT, vol. 101 (Göttingen: Vandenhoeck und Ruprecht, 1970), pp. 174-175.

[137] Von Rad, Old Testament Theology, 2:54-55, 59-60; Wolff, "Hauptprobleme alttestamentlicher Prophetie," EvT 15 (1955): 455; and Fichtner, "Berufung," p. 1085.

[138] Fohrer, "Die Gattung der Berichte über symbolische Handlungen der Propheten," ZAW 54 (1952): 101-120. He perceives this Beruf, Bericht, Deutung pattern in I Kings 11:29-39, 19:19-21, 22:11, II Kings 13:14-19, Hosea 1, 3, Isaiah 7:3, 8:1-4, 20, Jeremiah 13:1-11, 16:1-9, 19:1-2, 10-11, 27:1-3, 12, 28:10-11, 32:1-15, 43:8-18, 51:59-64, Zechariah 6:9-15, and extensively in Ezekiel; and Klaus Baltzer, "Considerations Regarding the Office and Calling of the Prophet," HTR 61 (1968): 567-581, finds parallels in Egyptian literature to demonstrate that the prophet is like the vizier who is called to bring justice.

[139] Ernst Kutsch, "Gideon's Berufung and Altarbau Jdc. 6:11-24," TLZ 81 (1956): 75-84.

[140] Fichtner, "Berufung," pp. 1084-1086.

[141] Richter, Traditionsgeschichtliche Untersuchungen zum Richterbuch, BBB, vol. 18 (Bonn: Hanstein, 1963), p. 153.

[142] Habel, "The Form and Significance of the Call Narratives," ZAW 77 (1965): 297-323. Hubbard, "Commissioning Stories," pp. 103-126, uses these categories to classify a large number of stories in the ancient Near East, Old Testament, and New Testament. Long, "Prophetic Call," pp. 494-500, believes this genre shares the same common roots with dream experiences and other epiphanies, so that one should not make a distinction between them.

[143] Habel, "Form," p. 317, raises the suggestion that the account in Genesis 24:34-48 may originally be the format used for the prophetic call narrative accounts. For here the relationship between Abraham and his servant is very similar. We have: 1) introductory word, 24:34-36, 2) commission, 24:37-38, 3) objection, 24:39, 4) reassurance, 24:40-41, and 5) sign, 24:42-48. Since Habel considers the epic literature to have arisen prior to the prophetic material, this account could have served as a format. However, the patriarchal material may be after the prophetic proclamations if the evaluations of Van Seters are correct, Abraham, passim. In the latter case

Genesis 24:34-48 would exemplify the utilization of a prophetic call narrative by exilic epic literature.

[144] Richter, Berufungsberichte, p. 139; and Thompson and Irwin, "Moses and Joseph," pp. 200-209, provide a thorough evaluation of this pattern in their consideration of Moses as a "savior figure."

[145] In I Samuel 3:10 the text reads, "The Lord came and stood," which implies visual phenomena. Newman did not address this text, but he is at least partially correct, since the text stresses the auditory.

[146] Our own textual analysis indicates that the double vocative is an intrusion into the text of I Samuel 3:4; the Septuagint has added it due to its presence in 3:10. The double vocative in 3:10 is original to the Hebrew, but it may have arisen in the transmission of the traditions due to the influence of Moses' call, and thus it may not be due to common origins in the Elohistic traditions.

[147] Newman, "Call of Samuel," pp. 86-97.

[148] Jenks, Elohist, p. 89, and "The Elohist," p. 221. Several scholars have noted the use of the double vocative and the reply, "Here am I," as similarities between the experiences of Moses and Samuel, Joseph Bourke, "Samuel and the Ark," Dominican Studies 7 (1954): 73-74; and Muilenburg, "The Form and Structure of the Covenantal Formulations," VT 9 (1959): 91.

[149] Jenks, Elohist, p. 89.

[150] Ritterspach, "I Samuel 1-15," pp. 235-240; and Hubbard, "Commissioning Stories," p. 107.

[151] Ritterspach, "I Samuel 1-15," pp. 240-241.

[152] Richter, Berufungsberichte, pp. 174-175.

[153] Caird, "Samuel," p. 893; Resch, Traum, pp. 111-112; William McKane, I and II Samuel, Torch Bible Commentary (London: SCM Press, 1963), p. 46; and John Mauchline, 1 and 2 Samuel, New Century Bible (London: Oliphants, 1971), p. 59, all call his experience a vision rather than a dream.

[154] Möhring, "Theophanien und Träume in biblischer Literatur" (Th.D. dissertation, n.p., 1914), p. 40, believes that Samuel was talking in his sleep as he saw the vision with an inner eye.

[155] Some scholars attach this text to the Elohist epic narrative, which they feel extends through the historical literature. The dream theophany is evidence that the text belongs to the Elohist, Budde, Samuel, KHAT, p. 26.

[156] E. Ehrlich, Traum, p. 47; and de Vaux, Samuel, p. 13.

[157] Klostermann, Samuelis, p. 11; Kennedy, Samuel, p. 54; Hölscher, Profeten, p. 84; Solomon Goldman, Samuel, Soncino Books of the Bible (London: Soncino, 1951), p. 18; Aubrey Rodway Johnson, The Cultic Prophet in Ancient Israel (Cardiff: Wales, 1962), p. 13; Lindblom, "Theophanies," p. 101, and Prophecy in Ancient Israel (London: Blackwell, 1962; reprint ed., Philadelphia: Fortress, 1973), pp. 55-56, believes the text uses a literary category of a dream experience, but in actuality it is not a dream but a real theophany; Resch, Traum, p. 112, believes that the objective visible appearance excludes the possibility of a dream; and Ackroyd, Samuel, p. 43.

[158] Long, "Prophetic Call," pp. 494-500, develops his argument with particular reference to Exodus 3-4 and the call accounts of Moses, which seem to have a common visionary form beneath both the Yahwist and Elohist versions of the call. In his article, "Prophetic Authority and Social Reality," Canon and Authority: Essays in Old Testament Religion and Theology, eds. George Coats and Burke Long (Philadelphia: Fortress, 1977), pp. 11-13, he maintains that prophetic call narratives are merely editorial creations designed to summarize the major themes of a particular prophet's ministry.

[159] Jensen, Nabi, pp. 48-52, calls is a night vision, but he then admits there is not much difference between a dream and a night vision; Schulz, Samuel, 1:62; Hertzberg, Samuel, p. 42; Hans-Joachim Kraus, Worship in Israel: A Cultic History of the Old Testament, trans. Geoffrey Buswell (Richmond: John Knox, 1965), pp. 110-111; and Fohrer, History of Israelite Religion, trans. David Green (New York: Abingdon, 1972), p. 107.

[160] E. Ehrlich, Traum, p. 47; Ralph David Gehrke, 1 and 2 Samuel, Concordia Commentary (St. Louis: Concordia, 1968), p. 44; and Mauchline, Samuel, p. 57.

[161] Budde, Samuel, KHAT, p. 26; Hertzberg, Samuel, p. 42; and Maly, Samuel, p. 19.

[162] ANET, pp. 143, 149, 451, 606, 449.

[163] Ibid., p. 30.

[164] Ibid., p. 449.

[165] E. Vogt, "Novae inscriptiones Nabonidi," Bib 40 (1959): 93.

[166] UT, pp. 247, 250.

[167] Oppenheim, Interpretation, pp. 187, 225.

[168] Vogt, "inscriptiones," p. 93.

[169] ANET, p. 449.

[170] Ibid., and Oppenheim, Interpretation, p. 251.

[171] UT, p. 250.

[172] Vogt, "inscriptiones," p. 93.

[173] ANET, p. 451.

[174] UT, p. 250.

[175] Oppenheim, Interpretation, p. 189.

[176] The ancients, however, may have based this motif in their literary format upon the actual observation of dreaming individuals. When a person dreams, the eyes will flutter in a manner which is technically described as a rapid eye movement (Klein, "Dreams," p. 665). If the ancients observed this phenomenon in a sleeping person, it would seem to them that the individual is actually seeing and hearing something from another realm, a divine communication. The dreamer sees something the person who is awake does not observe, so it appears that the dreamer is awake to another realm. Its formal expression in stylized literary categories would naturally have the dreamer awakened by the deity who is delivering the message from the other realm.

[177] ANET, p. 450.

[178] Oppenheim, Interpretation, p. 254.

[179] UT, p. 250.

[180] ANET, pp. 32, 449; and Oppenheim, Interpretation, p. 251.

[181] Oppenheim, Interpretation, p. 249; however, ANET, pp. 451, 606, merely translates the text as "Fear not!"

[182] Oppenheim, Interpretation, pp. 188-189; and ANET, pp. 309-310.

[183] Vogt, "inscriptiones," p. 93.

[184] ANET, p. 32.

[185] Oppenheim, Interpretation, p. 251.

[186] ANET, p. 449.

[187] UT, p. 250.

[188] G. Driver, Canaanite Myths, pp. 48-49; but Pardee, "Emendation," pp. 53-56, reads "El takes a cup in one hand," thus removing the possible physical manifestation by the deity.

[189] Oppenheim, Interpretation, pp. 188-189.

[190] Good examples are the several dreams to Nabonidus commanding him to rebuild the temples, Vogt, "inscriptiones," pp. 93-94. Biblical passages record imperatives given to Abimelech (Genesis 20:7), Laban (Genesis 31:24), Jacob (Genesis 46:2), and Balaam (Numbers 22:12, 21).

[191] Oppenheim, Interpretation, pp. 249-250; and ANET, pp. 451, 606.

[192] ANET, pp. 449-450.

[193] Oppenheim, Interpretation, p. 254.

[194] UT, p. 250.

[195] Oppenheim, Interpretation, p. 250.

[196] Ibid., p. 251.

[197] Ibid., p. 255.

[198] Ibid., p. 191.

[199] Ibid., pp. 251-252.

[200] ANET, p. 32.

[201] Ibid., p. 449.

[202] UT, p. 250.

[203] Oppenheim, Interpretation, p. 191.

[204] Budde, Samuel, KHAT, pp. 25-26, maintains the section is late, and although the account implies incubation, it was not the practice of Samuel's time; Nowack, Richter, Ruth und Samuelis, pp. 17-18; Stade, Theologie, 1:130-131; Gressmann, Geschichtsschreibung, pp. 6-7; Jirku, "Inkubation," p. 153; Eichrodt, Theology of the Old Testament, 1:105, maintains that since Shiloh was a shrine, this is the natural place for dream incubation to occur, just as at Bethel and Gibeon; Gaster, Thespis, p. 271; Kraus, Worship, pp. 110, 175, believes that Samuel was undergoing a natural incubation process, which any dedicated youth had to experience. The service by which Samuel ministered to the Lord (I Samuel 2:11, 18, 3:3) was a process of incubation, by which he sought to obtain an oracle. Receiving an oracle verified the recipient as a charismatic leader in Israel. Due to the importance of this event Eli had to be told the oracle in order to verify Samuel as a charismatic leader. Thus the reception of the oracle explains the conclusion of 3:19-4:1a; Gino Bressan, Samuele, Vecchio Testamento, La Sacra Bibbia (Torino: Marietti, 1954), p. 100; Hertzberg, Samuel, p. 41; Maly, Samuel, p. 19; Macholz, "Überlieferungen," pp. 92-93; Merrill, "I Samuel 1-15," p. 41; and Ackroyd, Samuel, p. 43.

[205] Maly, Samuel, p. 19.

[206] Loring W. Batten, "The Sanctuary at Shiloh, and Samuel's Sleeping therein," JBL 19 (1900): 33; Kraus, Worship, p. 176; and Hertzberg, Samuel, p. 41.

[207] Smith, Samuel, pp. 27-28, maintains that instead of being an example of incubation, this text merely indicates that a shrine is the best place to receive a revelation; Schulz, Samuel, 1:58, points out that only the burning lamp can be construed as evidence of incubation, for it indicates the time is in the early morning hours, the time when incubated dreams may come, but such evidence is too little to call this an incubated dream; A. Ehrlich, Randglossen, 3:178, points out that the lamp, the best evidence for incubation, is an object required for light in a dark tent, and thus its presence does not directly imply an incubation process; Dhorme, L'evolution, p. 232; E. Ehrlich, Traum, pp. 45-48, maintains that only I Kings 3:4 contains legitimate reference to incubation rites; Gaster, "Dreams," p. 208, changed his mind from his earlier work, Thespis, p. 271, and now rejects the idea of incubation; and Stoebe, Samuelis, p. 124. A mediating position is taken by Mendelsohn, "Dream," p. 868, who calls this an unintentional incubation dream. Such an experience is caused by the sleeper's inadvertently sleeping in a sacred place, which then

causes the deity to appear. The dreamer does not expect the theophany and does not perform incubatory rites. Thus Samuel slept in the shrine, and that alone incubated the dream unknowingly.

[208] Kennedy, Samuel, p. 53; Schulz, Samuel, 1:58; and Batten, "Samuel's Sleeping," pp. 32-33.

[209] Stoebe, Samuelis, pp. 123-124.

[210] Mendelsohn, "Dream," p. 868; and Oppenheim, Interpretation, p. 190.

[211] ANET, p. 449; and Oppenheim, Interpretation, pp. 249-251.

[212] Hölscher, Profeten, p. 58.

[213] Menahem Haran, "Shiloh and Jerusalem: The Origin of the Priestly Tradition in the Pentateuch," JBL 81 (1962): 22.

[214] Goldman, Samuel, p. 16.

[215] The auditory message dream formula may not have become popular in Israel until after its increased usage under Ashurbanipal in the late Seventh Century. This would indicate a late date for this passage, and imply that the Deuteronomistic Historian was its creator. However, the use of the dream pattern by the Elohist might tempt us to move the date back, even though the dream pattern of the Elohist differs from I Samuel 3.

[216] A. Ehrlich, Randglossen, 3:178; and Goldman, Samuel, p. 16.

[217] Wellhausen, Samuelis, pp. 51-52; Klostermann, Samuelis, pp. 17-18; Nowack, Richter, Ruth und Samuelis, p. 10; Schlögl, Samuelis, p. 20; and McCarter, Samuel, p. 98.

[218] Caspari, Samuelbücher, p. 54.

[219] Stoebe, Samuelis, p. 123.

[220] One might wish to postulate that in the traditions there was an earlier version of this story in which Samuel did lie by the ark to perceive a dream vision, hence incubation. Our present author would then have muted this aspect of the story for theological reasons. This kind of hypothesis cannot be verified, however.

[221] Batten, "Samuel's Sleeping," pp. 30-31.

[222] Ibid., Haran, "Shiloh," pp. 22-24, thinks the addition of these words illustrates a priestly editing of the chapter at a later date; Mauchline, Samuel, p. 7, sees this as proof for a prophetic editing.

[223] Schulz, Samuel, 1:13-14, 58; Haran, "Shiloh," pp. 22-24; R. Brinker, The Influence of Sanctuaries in Early Israel, (Manchester, England: University of Manchester Press, 1946), p. 165; and Mauchline, Samuel, p. 57.

[224] Goldman, Samuel, p. 17.

[225] McKane, Samuel, p. 42, points this out in response to earlier scholars who equated this lamp with the temple Menorah lamp in the tabernacle. Such scholars include Schlögl, Samuelis, p. 20; Smith, Samuel, p. 26; and Frederick Moriarity, The First Book of Samuel, (New York: Paulist, 1971), p. 14.

[226] Merrill, "I Samuel 1-12," pp. 38-40.

[227] E. Ehrlich, Traum, pp. 48-51.

[228] Thenius, Samuelis, p. 16; and Stoebe, Samuelis, p. 125, both see the purpose of the calling to contrast righteous Samuel with unrighteous Eli, who is so far removed from his contact with the Lord, he does not even give revelation his initial consideration. Caspari, Samuelbücher, p. 51, calls it a liturgical motif; and Merrill, "I Samuel 1-12," p. 40, thinks it is part of an important, but lost, pattern of divine revelation.

[229] Eichrodt, Theology of the Old Testament, 1:160, 2:445-447; Maly, Samuel, p. 20; and Stoebe, Samuelis, p. 125.

[230] Veijola, Dynastie, p. 38; and McCarter, Samuel, p. 98.

[231] Hertzberg, Samuel, p. 42.

[232] Ackroyd, Samuel, p. 44.

[233] Noth, "Samuel und Silo," p. 400, uses a different logic. He sees 3:21 as a true summary of chapters 1-3. Since these chapters occur in Shiloh, then the origin of these traditions must be Shiloh. I Samuel 3:19-4:1a was a conclusion to this short cycle of traditions, which were later taken into the greater cycle of Samuel traditions by the Deuteronomistic Historian. Since Shiloh was gone by Jeremiah's day, these Shiloh traditions must have taken their form at an early date.

[234] Lindblom, "Theophanies," p. 101.

[235] Hertzberg, Samuel, p. 42.

[236] Press, "Samuel," p. 189.

[237] Noth, "Samuel und Silo," pp. 399-400.

[238] Stoebe, Samuelis, pp. 86, 126.

[239] Hölscher, Geschichtsschreibung, p. 364; and Mauchline, Samuel, pp. 59-60.

[240] Bourke, "Samuel and the Ark," pp. 85-86, has drawn several interesting parallels: Eli is strong, Samuel is weak; but Eli sleeps in the dark, while Samuel is in the light; Samuel perceives what Eli cannot, Samuel "opens the doors," for he restores the Word of the Lord, and he alone can tend to the "still burning lamp." These literary motifs all further demonstrate to this author that the account is a literary creation.

[241] Kraus, Worship, pp. 109-111.

[242] Newman, "Call of Samuel," pp. 88-94.

[243] Lindblom, Prophecy, pp. 79, 82.

[244] Mauchline, Samuel, pp. 59-61.

[245] Gressmann, Geschichtsschreibung, p. 6.

[246] Stoebe, Samuelis, pp. 123-124, criticizes the historio-graphical presuppositions and reconstructions of Kraus, Newman, and Martin Cohen, "The Role of the Shilohite Priesthood in the United Monarchy of Ancient Israel," HUCA 36 (1965): 59-98.

178

CHAPTER V

ANALYSIS OF I SAMUEL 1-3

I Samuel 3 initially belongs to the context of I Samuel 1-3. Consideration of these three chapters needs to be undertaken to discover their form, content, meaning, relationships, origin, and theology. This will further explain the purpose of I Samuel 3. It will also assist in showing the development of this text, the reason for its creation, and the greater theological purpose behind it. We shall first consider the various form critical units of I Samuel 1-3 and then the greater unity of the material.

Form Critical Units

The material in these three chapters falls into fairly distinct form critical units. Once these units have been identified and discussed, their relationship to each other may be observed, and the literary structure of the chapters will emerge. The essential form critical units are: 1) the birth and dedication of Samuel, 1:1-28, 2) Hannah's Song, 2:1-10, 3) the behavior of Eli's sons, 2:12-17, 22-26, which is interwoven with Samuel's exemplary service, 2:11, 18-21, 4) the judgment speech directed toward an individual, 2:27-36, and 5) the dream experience of Samuel, 3:1-4:1a.

The Birth and Dedication of Samuel

Hannah's request for a child and her ultimate fulfillment is part of the common folktale motif of the barren mother who has a child, a type of story found in many societies. For Old Testament women like Sarah (Genesis 21), Hannah, and the wife of Manoah (Judges 13), the birth of a son brought great joy after being barren. This is the common folktale motif of the reversal of the fates.

The announcement of the birth of Samuel does not correspond to the pattern of birth announcements found elsewhere. Birth announcements are found in Genesis 16:11-12

179

(Ishmael), Genesis 17:15-21, 21:2 (Isaac), I Kings 13:2 (Josiah), Isaiah 7:14-17 (Immanuel), and I Chronicles 22:9-10 (Solomon). The form of these announcements includes: 1) declaration of the coming birth, 2) designation of his name, and 3) the role of the child in the future.[1] Samuel's birth follows a different pattern. Hannah is told by Eli that she would have a son, and Eli thus replaces the divine messenger. Hannah names the boy, for no name is given in the announcement. Nor is there a prediction of the child's greatness.

Samuel's birth narrative corresponds to Samson's birth narrative in Judges 13. In both there is the promise of a son (Judges 13:3-4, 7, I Samuel 1:17) and dedication of a son (Judges 13:5, 7, 25, I Samuel 1:24-28). The mothers are barren (Judges 13:2, I Samuel 1:15), there is a command to refrain from strong drink (Judges 13:4, 7, I Samuel 1:15), and it is said of both that "no razor shall touch his head" (Judges 13:5, I Samuel 1:11). Samson and Samuel fight the Philistines, they are tribal heroes or local judges, and both men are capable of personal rage. They are also in harmonious contrast, for Samuel is pious and Samson is mischievous, Samuel succeeds where Samson fails, and Samuel is the prototype of the true deliverer Samson fails to be.[2]

The reference to the unshaved head may imply that a Nazirite vow is involved. It is difficult to include the command to abstain from strong drink, for in the Samson account this is enjoined upon the parents. If Samson and Samuel are Nazirites, their vow is different from the one described in Numbers 6:1-21. In that passage the Nazarite is chosen by God, the vow is temporary, and the occasion of the vow is for time of war. But Samson and Samuel were called to life long service from birth, and they function during periods of peace. Samuel is chosen by his mother, not by God. Some scholars believe that these two narratives of Nazirite vows indicate a later historical development in the vow.[3] Others view Samuel's vow as a variation[4] a limited form of the vow, since he was not chiefly a warrior.[4] But it is more likely that the similarity between Samson and Samuel is due to literary dependence rather than some hypothetical historical development of the Nazirite vow. The account of Samuel's birth deliberately parallels the Samson version in respect to certain details like the childless mother and the uncut hair. Furthermore, Samuel is never again viewed as a Nazirite after I Samuel 1, which makes the birth story appear even more as a literary creation. The attribution of Nazirite functions to Samuel seems to be part of the tradition's development. This process continues down to the Septuagint's translation, for the Greek version also ascribes the abstention from alcohol to Samuel. It is possible that the birth story may intertwine two traditions about Samuel, his birth as a Nazirite and as a priest.[5]

These similarities between Samson and Samuel are dwarfed by the similarities between Saul and Samson. Dus has several parallels between Saul and Samson. 1) Both men warred against the Philistines until their death. 2) They experienced disgrace, a fall from God's favor because of their actions. An evil spirit took the place of the good spirit which they formerly possessed. 3) Suicide was the ultimate cause of death for both. 4) The power of the spirit of God came upon both men. The phrase "spirit of the Lord came over him" occurs in Judges 14:6, 19, 15:14-15, 16:20, I Samuel 10:6, 18:10, 19:9. 5) A hot temperament was characteristic of both. 6) As Samson tore a lion apart in Judges 14:6, so Saul cut two oxen in I Samuel 11. 7) The angel said, "he will deliver my people from the power of the Philistines" in Judges 13:5, and God tells Samuel that Saul will do likewise in I Samuel 9:16. 8) Individual acts of heroism are performed by both, and they come to the aid of helpless people. 9) "God was with him" is a phrase attributed to both men, Judges 13:24, I Samuel 10:7. And, 10) at the time of their death both men cried to the Lord, Judges 16:28, I Samuel 15:31.

Dus concludes that the birth story of Samuel really belongs to Saul, and thus the motifs of a barren mother and the uncut hair of the Nazirite belong to both Saul and Samson. When this transition occurs, new similarities arise. As the story of Samson's birth leads immediately to an account of his heroic acts, so also the birth story of Saul in I Samuel 1:1-11 may have led to his anointing in 9:1-10:16 and combat leadership in 11:1-11. Samson went down to look for a wife and began his career. Saul went to look for asses and ran into Samuel, who started him out as Israel's new king. Dus believes the original story of Saul was meant to be apologetic for this northern hero who fell from grace. It demonstrated the similarity of Saul with the southern hero, Samson. Thus Saul's reputation was being rehabilitated by this account after the Davidic criticism of Saul emanated from the south. Later Saulide traditions were woven with the very critical material, and Saul's birth was attributed to Samuel.[6]

Dus did not originate the idea of the birth legend originally belonging to Saul. The etymology of Samuel's name in I Samuel 1:20 led many to suspect this. The meaning of the name given by Hannah when she says, "I asked the Lord for him," implies the text should read šā'ûl instead of š^{e}mû'ēl. Samuel's name may mean "his name is El," or "the name of God," which has no relation to Hannah's etymology. Thus many scholars have deduced that Saul's name originally belonged here.[7] Hylander has most thoroughly developed this theory. He feels that the birth accounts of both Samson and Samuel originally belonged to Saul. There were two original versions of Saul's birth. Version A was the story of how Saul's birth

181

was first announced to the wife and then to the husband by the angel. The husband ultimately kept the Nazirite vow. Version A included Judges 13:2, I Samuel 1:6a, 5b, 11, 19b, Judges 13:3, 9bβ, 3b, 4, 5aβ, 6a, 7, 6b, I Samuel 1:20, 21, 22a, Judges 13:8, 9a, 11b, 12, I Samuel 1:28a, 22bα, 23aβ, 22b, 23a, Judges 13:24a, I Samuel 1:28aβ, Judges 13:5b, 17-18, 21b, I Samuel 1:28b, 2:11a, Judges 13:24b. Version B was the account of the cultic promise in the shrine by the wife and her fulfillment of the vow. It was composed of I Samuel 1:1-2, 4-5a, 6b, 7b, 9, 13-15, 17-18, 19bα, 20aβ, 23b, 24-25, 26a, 26bα, 27b, 2:11a, 20-21. These two accounts of Saul's birth were local traditions in Dan and Benjamin. This material was taken up and reconstructed to make the Samson and Samuel birth accounts of our present text. Our present text belies such a transformation not only because of the etymology in I Samuel 1:20, but also by the fact that I Samuel 1 and 3 perform the same function of showing Samuel as the servant of the Lord.[8]

This theory has not gained consensus among scholars, however. Hylander and others have placed too much evidence on too little data, for the beginning point of their theories is often the strange etymology in I Samuel 1:20. Explanatory etymologies among the Hebrews were often popular, inaccurate, and dependent upon sound rather than good linguistic meaning.[9] The intention of the text might be to demonstrate the relationship between "Samuel" and the meaning, "I have asked," by way of assonance.[10] Some have followed Rabbi Kimchi's medieval suggestion that the name simply means "asked of God."[11] It might be a subtle pun by the author, who seeks to indicate that Samuel will lead to Saul, and that Samuel is the more important figure of the two.[12] Perhaps, the rival traditions of Samuel stole the etymology from the Saul traditions at an early date in order to deprecate Saul.[13] This word play might be a literary technique to link the Samuel traditions to the Saul traditions by an effort of foreshadowing.[14] One unusual possibility is to maintain that Samuel's name is an abbreviation of a longer name, which may have equated with the etymology, such as ʾašer min ʾēl.[15] Another option is to state that this etymology refers to another name of Samuel.[16] Thus the highly complex theory of Hylander is rendered improbable by the complexity of his reconstruction, for he cannot explain how or why this process occurred in this peculiar fashion. It is improbable that a birth tradition could be so completely lost from the Saulide traditions.[17] It is likewise difficult to perceive how a dedication at Shiloh could relate to Saul.[18]

The significance of the debate for I Samuel 3 is in terms of the date. If I Samuel 1 originally belonged to the life of Saul and was connected to chapters 9:1-10:16, 11:1-15, and if this was a northern version of Saul's life after the division of

the monarchy, then the date of I Samuel 1-3 in its present form is late. The author of I Samuel 1-3 took northern traditions, altered them radically, added his own material, and probably created material to embellish the life of Samuel. In that case, chapter 3 would be late creation worked in with material in I Samuel 1-2.[19]

In this tradition Samuel is described as an Ephraimite. However, in I Chronicles 6:33 he is called a Levite. This is probably a later accretion to the reputation of Samuel, although some scholars believe he was a Levite by profession or adoption into the tribe.[20] Others are convinced of the historicity of his Ephraimite background in I Samuel 1:1-2.[21] However, there are problems with the location of the city of his origin. Schunck believes the original idyll comprised I Samuel 1:1-19a, 20-28, 2:18-21, and in this section Samuel was a man from Ramathaim in Ephraim. He was a Zuphite, and would become a seer in Ephraim. Later redaction added extensive Samuel traditions, including Elide material in chapter 2, and converted Samuel traditions, including Elide material in chapter 2,[22] and converted Samuel into a man from Ramah of Benjamin.[22] The redactor converted the seer-priest Samuel into the king-maker of the anti-monarchical source, and the modification of the name of his city is part of this. Wallis also believes that Samuel is a prophet, and the Samuel of Ramah is found in a separate cycle of traditions, where Samuel is a judge. Saul of Benjamin went up to Ephraim to meet Samuel the prophet in 9:1-10:16. In one cycle of tradition Samuel the prophet-seer in Ramathaim anointed Saul, and in the other Samuel the judge from Ramah rejected Saul and the kingship. Prophetic circles remembered Samuel as a prophet; circles at Mizpah recalled him as a judge.[25] However, Stoebe thinks the form of the word in I Samuel 1:1-2 for Samuel's city is harāmātah, which serves to indicate that Elkanah moved to that city. It is Ramah in Benjamin to which the family had moved from Ephraim. Therefore, no great conclusions may be drawn from this particular text.[24]

The issue of the family's origin is compounded by the nature of the festival they attended. It may have been merely a local festival for the Zuphites.[25] I may have been only a private festival for Elkanah and his family.[26] But most scholars believe it was the festival of harvest or some version of it. The question remains whether it was tribal or national. If it was merely attended by people from the local tribe of Benjamin, why would this family come from Ephraim? Various answers are given: the family really was from Ramah of Benjamin, or perhaps they moved and still attended this shrine, or their dislocation from the shrine may reflect tribal movements, or they merely came to this shrine out of preference.

183

Was Shiloh a significant shrine so as to attract Elkanah and his family on such a pilgrimage every year? Nothing may safely be deduced about Shiloh from other traditions in this regard. The earliest traditions are in Joshua 18:1, 8-10, 19:51, 21:2, where meetings and land distribution occur. These texts may have the name Shiloh inserted secondarily, and Gilgal may have been the original name.[27] This tendency to insert Shiloh is continued by the Septuagint, which places it in Joshua 24:1 instead of Shechem. Shiloh may not have been an important shrine for the celebration of the harvest festival. The site may have been a Canaanite cult center, which was taken over by Benjamin and then by Ephraim, and thus it was a shared tribal shrine. The tradition about Shiloh and the Benjaminites in Judges 21 appears to be an old and authentic tradition. In that account there is an allusion to a yearly festival in Judges 21:9. The shrine died out in importance before the patriarchal narratives were formed, and thus none of the patriarchal stories seeks to legitimate it as a shrine.[28] This yearly festival was a harvest festival, for there was drinking involved in it as Judges 21:20-21 and I Samuel 1:13-15 imply.[29] Whether it was a pan-Israelite festival is difficult to determine, but it may have had some connection with the later development of the Festival of Tabernacles. The Canaanite influence may be observed in the drinking, the possible sacred prostitution (I Samuel 2:22), and the worship of El, if Eli's name is derived from that theophoric title.[30] The presence of the ark at this shrine may be a secondary literary motif meant to unite the stories in I Samuel 1-3 with the narrative of the ark in chapters 4-6.

Archaeological research has found no evidence of a shrine at Shiloh.[31] Shiloh was at first believed to be at Beit-Sila,[32] but Kjaer dug at Seilūn and identified it as Shiloh in 1926. He believed that a later Arab shrine replaced the old Israelite shrine.[33] Later opinion, however, challenged whether the site contained a shrine. City and shrine may have been separate, or there may have been no shrine at all.[34] Shiloh was inhabited prior to the Iron Age, 1600-1440 B.C., but the site exhibits peak development during the Iron Age. Kjaer dated the material to Iron I with Albright's encouragement, and the consensus arose that the termination of Iron I came with the Philistine destruction in 1050 B.C.[35] However, I Samuel 4 does not record the actual destruction of the city. Kjaer's date of Iron I and 1050 B.C. was later challenged by Marie Louis Buhl, who edited Kjaer's work. She discovered pottery from the Iron II period, which Kjaer had dated as Iron I. This pottery indicated that the peak development of the city was in Iron II until its destruction in 700 B.C.[36] This would indicate there was no major Philistine destruction in 1050 B.C. But Buhl has also been challenged by later scholars. Yigal Shiloh disagrees with her classification of the collar rimmed jar at Shiloh as an

Iron II type like those at Hazor, so he maintains that these are truly Iron I collar rim jars at Shiloh.[37] This would push the date of destruction back to 1050 B.C. At present one can conclude that the archaeological evidence is ambiguous.

The literary tradition of Ahijah of Shiloh in I Kings 14:4 implies a continued prophetic activity there, even if there were no shrine, and that implies habitation, which supposedly ceased after the destruction. This implies that perhaps the major destruction was after 1050 B.C. Finally, the reference of Jeremiah to the destruction of Shiloh in Jeremiah 7:11-12, and the reference in Psalm 78:60 to the Lord's desertion of the city may imply a destruction closer to Jeremiah's day.[38] Shiloh simply faded in importance after the loss of the ark, and the transfer to Jerusalem of the significant religious activity caused the city's decline. Perhaps with Assyrian activity in the late Eighth Century the shrine and city were actually destroyed. Concerning this possibility archaeology gives ambiguous evidence, and concerning the importance of the shrine during the pre-monarchical period there is no evidence.

Later Rabbinic tradition views Shiloh as an important forerunner to Jerusalem. It was the central shrine for 369 years as opposed to 14 years for Gilgal and 57 years for Nob and Gibeon.[39] Although this tradition sees Shiloh as a major shrine, this viewpoint may be a later theological elaboration.

Some scholars have advocated that the city was important in the pre-monarchical period and the transfer of theological authority from Shiloh to Jerusalem was an important task for David. The passage in Genesis 49:10, "When he comes to Shiloh," is seen as a reference to David's assumption of authority in the north, for Shiloh is seen as the symbol for religious and political unity in the north.[40] But this argument has gained little consensus, for it is too speculative.

It is impossible to determine whether Shiloh was an important cult site to which pilgrims came for the annual festival of Tabernacles or a festival of harvest. It seems more logical to assume that it was a local shrine with a harvest festival emphasis that embodied many Canaanite elements. It may have been a wine festival, for this is the implication in Judges 21 with the reference to dancing and vineyards. The activities of the women in Judges 21 may somehow be related to the women in I Samuel 2:22, and such possible ritual prostitution may not have been offensive at that time. The present literary construction of our text has toned down such offensive references. The text also tries to give the impression that the festival is important like the later festival of Tabernacles.

The Song of Hannah

Many critics concede that this psalm is late, perhaps the latest addition in I Samuel 1-3. The reference to the "anointed" or the king in 2:10 implies that the song comes from the time of the monarchy. The mention of the king has caused critics to call this a Royal Psalm, a Thanksgiving Psalm of the King, or an Eschatological Psalm.[41] On the basis of some superficial relation to older psalmic material in the Old Testament, some critics conclude that Hannah's Song goes back to the time of the United Kingdom. Nyberg claims to have found the ancient name ^{c}Alu in the song, which is the short version of Elyon and El Elyon, which is also the basis of Eli's name.[42] Wright believes that Hannah's Song is the southern version of Deuteronomy 32:1-43, and both are to be associated with the destruction of Shiloh.[43] Some scholars believe the song originally referred to Saul's kingdom, but it was transferred to Samuel when it was added to chapter 2.[44] Zannoni tries to relate it to the defeat of the Philistines.[45] Others think the psalm may be an early song used in the Shiloh cult.[46] Goslinga assumes that if the tradition assigns this song to Hannah, there must be a good historical reason for doing so.[47] All of these scholars build their arguments on very slim and sometimes debatable observations. Nevertheless, they may be correct, and the song may be early in date. But this does not change the probability that the song was placed into this context at a late date. No one has effectively responded to the early literary critics who pointed out that the psalm does not really fit in the context. It intrudes into the middle of a sentence.[48] The psalm does not really refer to Hannah's circumstances, for the phrase "anointed" implies the psalm concerns the king. The reference to "barren" caused the editor to include this material in the story as a typical response of the once barren Hannah.[49] The only question remaining is whether this psalm was inserted after Deuteronomistic redaction, as Stoebe claims.[50] As a form critical unit it is very distinct.

Samuel and the Elides

I Samuel 2:11-26 appears to be a composite of two narrative strands. This was first noted by Samuel Driver when he perceived that in 2:11 Samuel ministers to the Lord before Eli, but in 2:18 he ministers before the Lord.[51] Two accounts were woven together. The abuses of the Elides are portrayed in I Samuel 2:12-17, 22-25, while I Samuel 2:11, 18-21, 26 contrasts with that material by demonstrating the righteousness of Samuel. The material was worked together to produce such an alternating contrast in order to justify the destruction of the Elides in I Samuel 4 and Samuel's ascendancy in 3:19-4:1a. The artificial relationship of Samuel and the Elides dissolves

when the two strands are separated, and Samuel's relationship to Shiloh is rendered very tenuous, for never again does he appear in the city.[52]

The material in these two strands has connections with material outside of this chapter. The Samuel references in 2:11, 18-21, 26 apparently continue the birth and dedication story of I Samuel 1 and culminate in I Samuel 3. This material is part of the Samuel idyll and appears to be younger than the Elide material which has been absorbed into its structure. The account of the Elides in I Samuel 2:12-17, 22-25 may have originally been connected with material in the ark narrative of I Samuel 4-6, especially chapter 4.[53] Some have noticed discontinuity between the Elide material in chapter 2 and 4.[54] The latter chapter seems to portray the sons of Eli in a more heroic role, as if the abuses were unknown. It may well be that the material in chapter 2 was created to reinterpret the account in chapter 4, and thus give a pejorative understanding to the defeat by making it appear as a punishment for cultic abuse.[55] The death of Eli and his sons requires the reader to ask why this happened, and I Samuel 2:12-17, 22-25 seeks to answer that question. The apprehension of Eli in chapter 4 seems to imply the existence of events described in chapter 2. If this material was a unity, it might have circulated at Nob during the days of the United Monarchy, and it may have been used to justify the exclusion of Abiathar from the court of Solomon. Zadok may be the one who is implied in I Samuel 7:1 as the son of Eleazar, who with his father then cared for the ark in Kirjath-jearim, or at least I Chronicles 24:3 tries to make the identification. The story was then woven into I Samuel 1-3, which continues this anti-Abiatharide polemic.[56]

The nature of the sins of the sons is subject to various interpretations. The relationship of Hophni and Phinehas to the women may indicate the Canaanite practice of sacred prostitution at this shrine,[57] or the sons may be taking sexual advantage of women who come to sacrifice.[58] Their demands for meat appear to violate some cultic regulation, but the actual violation is vague. It may be offensive to demand raw meat, to select the choice portions, and to interrupt the burning. However, it could well be that they are performing legitimate ancient cultic practices, but the Deuteronomistic Historian misunderstood them and interpreted their actions as evil.[59] This would accord well with the idea that the Elide material is an old tradition. Perhaps, they were performing an old Canaanite custom in boiling the meat, which later became viewed as evil according to Exodus 12:9.[60]

The sins of the Elides in this chapter are the highpoint in a sequence of many failures. Eli mistook Hannah to be drunk in I Samuel 1:12-18, and he forgot about her oath in

187

1:26-28. That Hannah could be accused of drunkenness may indicate that the presence of drunken frenzy was common, another[61] failure on the part of the administrators of the shrine. The sins of the Elides stand forth in both relief to Samuel's obedience and Hannah's patience. When rebuked Hannah is patient. Samuel personally served Eli in 1:24-28, 2:11, 3:1. He runs first to Eli when he is called by the Lord in 3:4-8, and he is fearful to tell Eli the prophecy because he respects Eli. The literary nature of the text is designed to magnify the nature of the sins, but it is not too clear what the actual abuses were. The author might be drawing a distinction between sins against God and sins against people; and if so, he[62] betrays a theology prior to the classical prophetic idea of sin. The clearest failure is Eli's inability to control his sons. Their abuses and his leniency bring the prophetic words of I Samuel 2:27-36 and 3:11-14 and cause the Word of the Lord to become rare according to 3:1.

The criticism of the Elides is probably exaggerated by the later editor of I Samuel 1-3 for theological reasons. The Canaanite influence at Shiloh was probably accepted in the pre-monarchical period, and a later prophetic perspective condemned early sacrificial practice, sacred prostitution, and cultic drunkeness. Despite its pejorative overtones the text reveals Eli and his sons lived in rustic simplicity, and people still came to them. Their demand for the meat may have been a justifiable practice in the early period, for that was their only source of livelihood.[63] This contrasts vividly with the luxury of the later Jerusalem priests. Practices condemned in I Samuel 2 also appear to be part of the festival in Judges 21, and no pejorative interpretation is put on them in that text.

The fact that the text also reveals these positive aspects may indicate the older origin of the Elide traditions. Some scholars point to the names of Hophni and Phinehas as having Egyptian etymology. Hophni, in particular, is an uncommon name, found only twice during the Middle Kingdom, and thus not likely to be a creation.[64] So if there are old traditions in this text, they have been reinterpreted by the present form and context to give a bad outlook on the house of Eli.

A significant issue arises concerning the role of Samuel. Some perceive that he is a priest because he wears the linen ephod and ministers before the Lord.[65] In I Samuel 22:18 and II Samuel 6:14 it is priestly garb, and it is probably comparable to the linen garb worn by Egyptian priests.[66] Many think that Samuel's ephod was different from the priestly ephod. It may simply be a "costly garment," as a similar word in Canaanite and Assyrian may suggest.[67] David also wore an ephod when he danced before the ark. It may have been priestly garb which laity could wear.[68] Thus it is probable that this text

describes Samuel as a server, a temple assistant, rather than a priest.[69]

This section may demonstrate how theological priorities have determined the structure of I Samuel 1-3. The sins of the Elides contrast with the righteousness of Samuel, and the reader is prepared for Samuel's reception of the word of judgment in the dream theophany. The reader also senses the artificial nature of Samuel's presence in Shiloh. He is a prophet, who as a child contrasts with the evil priests and thereby condemns them. Nowhere else does Samuel have connection with Shiloh or the priests of Nob. This appears to be a late literary creation meant theologically to condemn the Elides and their later representatives.

Individual Word of Judgment

The form of I Samuel 2:27-36 is a judgment speech directed against an individual. Claus Westermann has outlined the categories of the genre into which the pericope may be divided, and other scholars have followed his guidance in analyzing this text.[70]

Commissioning of the Messenger: This part of the genre may be missing. In verse 27 there is reference to the man of God, whose very title may imply that he has received a divine commission to bring this message. Thus the commission may be found in the formula, "the man of God came to Eli."

Summons to hear: In verse 27 the messenger proclaims, "this is the Word of the Lord," before Eli.

Accusation: With a historical prelude in verses 27b-28 the accusation comes in verse 29. Accusations often come as a question, and here we have three questions, "Why do you show disrespect for my sacrifices and offerings, which I ordained? Why do you resent them? Why do you honor your sons more than me by letting them take the choicest offerings of my people Israel?" This accusation takes into account both Eli's permissiveness and the sacrilege of Hophni and Phinehas.

Announcement: This is introduced by the formula, "therefore the Lord, the God of Israel, says." The particular form of this announcement is the contrast motif.[71] The prophet states the former conditions, and the announcement reverses those conditions. In verse 30 he declares, "I promised your house and your father's house would serve forever, but now the Lord declares, 'I will have no such thing.'" The message continues through verses 31-36. It is the announcement to an individual, but because he owns a hereditary office, the curse is upon his

189

house, and it includes a greater number of people. The punishment also carries a sign, which is in verse 34. The impending death of the sons in battle is a sign of the future punishment. But this is also part of the punishment itself, so the punishment comes in several phases. For this reason many scholars believe there are some expansions in the accusation, which update the punishments of the Elides from Abiathar's expulsion to the Josianic reform.

Many scholars consider the entire passage to be a later insertion into this text.[72] Pfeiffer maintains it is a late gloss because the editor misunderstood the use of the ephod when he added the phrase "before Yahweh" in verse 28, for a divinatory device like the ephod was not connected with any sacrifice.[73] With the confusion of the genealogies, Eli is made into the ancestor of all Levites, and coupled with the anonymity of the prophet, the late date of the text is indicated.[74] The image of the priest following the king is late, and it betrays a theology of priestly subservience unfamiliar to the rest of the practices in the books of Samuel.[75] Veijola points out the Deuteronomistic affinities of the language: 1) verse 30, "Lord God of Israel" is a Deuteronomistic expression, 2) verse 33, "I will not cut off a man from my altar" is comparable to II Samuel 3:29, I Kings 2:4b, 8:25, 9:5, 3) the idea of "eternal election" in verses 30, 35, and the "house" in verses 27, 28, 30, 31, 32, 35, 36 are both Deuteronomistic expressions.[76]

Some scholars maintain this passage has an integral connection to the previous material in chapter 2. Smith feels that 2:27-36 responds to the evils listed in 2:12-17, 22-25, and all of the verses were an original unity. This material was united to I Samuel 4:1b-7 and only later did other material intervene. The passage could not be a later insert because it would then reduplicate the oracle in chapter 3.[77] Although one might call this a foreshadowing technique,[78] many point to the reduplication as a sign of the secondary nature of 2:27-36, and thus turn Smith's argument back on him.[79] It may be possible that this secondary passage about the anonymous prophet is really about Samuel's prophecy as an adult, in which case 2:27-36 is a doublet for all of chapter 3.[80] Some would reply to Smith that the condemnation of Eli in 2:27-36 is different than the material in 2:12-17, 22-25, for the oracle in 2:27-36 condemns Eli for active participation, but in the earlier material he was guilty only of passive permission.[81] Given all the arguments, it appears that 2:27-36 does reinterpret the previous material, and thus it was separate at some stage in the development. Most of the material in I Samuel 1-3 is really concerned with Samuel, but the oracle in 2:27-36 shifts the interest away entirely. Its concerns are very much with the history of the priesthood as it stood under prophetic judgment, whereas most of the Samuel material is a created literary

idyll.[82] Furthermore, its proclamation of judgment contrasts with the unexpected oracle which comes in chapter 3.[83] This passage does have discontinuity with its context, both with the Samuel material and the Elide material.

Dus proposes that all of these fragments were indeed separate, and this explains their discontinuity with each other. They were all brought together by a final editor of all three chapters. He proposes that originally 2:27-30 was a separate tradition about the Elides, as was 1:3b, 2:12-16, 22-25, and 3:11-14. Not until the final edition of I Samuel 1-3 were they combined. In 2:27-30 Eli is godless and responsible for the sin, but the sons are not cursed; in 1:3b, 2:12-16, 22-25 Eli is pious and not responsible for the evil, the sons are priests and they cause the evil; and the ultimate effect of I Samuel 1-3 as a unity is to show that Eli is pious but responsible for the irresponsibility of his sons.[84] In this analysis all the anti-Elide elements are initially unrelated until the final edition, and the discontinuity between 2:27-36 and the rest of the chapter is explained. It does seem that 2:27-36 is a separate creation, perhaps brought into existence by the final editor along with chapter 3, while 2:12-17, 22-25 might represent the remnants of earlier material.

The date, integrity, and purpose of the text are dependent upon the meaning of the various components in the text. Most scholars concur that the prophecy refers at least to the explusion of the priest Abiathar from the court of Solomon in favor of Zadok, the faithful priest. I Kings 2:27 makes this connection by indicating that Abiathar's explusion fulfilled the prophecy at Shiloh. The slaughter of the house of Eli in I Samuel 2:31 refers not only to the Philistine victory at Shiloh but also to the massacre at Nob described in I Samuel 22. The survivor mentioned in verse 33 is Abiathar, who escaped that slaughter, and the faithful priest in verse 35 is probably Zadok. The anointed one may be David, or any king of the house of David. Finally, the begging family members in verses 35-36 may[85] refer to the Levites who are displaced by Josiah's reform. Some think the faithful priest originally may have meant Samuel, but in later development it came to be seen as Zadok.[86] The oracle therefore has two disasters for the Elides, the slaughter at Nob, and the later degeneration of the line until the final humiliation at the hands of Josiah.[87] The defeat at Shiloh is a foreshadowing, and it could be seen as a third disaster, but the prophecy really looks beyond that defeat. Ironically, the oracle in 3:11-14 seems to point more toward the defeat near Shiloh. Thus the two oracles need not be seen as duplications. The oracle is vaticinia ex eventu and reviews events from the Shiloh defeat down to Josiah's reform. If the text is a unity, then it must be dated to the time of Deutero-nomistic redaction. Tsevat, however, maintains that the

191

prophecy may have been before the event, since the prophecy is vague and parts of it did not come true exactly according to the words of the prophet. For in verses 31b and 32b it says there never will be an old man in the house of Eli, and the verb krt implies premature death. Since Abiathar lived to be an old man, the prophecy did not really come true as it was told.[88] Tsevat may be drawing too fine a distinction, for the prophecy may refer to the general destruction of the house of Eli accomplished at Nob, which did indeed prevent almost all the men from reaching old age.

Since the events which are prophesied in this oracle came true over a three-century span, the possibility arises that the oracle is not a unity, but has grown as the years progressed. The oracle in its earliest form may have referred to events at Nob and the expulsion of Abiathar, and only later were verses 35-36 added to update the history of the Elides to the time of Josiah. There is evidence of addition and growth in this passage. Wellhausen first noticed that verses 31b and 32a were glosses, a parallel of 32b. With the aid of the Septuagint he determined that verse 32b is more original than 31b because it allows for survivors, whereas the latter does not. Verse 33a is original, for it continues the thought of 32b, and in its earliest form the oracle referred only to the faithful priest, and the original text was 2:31a, 32b, 33-34. The text was reinterpreted by I Kings 2:27, which made Abiathar the survivor, and Zadok the faithful priest. The addition of 2:31b and 2:32a brought in the massacre of Nob as part of the prophecy. Finally, 2:35-36 extended the curse to include the dislocations of Josiah's reforms.[89] These three stages of development were fairly well accepted by other scholars.[90] Nowack deleted 2:29a, 32, 35-36 and called the rest original. Steuernagel built upon Wellhausen in seeing these levels of development and Deuteronomistic influence on the passage, but he thought only 2:31a, 33aα, 33b were original.[91] Others modified the consensus by postulating that the Septuagint was in error, and hence the basis of Wellhausen's reconstruction was incorrect. The text of 2:31-34 is original in its totality, and the prophecy first referred to the massacre at Nob and the expulsion of Abiathar.[92] Thus there are two stages in the development of meaning, the addition of verses 35-36 then extend the curse upon the Elides to include the later Josianic reform.[93] The original oracle in 2:31-34 would date back to Solomon's day, and 2:35-36 would be Deuteronomistic editing.[94] Segal departed from this consensus by claiming that the triplet in verses 31b, 32b, and 33b is late and should be omitted; he also felt that 3:35-36 is early, since the Zadokites are already in decline by the end of the monarchy, while these verses assume they are still in good standing, and the Levites of Josiah's day are totally unrelated to the earlier Elides.[95] More recently Dus introduced a new idea for the development of

the passage. Verses 27-30 form a structural unity, and they are the earliest oracle, which refers only to the defeat in chapter 4. After this battle at a later date verses 31-34 were added and verses 35-36 were attached as an even later reflection of Abiathar's expulsion.[96] In a similar fashion Merrill felt that 2:27-31 is original to the rest of the chapter, 2:32-34 was created to bridge the existing account to chapter 4, since it foresees the disastrous defeat, and 2:35-36 was added with the overview of the Deuteronomistic History, for it refers to the time of Josiah.[97]

The dating of the pericope varies according to the views concerning its integrity and development. The basic consensus is that 2:31-34 is as early as the time of Solomon or at least pre-Deuteronomistic, while 2:35-36 is a Deuteronomistic addition. Some would say that 2:35-36 is still pre-Deuteronomistic, however[98] Others think both phrases are late and Deuteronomistic.[99] But the general consensus is that the incorporation of the pericope with the rest of the material came late even though the material had a long prehistory.

I Samuel 1-3 as a Unit

With the consideration of the various form critical units of I Samuel 1-3 completed, the question arises concerning their relationship to each other, the date of their integration, and the theological purpose of this greater literary structure. The entire structure has frequently been called an idyll. This is evidenced by the full personality development and the strong emphasis on personal piety.[100] This contrasts with the material in I Samuel 4-6, sometimes called historical legends.[101] Other scholars would call I Samuel 1-3 "cultic legends,"[102] or "priestly legends."[103] Only a few would try to maintain the historicity of parts of the accounts.[104] The majority feel this material is primarily a literary creation, not history.

Sources

Many theories are given for the origin of this material and the sources from which the various form critical units arose. Early literary critics and some modern scholars consider the chapters to be part of the Elohist.[105] Many scholars consider the greater part of it to come from the Elohist. Mowinckel calls I Samuel 1:1-38, 2:11-17, 19-26, 3:1-11, 14-21 Elohistic; Hölscher limits it to 1:1-3a, 4-6a, 7-28, 2:11-22abα, 23-26, 3:1-11, 13, 15-18, 19abα, 20-21a; and MacLaurin sees it as 1:1-38, 2:11-26, 3:1-11a, 15-20.[106] A reluctance to use Pentateuchal nomenclature causes some to refer to it as the anti-monarchical source.[107] Others view it as a mixture of

193

Yahwist and Elohist. Eissfeldt calls 2:12-17, 22-25, 27-36 Yahwist and 1:1-28, 2:11, 18b-21, 3:1-21 Elohist, while Stahelin calls 1:1-2:36 Elohist and 3:1-21 Yahwist.[108] It has been designated as a special Samuel Source.[109] Press sees three different sources within the chapters, a cultic source in 1:1-28, 2:11, 18b-21, a prophetic source in 2:12-18a, 22-36, 3:19-4:1a, and the special theophany in 3:1-18.[110] But though there is disagreement on the exact divisions, there seems to be a consensus in trying to separate Samuel material in chapters 1, 3, parts of 2 from Elide material in 2.[111]

Most modern scholars are reluctant to speak of sources. They prefer to describe the segments as units of tradition, which have been assembled at some time. Fohrer believes the components were the birth and dedication, the Elide material, the judgment oracle, and the theophany of Samuel, which were all compiled by the editor who used them as a supplementary stratum in a pre-Deuteronomistic edition of Samuel.[112] Hertzberg believes the final compiler wove the traditions about the Elides in 2:12-17, 22-25, 27-34, and the rise of Samuel in 1:1-28, 2:11, 18-21, 26, 3:1-10, 15-21, and then he added the hymn in 2:1-10 and created 2:35-36, 3:11-14.[113] Noth feels there were two cycles of tradition, 1:1-28, 2:11, 18-21, and 2:12-17, 22-36, which were brought together, while 3:1-21 was either a creation by the editor, or it was drawn from other circles who had kept the tradition.[114] Dus believes that a modified birth story of Saul in 1:1-11 was combined with three anti-Elide elements in 1:3b, 2:12-16, 22-25; 2:27-30, 31-34, 35-36; and 3:11-14. Material was created in 1:12-28, 3:1-10, 15-18 to produce a literary account in chapters 1-3, and then chapters 4-6 were added to this.[115] Macholz is reluctant to give specific verses, but he believes the earliest components were the birth account, the connection of Samuel to Shiloh, and the various genealogies. The final editor gave chapters 1-3 its final form by creating the rest of the material, although he may have taken 3:2-18 from elsewhere.[116] Zannoni believes the form critical units of the birth and dedication, the wickedness of the sons, and the revelation to Samuel were taken by a Deuteronomistic editor from their oral setting in Ramah and brought together with editorial additions in 2:1-10 and 2:27-36.[117] Miller and Roberts see chapters 1-3 as a creation out of old Samuel and Elide material, but the Samuel material in chapter 2 is part of the created account.[118]

Some scholars advocate that these units should be viewed as a coherent unity. Bourke omits 2:1-10, 27-36 and calls the rest a unified Ephraimite source.[119] Willis offers extensive arguments that these chapters are a literary unity. He finds an underlying structural unity in the contrast of the Elide downfall and Samuel's ascent. The piety of Samuel and Hannah contrast with the Elides in an alternating pattern:[120]

194

Samuel's ascent:	2:11	Elide descent:	2.12-17
	2:18-21		2:22-25
	2:26		2:27-36
	3:1-10		3:11-18
	3:19-4:1a		4:1-22

He also points to recurring words and themes as proof of unity. These include: 1) reference to an annual festival, 1:3, 21, 24, 2:19; 2) Samuel's progress, 1:22, 24, 2:19, 21, 26, 3:19; 3) the pun on Saul's name, 1:17, 20, 27, 28, 2:20; 4) Hannah's barren condition, 1:5, 6, 11, 2:5, 7-9, 20-21; 5) Elide sin, 2:13-16, 29; 6) divine providence, "may the Lord do what seems best," 1:23, 3:18; 7) the judgment, 2:27-36, 3:12; 8) reference to sacrifice, 2:13, 17, 29, 3:14, and 9) the phrase, "house of Eli," 2:27, 28, 30, 31, 32, 33, 35, 36, 3:12, 13, 14.[121] Most of these observations are superficial. Many of them demonstrate the unity within the various segments or sources, but they do not convincingly show an over-all unity. Finally, one would expect an editor to bring together material that is related, and these motifs are the points of connection for these various materials. Material created by the editor would also refer to accounts already in existence in order to link the stories together by common themes. The editor has the right to receive some credit for artistic talent. The demonstration of unity by the indication of a few superficial similarities is not as significant as the discontinuities. Merrill also attempts to show an underlying structural unity in I Samuel 1-7, which he parallels to Exodus 1-15. Both texts have a pattern of bitter life for God's people, the birth of a deliverer, a hymn of victory, theophany, commission, conflict, deliverance, and a festival. But he attributes this to the work of an editor who skillfully wove Samuel material in 1:1-28, 2:11, 18-21, 26, 3:1-21, Elide material in 2:12-17, 22-25, 27-36, and independent material in 2:1-10 together.[122] Merrill's observations, though not necessarily accepted totally by this author, serve to demonstrate that structural unity does not indicate unity in the original account. An even better critical response to Willis is provided by Garbini. He affirms the established divisions into sources as outlined by Dus and Noth. He makes several stylistic observations about material peculiar to each particular source.[123] Although his evidence is not conclusive, it is a good response to the position of Willis, for it demonstrates that there are discontinuities between the various parts of these chapters.

The consensus is that there are various sources or traditions in I Samuel 1-3. However, all of this material was probably brought together by an editor at a certain point in time. If this is the case, the date would be late, perhaps Deuteronomistic in origin. There is also consensus that

chapter 3 is a literary creation composed at the time when these other elements were brought together. This author would maintain that 2:27-4:1a took its present form in this late stage, and that it was a creation by the editor. Although 2:27-30 or 2:27-34 may have had some prior form, these verses were brought together at the latest stage to serve as a prelude to chapter 3. For 2:27-36 and 3:11-14 serve to reinforce each other. These three chapters were created to serve as a prelude to the rest of the book of Samuel. Only a few scholars believe that these three chapters had a definite separate existence apart from the rest of the book before their attachment to it.[124] The material they contain is so distinct from the rest of the book of Samuel, they claim it had to have been separate. However, most scholars, including this author, concur that its distinct nature is due to the fact that these three chapters were created at a late date in order to serve the express purpose of being a prelude.

Relation of the Samuel Legends to the Ark Narrative

There is debate as to the relationship of I Samuel 1-3 to the ark narrative in chapters 4-6. Early critics often stated that Elide material in 2:12-17, 22-26 and perhaps 2:27-36 was part of a prelude to the ark narrative before its incorporation into our present text.[125] Even modern traditio-historical critics believe there was some connection in the oral setting before the late editor worked it all together.[126] The evil actions of the Elides in chapter 2 seem to lead to their punishment in chapter 4. Many critics disclaim such an original relationship, for the references in 4:4b, 15 hardly justify a prior segment of material like chapter 2, nor does chapter 4 picture the Elides as godless, as chapter 2 implies.[127] Chapter 4 seems to be unaware of most of the material in the first three chapters; Samuel is the important figure in the first three chapters, but he is totally lacking in the last three.

I Samuel 1-3 was created with I Samuel 4-6 in mind; and it also looks forward to chapter 7, which connects the first three chapters with the material in I Samuel 7-15. For this reason some would see I Samuel 1-3, 7 as part of the same source.[128] I Samuel 1-3 is an idyll, which uses Yahweh as the divine name while I Samuel 4-6 are historical legends, which use Elohim.[129] Chapters 4-6 are unaware of 1-3, but the latter serve as prelude to the former. It seems logical that 1-3 was written at a later date to foreshadow and interpret the material in both 4-6 and 7-15.[130] Samuel never again appears in Shiloh, nor is he viewed in the same manner as in those three chapters.

The ark narratives may have originally been connected with the Samson narratives rather than the Shiloh legends. As in the Samson narratives there is comical derision of Philistines in the ark narratives. Some believe the Samson stories to have formed a literary unit with the ark narratives at some time.[131] Judah viewed Aphek's defeat as divine judgment upon sinful Ephraim, which event also brought the ark to Judah. Judah's version of the story was I Samuel 4-6. The northern version of the same story was I Samuel 1-3, 7, where the defeat is seen as judgment only on the house of Eli, and Samuel arises out of Ephraim to replace Eli. So Bourke sees chapters 1-3 describing men as individuals, whereas 4-6 tells the story of God, and in this account "man proposes, but God disposes." The two stories were united by virtue of their common themes: God brings life to His people, whether it be Hannah or the nation. The story of Samuel becomes a connecting link between the covenant of Sinai and the covenant of David, for Samuel is the second Moses.[132]

Some scholars feel that the Samuel stories and the ark narratives are an essential unity in regard to the history of the ark. Fruin sees I Samuel 1-4 as a unity written by the Zadokites after 721 B.C. The fall of Israel brought refugee Israelites to Judah, among whom were priests and Levites. The Jerusalem people told this story to disinherit them. Eli is short for Eliezar, son of Aaron, who was Shiloh's first priest. In Numbers 25:6-13 Phinehas, son of Eliezar is a hero, but I Samuel 2 seeks to dishonor both of them, thus discrediting the whole northern priesthood.[133] Paul Dhorme also maintains that chapters 1-4 are an integral account of evil, prophecies, and punishments brought against the Elides centered around the affairs of the ark. Chapters 1-4 are Elohist, while chapters 5-6 are Yahwist. Together these two segments form a pattern with chapter 7 that is imposed upon them by the Deuteronomistic redactor. The pattern consists of a cycle of sin, oppression, return, and salvation.[134] But Dhorme's argument can be used against him, for the pattern he sees imposed upon chapters 1-7 might likewise indicate that the pattern in 1-4 was also imposed by editorial work. Cohen uses the argument that there must be historical connections between 1-3 and 4-6 for later editors to bring them together.[135] But he offers no real data to substantiate this idea. Willis builds upon the idea that chapters 1-7 are a complete source, which the Deuteronomistic editor took intact. He perceives a pattern in which chapters 1-3 describe the hero, chapters 4-6 describe the crisis, and chapter 7 shows how the hero meets the crisis. This same pattern is found in stories about Saul, Samson, Jephthah, and David. Willis gives an outline of this pattern:

	hero	crisis	solution
Jephthah:	Judges 11:1-3	11:4-28	11:29-33
Samson:	Judges 13:2-5	14:1-18	14:19-20
		15:1- 6,	15: 7- 8,
		9-13	14-20
		16:1-27	16:28-31
Samuel:	I Sam. 1-4:1a	4:1b-7:1	7: 2-17
Saul:	I Sam. 9:1-10:16	11:1- 4	11: 5-11
David:	I Sam. 16:1-23	17:1-30	17:31-54

This is a pre-Deuteronomistic pattern, which would later be modified for other heroes and become the well know pattern of apostasy, oppression, repentance, and deliverance. Samuel's birth is patterned after Samson's as a demonstration of this parallel narrative structure. Samuel is not mentioned in chapters 4-6 to demonstrate how bad the situation was; this prepares for the deliverance in chapter 7. Thus I Samuel 1-3 prepares us for the punishment of 4-6 and the deliverance of 7. All three parts are essential to each other.[136]

Willis offers the most thorough defense for the unity of these seven chapters. His observations are comparable to the defense he made for the unity of chapters 1-3. As with his earlier arguments there are also weaknesses here. He has been criticized by Miller and Roberts, who ask why Samuel is not mentioned in chapters 4-6. All the other heroes are consistently mentioned throughout their narrative; why is Samuel omitted in this key section? How can a "judge," Samuel, replace a "priest," Eli, according to the final perspective given to us by the text? Evidence indicates that varying materials have been merged.[137] This author has several criticisms. The fact that there is a pattern in I Samuel 1-7 is a probable demonstration of the work of an editor who brought these traditions together. Willis' observation of the so-called pre-Deuteronomistic pattern is really an inadequate assessment of the material in chapters 1-7. In actuality, the Deuteronomistic pattern of sin, oppression, repentance, and deliverance is discernible in the text. The sin of the Elides in chapters 1-3 is followed by defeat and loss of the ark in chapters 4-6, and repentance and deliverance come with Samuel in chapter 7. The argument for a pre-Deuteronomistic pattern is found in the other hero stories, but not here. The connecting motifs are either superficial coincidences or the result of a good editor. Many of the significant corres- pondences, such as the reference to the ark and Eli's poor eyesight in chapters 1-3, are mentioned only once or twice.

This gives the impression that they were deliberately included by the editor who created chapters 1-3 in order to make the connection with 4-6. The reference to the "hand of the Lord" occurs only once outside of chapters 4-6 in 7:13, where it again is meant to be an editorial connecting link. Ebenezer is used in both sources, but it is found in a contradictory fashion. Both of these points indicate that chapter 7 was written with the intent of following chapters 4-6. Common themes like the Philistines, judgeship, idolatry, and fear are so common in all the early stories of the judges that they cannot be viewed as valid evidence. The evidence he offers indicates more clearly that I Samuel 1-3, 7 was created with I Samuel 4-6 already in existence, and a very creative editor has brought these traditions together and related them with reworked motifs. Willis cannot answer the questions previously raised by literary critics as to why I Samuel 4-6 is unaware of 1-3 and why certain basic textual and theological discontinuities appear.

For the last generation the weight of scholarship has affirmed that I Samuel 4-6 and II Samuel 6 constitute a unified source, which had a prior existence before its utilization in Samuel. Any theory which seeks to postulate that chapters 1-4 or 1-7 constitutes a unity must overturn this established scholarly consensus.[138]

Thus we conclude that I Samuel 1-3 is a late literary creation written to be a prelude to I Samuel 4-6 and to link both segments to I Samuel 7. The editor has masterfully woven and created material in these first three chapters to offer an introduction to the historical books of Samuel.

Theology of I Samuel 1-3

The chief purpose of this material appears to be the condemnation of the house of Eli and the justification of Samuel's replacing them. This was the intention of the editor who wove negative Elide traditions with Samuel material in chapters 1-2 and then created chapter 3 as the fitting climax.[139][140] Samuel then appears as the great prophet and priest. The story portrays Samuel as the prophet who bears judgment against this corrupt priestly house.[141] He is able to do this even as a mere child, but this is part of the theology, for it condemns the Elides even more. Thus there is a prophetic bias in the story. The whole section functions as a pre-history to the history of the kingdom, as Genesis 1-11 functions for the patriarchal history.[142]

Where would this prophetic criticism originate, and where would old traditions in chapter 2 have been remembered? It is probable that the traditions were kept in prophetic circles at

some shrine, perhaps one mentioned in the greater Samuel traditions. A natural response would be Shiloh, for this is where the Samuel's[143] prophetic activity occurs according to I Samuel 3:19-4:1a. The traditions would have been remembered by prophets, Ahijah of Shiloh and his followers. But the tradition of I Samuel 3:19-4:1a is probably a late creation, and all of I Samuel 1-3 is late. Since Samuel never again is connected to Shiloh, nor or the Elides who appear at Nob, this may be discounted as the locale for the traditions. Samuel is associated with Shiloh for the theological purpose of discrediting the Elides. Since Shiloh and its cult are the target of the polemic, one would not expect it to be the place where the traditions are cherished. Bethel and Gilgal are important shrines, but they are not mentioned. Mizpah is not mentioned until chapter 7; it occurs elsewhere, but more of these traditions are considered to be late. Ramah becomes the likely candidate for the site of the traditions, for it was Samuel's home and starting point for his activity in many of the old traditions. It is an otherwise unimportant city, whose only claim to fame is that Samuel came from there, and it is unlikely that an unimportant town would usurp another city's leading figure, Samuel. Ramah is the home of Samuel the judge in 7:17, the home of Samuel the seer in 9:1-10:16, his place of return after rejecting Saul in 15:34 and anointing David in 16:13, the site of the prophetic guilds under his tutelage in 19:18-24, and the place of his burial in 25:1. It seems likely that most of the Samuel traditions were first remembered in this town. The later edition of these elements was probably taken up by circles in Jerusalem because they justified the transfer of religious[144] authority from Shiloh in the north to Jerusalem in the south. Eventually the traditions were used in the Deuteronomistic History. Deuteronomistic theology is reflected in the emphasis upon faithfulness, the description of the Shiloh sanctuary as though it were the temple in Jerusalem, the anti-Elide and anti-Abiatharide bias, the attack upon syncretism and Canaanite influence, the rejection of foreign gods, the stress on retribution, the attack on cultic abuse, and the fulfillment of the prophetic word, for I Kings 2:26-27 records the fulfillment of I Samuel 2:35 and 3:11-14.[145]

The theological concerns are of a prophetic and cultic nature. The stress reflects a Deuteronomistic concern in its final form. The attack on abuses, so typical of the Deuteronomistic reform, has led some to conclude that the evaluation of this entire section must be understood in a cultic perspective that is concerned with reform undertaken or demanded throughout the divided monarchy until the time of Josiah. The author sought to attack the syncretism of Shiloh where Canaanite customs abounded. The author stressed the impotence of foreign gods like Dagon, lest the people be tempted to worship them. He warned against the manipulation

of God, which those who possessed the ark sought to accomplish. The work gives a theological interpretation of history by showing the transition from the period of the judges to the monarchy, and it indicates the continuity from Shiloh to Jerusalem. The need for such a transition is implied by the abuses which might occur at a local shrine. Fruin also believes the primary concern of this material is cultic. It is an attempt by southern priests to discredit the northern families of Shiloh after the fall of Samaria.[146] Lindblom believes that Shiloh was a symbol of the north. In the Shiloh oracle in Genesis 49 the phrase, "the scepter shall not depart from Judah until he comes to Shiloh," refers to David's unification of the south and the north. Reuben represents the kingdom of Ishbaal, Judah was David's kingdom, and the transfer of religious authority from Shiloh to Jerusalem reflects David's unification of all Israel. I Samuel 1-3 gives the cause for this transfer by showing the bankruptcy of the religious institutions in the north.[147] While some scholars maintain the cultic aspect of the polemic, others would argue that the chief thrust is prophetic. Jenks sees these chapters affirming the revolutionary transfer of authority from priest to prophet.[148]

The explication of the theological insights is done with consummate skill by the editor of these chapters. It has been seen how various parts have been skillfully woven together to contrast Samuel and the Elides. The material is constructed with the utilization of contrasts. Eli is very critical of Hannah in 1:12-18 and unaware of her vow in 1:26-28, but she is pious in 1:1-11 and faithfully dedicates her son in 1:19-25. This chapter has the same alternating pattern as does chapter 2 where the editor has brought together old Elide traditions and alternated them with observations about Samuel. Hannah's piety contrasts with the callousness of Eli, just as Samuel's obedience to God contrasts with the disobedience of the sons. The culmination is that Samuel receives the revelation which has become rare due to Elide abuse, and for this reason he inherits their prerogatives. This is tersely summarized in 3:19-4:1a, while the Elides are then destroyed in chapter 4. The Word of the Lord comes to a weak woman, Hannah, and a small child, Samuel, while the powerful and corrupt priesthood fails.[149] The contrasts also function in another fashion. The house of Eli is further shamed by the fact that the ultimate heir of the prerogatives is faithfully obedient to Eli, for Samuel ministers to Eli in 2:11, 18, 3:1; he runs first to Eli when called by the Lord in 3:4-5, 6, 8; he is so obedient after receiving the oracle that he fears to tell Eli the message in 3:15-17. In this respect Samuel relates to Eli as David would later relate to Saul. Samuel's rise parallels David's rise. David respected his predecessor as did Samuel, despite the evil. He was a personal servant to Saul as Samuel was to Eli, and like Samuel he perceived the ultimate downfall of Saul, if only because he had

201

previously been anointed by Samuel.[150] This all indicates a high literary skill in the formulation of these chapters.

The literary structure which alternates material, the parallel with the Davidic cycle, the lack of reference to Samuel's connection with Shiloh elsewhere, the relationship of chapters 1-3 to the ark narrative in 4-6 and chapter 7, the form critical structure of the dream theophany in chapter 3, and the Deuteronomistic theological emphases in this section all indicate that the material is late and a literary creation. Samuel is the idealized child in a setting to which he never returns, performing a role he never again fulfills, condemning a cult in prophetic fashion while he is still a child servant in that cult. The story is an idyll, and any historical reconstruction[151] based on this material sadly misses that observation.

Conclusion

I Samuel 1-3 is a late literary creation, perhaps brought into existence by the hand of the Deuteronomist. Traditio-historical and source critical evaluations have disclosed that some elements, especially the Elide material in chapter 2, may have a prior history. However, the text has been shaped and edited by a theologian with strong Deuteronomistic concepts. This editor may be responsible for the creation of significant segments of the section, of which chapter 3 is most likely such a literary creation. These three chapters serve as a prelude to the entire book of Samuel, they foreshadow and reinterpret chapters 4-6, and they anticipate chapter 7. The material is a late development in the traditions about Samuel, for it presents him as a child wonder, a prophet who does possible priestly service, a prophet who can condemn the entire priestly house of Eli, and the successor in a cult center in which the historical Samuel may never have been.

CHAPTER V

FOOTNOTES

[1] Robert Neff has isolated this form as the ABND pattern of announcement, birth, name and destiny, "The Announcement in Old Testament Birth Narratives" (Ph.D. dissertation, Yale University, 1969), pp. 55-81.

[2] Hannelis Schulte, Die Entstehung der Geschichtsschreibung in Alten Israel, BZAW, vol. 128 (Berlin: Gruyter, 1972), p. 89.

[3] De Vaux, Ancient Israel: Its Life and Institutions, trans. John McHugh (New York: McGraw-Hill, 1961), p. 467.

[4] Eichrodt, Theology of the Old Testament, 1:304.

[5] Fohrer and Ernst Sellin, Introduction to the Old Testament, trans. David Green (Nashville: Abingdon, 1968), pp. 223-224.

[6] Dus, "Geburtslegende," pp. 163-194.

[7] Jastrow, "The Name Samuel and the Stem š²l," JBL 19 (1900): 82-105; Ivar Hylander, Der Literarische Samuel-Saul-Komplex (I Sam. 1-15) Traditionsgeschichtliche Untersucht (Uppsala: Almquist und Wiksell, 1932), pp. 31-36; Adolphe Lods, Israel from its Beginnings to the Middle of the Eighth Century, trans. Samuel Hooke, The History of Civilization, ed. C. K. Ogden (New York: Knopf, 1932), p. 354; Press, "Samuel," p. 189; Leo Seeligmann, "Voraussetzungen der Midraschexegese," VTSup, vol. 1 (Leiden: Brill, 1953), p. 155; Dhorme, La Bible, 1:813; Fohrer, Introduction, pp. 223-224; and Macholz, "Samuel Überlieferungen," pp. 74-75.

[8] Hylander, Samuel-Saul-Komplex, pp. 31-36.

[9] George Anderson, A Critical Introduction to the Old Testament, Studies in Theology (London: Duckworth, 1959), p. 80; and Maly, Samuel, p. 13.

[10] Kennedy, Samuel, p. 40; Goldman, Samuel, p. 6; and de Vaux, Samuel, p. 24.

[11] George Cunninghame Monteath Douglas, Samuel and His Age: A Study in the Constitutional History of Israel (London: Eyre and Spottiswoode, 1901), pp. 44-45; however, Douglas himself prefers to read the phrase as "name of God."

[12] Gehrke, Samuel, p. 31; Merrill, "I Samuel 1-12," p. 20; and John Willis, "Cultic Elements in the story of Samuel's birth and dedication," ST 26 (1972): 53-54.

[13] Karl-Heinz Bernhardt, Das Problem der altorientalischen Königsideologie im Alten Testament: unter besondere Berücksichtigung der Geschichte der Psalmenexegese dargestellt und kritisch gewürdigt, VTSup, vol. 8 (Leiden: Brill, 1961), p. 148, and McCarter, Samuel, p. 62, 65.

[14] Ackroyd, Samuel, p. 26.

[15] Schulz, Samuel, 1:19.

[16] Gerhard Wallis, "Die überlieferungsgeschichtliche Forschung und der Samuelstoff," Geschichte und Überlieferung: Gedanken über alttestamentliche Darstellungen der Frühgeschichte Israels unter der Anfänge seines Königtums, Arbeiten zur Theologie, ser. 2, vol. 13 (Stuttgart: Calwer, 1968), p. 83.

[17] Ibid.; and Stoebe, Samuelis, p. 98.

[18] Noth, "Samuel und Silo," p. 395.

[19] Dus, "Geburtslegende," pp. 164-169, tries to find evidence that the story once was composed of I Samuel 1:1, 9:1-2, 1:4-7, 9-11, 18-20, 26, 28, 3:19abα, and the conclusion would read, "Saul grew and the Lord was with him." Dus maintains that in the original story Hannah's husband hated her, and she had to go on the pilgrimage to Shiloh alone. Saul's father could initially be seen as impious, but when he became Samuel's father, modification in I Samuel 1:3a and 1:9a made him into a pious pilgrim. With the creation of our present text Elkanah loves his wife and allows her to do as she wishes. The editor wishes to make everyone an example of good piety. Dus offers an attractive theory, and it reinforces this author's view of the late date for I Samuel 3. But beyond the textual evidence in I Samuel 1:5a, 1:6a, 1:9a, 1:18b, and 1:20 his theory is tenuous and fails to meet all the criticism previously cited.

[20] Caird, "Samuel," pp. 876-877; and William Foxwell Albright, Samuel and the Beginnings of the Prophetic Movement (Cincinnati: Hebrew Union College Press, 1961), pp. 10-11.

[21] Noth, "Samuel und Silo," pp. 396-397.

[22] Klaus Dietrich Schunck, Benjamin: Untersuchungen zur Entstehung und Geschichte eines israelitischen Stammes, BZAW, vol. 86 (Berlin: Töpelmann, 1963), pp. 102-104. Thus David fled to the more logical site of Ramathaim in I Samuel 19:18-24.

[23] Wallis, "Samuelstoff," pp. 84-85.

[24] Stoebe, Samuelis, p. 94.

[25] Budde, Samuel, KHAT, p. 4.

[26] Menahem Haran, "Zebah Hayammîm," VT 19 (1969): 11-12.

[27] Brinker, Sanctuaries, p. 164; Noth, Das Buch Josua, 2d ed., HAT, pt. 1, vol. 7 (Tübingen: Mohr, 1953), pp. 107-109; and Svend Holm-Nielsen, "Shiloh in the Old Testament," Shiloh: The Danish Excavations at Tall Sailūn, Palestine in 1926, 1929, and 1963 (Copenhagen: National Museum of Denmark, 1969), p. 57.

[28] Holm-Nielsen, Shiloh, pp. 57-58.

[29] Brinker, Sanctuaries, p. 166.

[30] Holm-Nielsen, Shiloh, p. 57.

[31] Despite this lack of archaeological remains, Cobbey Crisler, "The Acoustics and Crowd Capacity of Natural Theaters in Palestine," Biblical Archeologist 39 (1976): 130-134, has shown the possible existence of a major shrine in Shiloh by demonstrating that the area is acoustically conducive to large gatherings of people.

[32] A. T. Richardson, "The Site of Shiloh," PEQ 59 (1927): 85-88.

[33] Hans Kjaer, "Shiloh. A Summary Report of the Second Danish Expedition, 1929," PEQ 62 (1931): 78-79.

[34] Marie Louise Buhl, "Conclusion," Shiloh: The Danish Expedition, pp. 30-35.

[35] Kjaer, The Excavation of Shilo, the Place of Eli and Samuel, (Jerusalem: Beyl-Ul-Makdes, 1930), pp. 19-23 = JPOS 10 (1930): 87-174; and "Shiloh. A Summary," pp. 76-77.

[36] Buhl, "Conclusion," pp. 60-62.

[37] Yigal Shiloh, "Review," IEJ 21 (1970): 67-69, and "The Camp at Shiloh," Eretz-Shomron (Jerusalem: n.p., 1973), as cited in "Did the Philistines Destroy the Israelite Sanctuary at Shiloh -- The Archaeological Evidence," BAR 1 (1975): 3-5.

[38] Irving Gefter, "Shiloh: The Shrine that would not die" (address delivered to the Society of Biblical Literature, New Orleans, 20 November 1978), pp. 1-11, adheres to the 1050 B.C. date for Shiloh's destruction, yet he very thoroughly reviews the continued influence Shiloh exercised upon the religious tradition until the time of Jeremiah. One might use the same data to postulate a later destruction, for the material is subject to either interpretation.

[39] Brinker, Sanctuaries, pp. 168-169.

[40] Lindblom, "The Political Background of the Shilo Oracle," VTSup, vol. 1 (Leiden: Brill, 1953), pp. 78-87; and Otto Eissfeldt, "Silo und Jerusalem," VTSup, vol. 4 (Leiden: Brill, 1957), pp. 138-147.

[41] Bentzen, Introduction 1:95; Ivan Engnell, "Samuelsböckerna," Svenskt Bibliskt Uppslagsverk, 2d ed. (Stockholm: Nordiska Uppslagsbocker, 1962), 2:868-870; and "Hannaslovsäng," Svenskt Bibliskt Uppslagsverk, 1:879-880, call this a Royal Psalm. Merrill, "I Samuel 1-12," pp. 53-62, maintains it is a Royal Psalm because I Samuel 1:20 originally had Saul's name, and thus this hymn was given in his honor, which would then imply that the entire context deals with the birth of a royal figure. Mowinckel, "Samuelsboken," Det Gamle Testamente (Oslo: Aschehoug, 1936), 2:152; and Willi Staerk, Lyrik: Psalmen, Hoheslied und Verwandtes, 2d. rev. ed., Die Schriften des Alten Testaments, pt. 3, vol. 1 (Göttingen: Vandenhoeck und Ruprecht, 1920), pp. 70-71, call it a Thanksgiving Psalm. Gunkel, Ausgewählte Psalmen: übersetzt und erklärt, 2d rev. ed. (Göttingen: Vandenhoeck und Ruprecht, 1905), pp. 265-272, calls it an Eschatological Psalm.

[42] Nyberg, "Studien zur religionsgeschichtlichen Kampf im Alten Testament," ARW 35 (1938): 368-371.

[43] George Ernest Wright, "The Lawsuit of God: A Form Critical Study of Deuteronomy 32," Israel's Prophetic Heritage, pp. 57-66.

[44] Hylander, Samuel-Saul-Komplex, pp. 20, 234; and Ackroyd, Samuel, p. 32.

[45] Zannoni, "Call and Dedication," p. 102.

[46] Engnell, "Hannaslovsäng," p. 880; and Bourke, "Samuel and the Ark," p. 73.

[47] C. J. Goslinga, Het Eerste Boek Samuel, Commentar op Het Oude Testament (Kampen: Kok, 1968), p. 48.

[48] Caird, "Samuel," p. 862.

[49] Smith, Samuel, p. 14.

[50] Stoebe, Samuelis, pp. 106-107.

[51] S. Driver, An Introduction to the Literature of the Old Testament, 2 vols. (Edinburgh: Clark, 1891), 2:164.

[52] Smith, Samuel, p. 17; Press, "Samuel," p. 188; and Segal, "Books of Samuel," pp. 41-42.

[53] Dhorme, Samuel, pp. 50-56; Caspari, Samuelbücher, p. 14; Jepsen, Nabi, pp. 102-103; Eissfeldt, Die Komposition der Samuelbücher (Leipzig: Hinrichs, 1931), p. 6; Press, "Samuel," p. 180; Carl Steuernagel, "Die Weissagung über den Eliden," Alttestamentliche Studien für Rudolf Kittel zum 60. Geburtstag, BWAT, vol. 13, ed. Rudolf Kittel (Leipzig: Hinrichs, 1913), pp. 215-216; Theodore Christian Vriezen, "De Compositie van de Samuël-Boeken, Orientalia Nederlandica: A Volume of Oriental Studies (1948): 168, 188-189; Segal, "Books of Samuel," pp. 41-42; Stoebe, Samuelis, p. 86; Miller and Roberts, Hand of the Lord, pp. 19-21; and McCarter, Samuel, p. 85.

[54] Hertzberg, Samuel, pp. 46-47.

[55] Smith, Samuel, p. 17; Schunck, Benjamin, p. 10; Wallis, "Samuelstoff," p. 55. Budde, Samuel, KHAT, pp. 17, 32, 35, believes this occurred in the second edition of the Elohist.

[56] Dus, "Die Erzählung über den Verlust der Lade I Sam. IV," VT 13 (1963): 333-337.

[57] Ackroyd, Samuel, p. 36.

[58] Whiston, Josephus, 2:340.

[59] Miller and Roberts, Hand of the Lord, p. 28; and McCarter, Samuel, p. 83.

[60] Merrill, "I Samuel 1-12," p. 47.

[61] Willis, "Cultic Elements," p. 55.

[62] Caird, "Samuel," p. 889.

[63] Zannoni, "Call and Dedication," p. 161.

[64] Aelred Cody, A History of Old Testament Priesthood, AnBib, vol. 35 (Rome: Pontifical Biblical Institute, 1969), pp. 70-71. Pfeiffer thinks the names are merely creations, "Midrash," p. 315.

[65] Smith, Samuel, p. 19; and Maly, Samuel, p. 17.

[66] Wolf Graf Baudissin, Geschichte des Alttestamentlichen Priesterthums (Leipzig: Hirzel, 1889), p. 70.

[67] Kennedy, Samuel, p. 47; Schulz, Samuel, 1:38-40; and Moriarity, Samuel, p. 14.

[68] Goldman, Samuel, p. 12.

[69] A. Ehrlich, Randglossen, 3:172.

[70] Westermann, The Basic Forms of Prophetic Speech, trans. Hugh Clayton White (Philadelphia: Westminster, 1967), pp. 129-163.

[71] Ibid., pp. 155-158.

[72] Thenius, Samuelis, p. 15; Wellhausen, Samuelis, pp. 48-51; Budde, The Books of Samuel: A Critical Edition of the Hebrew Text, trans. B. W. Bacon (Leipzig: Hinrichs, 1894), p. 3; Nowack, Richter, Ruth und Samuelis, pp. 14-17; Schäfers, "I Sam. 1-15," pp. 9-11; Dhorme, Samuel, pp. 39-42, who diverges from the consensus that calls this material Deuteronomistic, for he views the emphasis upon Zadok as indicative of its origin in the Priestly source; Miller and Roberts, Hand of the Lord, p. 21; and Veijola, Dynastie, pp. 35-42.

[73] Pfeiffer, "Midrash," p. 315. However, Kennedy, Samuel, p. 49, offers a translation that weakens Pfeiffer's argument, for he reads the text as "carry the ephod," so that the ephod is seen to be an object, as in I Samuel 14:3, 18, 21:9, 23:6, Judges 8:7.

[74] Pfeiffer, Introduction to the Old Testament (New York: Harper and Brothers, 1941), pp. 368-369.

[75] Budde, Die Bücher Richter und Samuel, ihre Quellen und ihr Aufbau (Giessen: Ricker, 1890), pp. 199-200.

[76] Veijola, Dynastie, pp. 36-37, calls these verses part of the material belonging to DtrG.

[77] Smith, Samuel, pp. xix-xx, 21; also Stoebe, Samuelis, p. 86.

[78] Caird, "Samuel," p. 862.

[79] Nowack, Richter, Ruth und Samuelis, pp. 14-17; and Stoebe, Samuelis, p. 86.

[80] Press, "Samuel," pp. 187-189.

[81] Maly, Samuel, p. 18.

[82] Kennedy, Samuel, p. 48; and Steuernagel, "Weissagung," pp. 210-211.

[83] Steuernagel, "Weissagung," p. 211. Though he sees discontinuity with chapter 3, he would maintain along with Smith that 2:12-17, 22-25, 27-36 and chapter 4 were once part of a history, which he calls S^a, part of the cycle of the judges.

[84] Dus, "Geburtslegende," p. 185.

[85] Thenius, Samuelis, p. 15; Smith, Samuel, p. 23; Budde, Samuel, KHAT, p. 22; Schäfers, "I Sam. 1-15," pp. 9-11; S. Driver, Hebrew Text, p. 41; Eissfeldt, The Old Testament: An Introduction, trans. Peter Ackroyd (New York: Harper and Row, 1965), p. 270; Press, "Samuel," p. 190; Caird, "Samuel," pp. 891-892; de Vaux, Samuel, p. 29; Dhorme, La Bible, 1:818-820; Matitiahu Tsevat, "Studies in the Book of Samuel. I. Interpretation of I Sam. 2:27-36: The Narrative of Kareth," HUCA 32 (1961): 193; McKane, Samuel, p. 40; Maly, Samuel, p. 19; Ackroyd, Samuel, p. 40; Mauchline, Samuel, p. 56; and McCarter, Samuel, pp. 91-93.

[86] Maly, Samuel, p. 19; and Mauchline, Samuel, p. 56.

[87] S. Driver, Hebrew Text, p. 41.

[88] Tsevat, "Studies in Samuel," pp. 194-196.

[89] Wellhausen, Samuelis, pp. 48-51; Schulz, Samuel, 1:47-56, and Budde, Samuel, KHAT, p. 22.

[90] Nowack, Richter, Ruth und Samuelis, pp. 14-17.

[91] Steuernagel, "Weissagung," pp. 206-208, 220-221.

[92] Kennedy, Samuel, p. 52; S. Driver, Hebrew Text, p. 41; Steuernagel, "Weissagung," pp. 208-209; and Cody, Priesthood, p. 67.

[93] S. Driver, Hebrew Text, p. 41; and Stoebe, Samuelis, p. 119.

[94] Noth, "Samuel und Silo," p. 394; and Stoebe, Samuelis, p. 119.

[95] Segal, "Books of Samuel," pp. 41, 56.

[96] Dus, "Die altisraelitische amphiktyonische Poesie," ZAW 75 (1963): 49-54; and "Geburtslegende," pp. 182-184.

[97] Merrill, "I Samuel 1-12," p. 13.

[98] Noth, "Samuel und Silo," p. 394.

[99] Steuernagel, "Weissagung," pp. 209, 220-221.

[100] Gressmann, Geschichtsschreibung, p. 4; Gunkel, "Samuel," RGG, 2d ed., edited by Hermann Gunkel and Leopold Zscharnack (Tübingen, Mohr, 1931), 5:104; Pfeiffer, Introduction, p. 360; Hertzberg, Samuel, p. 22; Westermann, Handbook to the Old Testament, trans. Robert Boyd (Minneapolis: Augsburg, 1967), pp. 108-110; and Dus, "Geburtslegende," p. 163.

[101] Gressmann, Geschichtsschreibung, p. 11.

[102] Eissfeldt, Introduction, p. 45.

[103] Fohrer, Introduction, pp. 91-92; and Cody, Priesthood, pp. 72-80.

[104] Albright, Samuel, pp. 1-22; and Willis, "Cultic Elements," p. 61.

[105] Cornill, "Ein elohistischer Bericht über die Entstehung des israelitischen Königtums in I Samuelis 1-15 aufgezeigt," Zeitschrift für kirchliche Wissenschaft und kirchliches Leben 6 (1885): 130-131; Budde, Samuel, pp. 1-6, and Samuel, KHAT, p. 2; Dhorme, Samuel, pp. 43, 52; and Hylander, Samuel-Saul-Komplex, pp. 227-235.

[106] Mowinckel, Samuelsboken, p. 129; Hölscher, Geschichtsschreibung, pp. 142, 364; MacLaurin, Theocracy, pp. 122-123.

107 Plöger, "Prophetengeschichten," p. 10; Augustin George, "Fautes contre Yahweh dans les livres de Samuel," RB 53 (1946): 161; Caird, "Samuel," pp. 856-864; Maly, Samuel, pp. 8-9; and Ritterspach, "I Samuel 1-15," p. 134.

108 Eissfeldt, Komposition, p. 5; and Ernst Stähelin, Kritische Untersuchungen über den Pentateuch, die Bücher Josua, Richter, Samuelis und der Könige, 3 vols. (Berlin: n.p., 1843), 3:103-105.

109 Thenius, Samuelis, p. xv; Anderson, Introduction, p. 74; Smith, Samuel, p. xviii, includes chapters 1, 3, 7, 8, 10:17-27, 12, 15 in the source Sm; and Steuernagel, "Weissagung," pp. 212-214, includes 1-3 with 8 and 15 in the source s^b.

110 Press, "Samuel," pp. 178-180.

111 Jepsen, Nabi, p. 103; and Vriezen, "Samuël-Boeken," pp. 167-189.

112 Fohrer, Introduction, pp. 218-226.

113 Hertzberg, Samuel, p. 44.

114 Noth, "Samuel und Silo," pp. 390-400.

115 Dus, "Geburtslegende," pp. 163-194.

116 Macholz, "Samuel-Überlieferungen," pp. 73-75, 98.

117 Zannoni, "Call and Dedication," pp. 79-127, 195-199.

118 Miller and Roberts, Hand of the Lord, p. 114.

119 Bourke, "Samuel and the Ark," p. 73.

120 Willis, "Cultic Elements," pp. 38-39.

121 Willis, "An Anti-Elide Narrative Tradition," JBL 90 (1971): 293-294; and Dhorme, Samuel, pp. 51-52.

122 Merrill, "I Samuel 1-12," p. 118.

123 Giovanni Garbini, "Osservazioni linguistiche a I Sam. cap 1-3," Bibbia e Oriente 5 (1963): 47-52, notices the following: 1) ʾānōkî is found in 1:8, 15, 28, 2:23, 24, 3:11, but ʾanî is found in 1:26, 3:13. He declares that since the final -k is indicative of Ugaritic influence, it is demonstrative of older material. He feels that 3:12-14 is a later insertion into chapter 3. 2) The paragogic nun is found only in the Eli

source, 1:7, 14, 2:15, 16, and twice in 2:23. 3) The particle ʿîm is used with Samuel material in 1:24, 2:21, 26, 3:19, and ʾet is used with Eli material in 2:13, 19, 22. (It will be noticed that 2:19 and 2:26 are the reverse of what they should be, for the former is really in Samuel material and the latter in Eli material.) 4) The use of the hithpael tense in 1:12, 19, 28, 2:36 seems to be Deuteronomistic and late.

[124] Cody, Priesthood, p. 68.

[125] Cornill, Introduction, p. 185; Smith, Samuel, p. 21; Steuernagel, "Weissagung," p. 86; Hylander, Samuel-Saul-Komplex, pp. 64, 69; Caspari, Samuelbücher, p. 2; Eissfeldt, Komposition, p. 6; Jepsen, Nabi, p. 103; and Press, "Samuel," p. 180.

[126] Segal, "Books of Samuel, pp. 41-42; Schunck, Benjamin, p. 10; and Stoebe, Samuelis, p. 127, thinks that the Elide material was connected to chapter 4, but independent of chapters 5-6, and it belonged to a history of Shiloh traditions.

[127] Schäfers, "I Sam. 1-15," pp. 15-16; Cody, Priesthood, p. 66; and Ritterspach, "I Samuel 1-15," p. 134.

[128] Steuernagel, "Weissagung," pp. 214-215, calls it part of S^b; and Ritterspach, "I Samuel 1-15," pp. 138-139, considers it to be part of the anti-monarchical source.

[129] Wellhausen, Die Composition des Hexateuchs und der historischen Bücher des Alten Testaments (Berlin: Reimer, 1889), pp. 239-241; and Gressmann, Geschichtsschreibung, p. 11.

[130] Kuenen, Einleitung, p. 52; Baudissin, Einleitung in die Bücher des Alten Testaments (Leipzig: Hirzel, 1901), p. 242; Wellhausen, Composition, pp. 239-241; Kittel, A History of the Hebrews, 2 vols., trans. John Taylor, Theological Translation Library, vols. 3-4 (London: Williams and Norgate, 1895), 2:31; Budde, Richter und Samuel, pp. 193-196, and Samuel, KHAT, p. 2; Jepsen, Nabi, p. 102; Noth, "Samuel und Silo," pp. 391-392; Dus, "Geburtslegende," pp. 163-194; Stoebe, Samuelis, p. 127; and Miller and Roberts, Hand of the Lord, pp. 19-21.

[131] Mowinckel, Psalmenstudien, 2:109-111; Bentzen, "The Cultic Use of the Story of the Ark in Samuel," JBL 67 (1948): 37-53; Pfeiffer, Introduction, pp. 99, 111-112, 342; de Vaux, Samuel, p. 33; and C. R. North, The Old Testament Interpretation of History (London: Epworth, 1946), p. 33. Mowinckel and Bentzen include Psalm 132 in this source.

132 Bourke, "Samuel and the Ark," pp. 75-103.

133 R. Fruin, "Oudtestamentische Studien. I. Eli de priester te Silo," Nieuw Theologische Tijdschrift 20 (1931): 108-113.

134 Dhorme, Samuel, pp. 52, 69.

135 Cohen, "Shilohite Priesthood," p. 66.

136 Willis, "Anti-Elide Narrative," pp. 288-305, lists motifs which connect these chapters: 1) sins of Eli's sons and the subsequent punishment; 2) the presence of the ark in both accounts; 3) the reference to Eli's poor eyesight in 1:12-13, 2:22-24, 3:2, 4:15; 4) the sin of the sons in 4:10-11 connects with the idolatry described in 7:3-4, for they had made the ark into an idol; 5) the "hand of the Lord" is mentioned in 5:6, 7, 9, 11, 6:3, 5, 9, 7:13; 6) Ebenezer is mentioned in both accounts; 7) both Samuel and Eli are judges; 8) Philistines are found in both sections; and 9) the fear of Israel in 4:6-7 corresponds to the fear experienced by the Philistines in 7:7.

137 Miller and Roberts, Hand of the Lord, pp. 19-20.

138 Georg Stolsch, Alttestmentliche Studien, vol. 5: Die Urkunden der Samuels-geschichte (Gütersloh: Bertelsmann, 1901), pp. 58-72; Jared Judd Jackson, "The Ark Narratives: An Historical, Textual, and Form-Critical Study of I Samuel 4-6 and II Samuel 6" (Th.D. dissertation, Union Theological Seminary in New York, 1962), pp. 250-301; Antony Campbell, The Ark Narrative (1 Sam. 4-6; 2 Sam 6) A Form-Critical and Traditio-Historical Study, SBLDS, vol. 16 (Missoula, Montana: Scholars Press, 1975), pp. 6-54, 142-178; and Miller and Roberts, Hand of the Lord, passim.

139 Gressmann, Geschichtsschreibung, p. 5; and Cody, Priesthood, pp. 68-69.

140 Hertzberg, Samuel, p. 44; Mauchline, Samuel, p. 17; and Schulte, Geschichtsschreibung, p. 90.

141 Jepsen, Nabi, pp. 104-105; Caird, "Samuel," p. 896; Newman, "Call of Samuel," p. 93; Noth, "Samuel und Silo," p. 398; Cody, Priesthood, pp. 68-69; Mauchline, Samuel, p. 31; and Willis, "Anti-Elide Narrative," pp. 306-308.

142 Stoebe, Samuelis, p. 84.

143 Gads Danske Bibel Leksikon, s.v. "Eli," by K. T. Anderson, 1:423; Noth, "Samuel und Silo," pp. 395-398; and Merrill, "1 Samuel 1-12," pp. 34-35, makes the connection only because both Samuel and the Elide priests wear the ephod,

which indicates the use of the ephod comes from the Shiloh sanctuary.

[144] Macholz, "Samuel-Überlieferungen," p. 207.

[145] Willis, "Anti-Elide Narrative," pp. 306-308; and "Cultic Elements," pp. 54-55, outlines these motifs excellently even though he believes they are pre-Deuteronomistic.

[146] Fruin, "Eli," pp. 108-113.

[147] Lindblom, "Shilo Oracle," pp. 86-87; and Eissfeldt, "Silo," pp. 138-147.

[148] Jenks, Elohist, p. 88.

[149] Bourke, "Samuel and the Ark," pp. 81-89, provides examples of such contrasts.

[150] Willis, "Anti-Elide Narrative," pp. 289-290.

[151] Tomoo Ishida typifies the latest attempt to derive a historical reconstruction out of these chapters, The Royal Dynasties in Ancient Israel: A Study on the Formation and Development of Royal-Dynastic Ideology, BZAW, vol. 142 (Berlin: Gruyter, 1977), p. 33; and "The Leaders of the Tribal Leagues 'Israel' in the Pre-Monarchic Period," RB 80 (1973): 528-550. He believes these chapters reflect a new political stage in the history of the amphictyony. Prior to this time a charismatic military judge held the league together until his death. At Shiloh there arose a more stable leadership with hereditary priest-judges who functioned at the central shrine. This stabilizing move was prompted by the Philistine threat, but it was short lived, for Eli was the first and the last person to hold the office. Samuel inherited what was left of the position, but he had no central shrine due to the loss of the ark. His position would have gone to his sons, who were also judges in Israel, according to I Samuel 8:11. Samuel failed for lack of a central place of authority and due to his own lack of military capacity, for he was only a seer-priest judge, not a general. Hence, Saul and David ultimately replaced him. This entire view is intriguing, but it interpolates a great deal into the text.

CHAPTER VI

THE SAMUEL TRADITIONS

The last stage of this study should consider the totality of the Samuel traditions in I Samuel 1:1-16:13, 19:18-24. For the text in I Samuel 3 is an integral part of the entire Samuel idyll in chapters 1-3, which in turn contributes to the Samuel traditions by portraying the childhood images of Samuel. The view of Samuel which emerges in these first three chapters is not completely in harmony with the material in the later chapters. Throughout the Samuel traditions various images of Samuel emerge. Scholars have either accepted these diversities as clearly separate traditions or they have tried to merge the images into a unified and coherent picture. I Samuel 1-3 contributes specific images of Samuel to the greater complex. Thus after considering the material in I Samuel 1-3 it becomes necessary to turn to the remaining traditions in order to observe the relationship of these chapters to the greater whole and to consider how our conclusions regarding I Samuel 1-3 may affect the understanding of the entire corpus.

Samuel is seen as seer, prophet, judge, priest, and covenant mediator throughout these traditions. The images of priest and prophet in particular are reinforced by the material in chapters 1-3. However, if those chapters are a late literary creation, then their testimony to the nature of the historic Samuel is weakened. But then to denigrate their value in relation to the later chapters is too simple, for we must now study the remaining traditions to see if the quality of their testimony is firm under critical scrutiny. It may be that critical observations made concerning I Samuel 1-3 need to be made about the remaining material also. Then a more thorough evaluation of the person of Samuel may be produced than is possible with the limited study of I Samuel 3.

A quick survey of the history of research will expose both the issues and the complexity of the debate. It may reveal the futility of the entire enterprise.

215

History of Research

Early literary critics were the first to distinguish between the various traditions.[1] Two literary sources were separated on the basis of vocabulary, concepts, and theological development. Often the two sources were equated with the Pentateuchal sources, Yahwist and Elohist, but sometimes they were viewed as separate editions of the Elohist. The older pro-monarchical source was considered more authentic by virtue of its age, and therefore its view of Samuel as a local seer and Saul as a charismatic warrior in the succession of the judges was considered to be more historical. The younger anti-monarchical source was a later theological polemic against the already established institution of kingship, which of necessity rendered its historical credibility dubious. It denigrates Saul in favor of Samuel, gives to the latter great authority and insightful sermons in chapters 8 and 12, and offers the picture of the people demanding a king against God's will and Samuel's better judgment. The law of the king in 10:25 was alleged to be an allusion to material in Deuteronomy 17:14-20, which then confirmed a late date and a connection with Deuteronomic reform.

Subtle incongruities in the division of this material made these theories tenuous. Whether the two sources were independent or whether the later source was merely a supplement to the former could not be clearly resolved. Several scholars sought to resolve these problems by increasing the complexity of the sources and their development.[2] The discontinuities between the sources and their interdependencies could be explained only by a more complex history of literary development. As the various layers of literary strata were added, the characterization of Samuel became more complex. His appearance in the early strata was that of a humble local seer. Successive literary additions portrayed him as priest and prophet, and the final propagandistic touches of the Deuteronomic editors left him as a charismatic warrior judge who embodied all the previous offices in his person.

The precision with which scholars divided and subdivided texts became so extreme as to appear absurd. This engendered two responses in the scholarly world, which reacted against the literary critical method. Certain scholars began dogmatically to affirm the unity of the Samuel traditions, while others began to move in the direction of the newly developed traditio-historical methodology.

Advocates of unity for Samuel traditions generally maintained the historical veracity of all the roles attributed to Samuel.[3] Their usual argument was that the diversity noted within the text was exaggerated and often misinterpreted by the

216

other critics. The diversity in the texts reflects ambiguity in the historical period among the various witnesses and participants, perhaps the ambiguity in Samuel's own mind. Thus, two different historical viewpoints are being faithfully reproduced by the author. The pro-monarchical and the anti-monarchical sources both have authentic memories. Advocates of this position generally began with consideration of Samuel's person and role function, and textual considerations were subordinate to a holistic view of all the material. Rather than stressing differences in vocabulary, characterization, narrative plot, theology, writing style, and other discrepancies in the text, these writers observed the greater unity in the traditions. As a result they saw no need for the minute divisions given by literary critics. Therefore, the Samuel traditions were seen as an essential unity which accurately reflected the historical period.[4] However, it is interesting to note that the more thorough scholars who adhere to this position must still make concession to the idea of variant traditions or at least minimal secondary editing, for the presence of diverse theological stresses is irrefutable.

Although the argument for unity is a minority viewpoint, several scholars adhere to it. Recourse is often made to a theoretic construct which will bind the diverse images of Samuel together. Covenant mediator is the role model assigned to Samuel, which seeks to give all traditions equal consideration and then draws its verification from those texts. The argument is circular, and the texts and traditions receive equal consideration for the sake of the model with no prior verification or discrimination. To admit the presence of different theological stresses or existing sources prior to the creation of the unified account, which most of these men concede, leads the scholar to a necessary evaluation and discrimination of the texts which bear those stresses. For it is improbable that all traditions have the same degree of reliability in reconstructing an image of Samuel. Failure to take this into account will result in an uncritical utilization of the text, which may result in a naive evaluation of the textual and historical problems.[5] This awareness led scholars, who were likewise critical of the literary-critical methodology, to turn to another methodological approach to the Samuel traditions, the traditio-historical method.

After the pioneering work of Hermann Gunkel and Hugo Gressmann, scholars were able critically to approach the text without the problems engendered by literary criticism. No longer did they speak of sources, but a more organic process was envisioned. Early traditions were collected in an oral state, and as they precipitated into a fixed oral or written form, further material supplemented and correlated the traditions. Because the traditions were fluid in the oral state,

the continual growth and interaction between the various traditions caused the complex structure of interdependencies and discontinuities among the various texts as we have them now. Literary critics functioned in a linear dimension and were unable to perceive the complexity which an oral pre-history could bring into the text. Thus traditio-historical critics were able to hypothesize answers to problems that confounded literary critics or caused an increased complexity in the particular source theory. But the depth of the new dimension offered by traditio-historical criticism also increased the range of possible theories to explain the text. Early traditio-historical critics advocated that an early core of traditions arose and around them grew later traditions.[6] While some scholars viewed this process as gradual and fragmented, others considered the process to be the work of one author who brought all the traditions together, the Deuteronomist.[7] More recently traditio-historical evaluation has moved in the direction of a fragmentary hypothesis.[8] The various components of the early traditions were taken from the various shrines where they had arisen independently of each other. The editor gathered these fragments together and supplemented them with his own material, and perhaps later additions were made with succeeding editions. This would explain the difficulty that arises in trying to reconstruct an original source or core of traditions. We are left with the final product, and any material lost during this long process of development must be hypothesized by us.

Theologically the view of Samuel can move in opposite directions with various traditio-historical critics. Some scholars will maintain the historicity behind all the layers of tradition, especially those who endorse the fragmentary view, while others will seek only the oldest traditions or the primal core of the tradition in order to ascertain the historical view of Samuel and his times.[9] Numerous scholars have evaluated the Samuel traditions to discover the actual role of the historical Samuel, including scholars who were not directly dealing with the text of I Samuel. The majority have concluded that Samuel's historical role was that of a seer.[10] However, this raises a complex discussion of what is a seer and how is he related to the office of prophet.[11] It is evident from the debate that too little data are available for a reconstruction of the origin and history of prophecy. The allusions in the text are too vague to help place Samuel in this theoretic historical development. A strong minority affirm that the historical Samuel was a minor judge, an office in the pre-monarchical period which functioned under the auspices of the tribal league.[12]

The minor judge rendered legal decisions, officiated at covenant renewal ceremonies, and led the nation in an official, but limited capacity. This second theory is dependent upon the creation of a hypothetical office, whose existence is

debatable.[13] Furthermore, it requires the acceptance of the much disputed theory of an amphictyonic league in pre-monarchical Israel.[14]

Conclusion

The quest for the historical Samuel is bankrupt. Like the quest for the historical Jesus the scholars cannot penetrate through the layers of tradition to perceive Samuel as he really was. The various approaches all have their difficulties. Any attempt to take all the traditions at face value will produce a naive picture of Samuel comparable to what the final editor of the books of Samuel wished the reader to perceive. It must of necessity gloss over the contradictions and ignore the obvious historical development of the text. Any attempt to remove the layers of tradition and peel away the later accretions in order to perceive the earlier and more authentic traditions runs two risks. Removing later traditions may actually ignore some authentic historical data, and it is difficult for the historian to perceive which aspects this might entail. The end result may produce only a shadow of the real Samuel, and there may be no historical core left at the end of the process. Any attempt to cut through the traditions and find a special office for Samuel, such as minor judge, must use some particular text as its starting point, and this is a highly subjective procedure. One can create models like seer-priest, minor judge, or covenant mediator, but the texts which are selectively chosen by the author to reinforce this model only create a hermeneutical circle. The model leads us to interpret the texts, which are then used to verify the model. A good word of warning for the Samuel traditions in this respect was issued by Kessler, who demonstrated the danger of emphasizing one text to the exclusion of others. A reading of I Samuel 16:1-13 out of context would lead the reader to believe that Samuel was a lowly and slow-witted prophet who needed to be continually prodded along on the assigned task.[15] Were the process of development different for the Samuel traditions, and this were one of the few accounts to survive, our picture of Samuel might be highly modified. Any particular aspect which might be emphasized to the exclusion of others will produce a distorted picture. This problem is compounded by the good possibility that in the developing process of oral tradition some of the accounts and narratives about Samuel may have been lost.

The primary problem is the lack of data. The few passages which may be utilized are found only in Samuel, Kings, and a few scattered references elsewhere. Any reconstruction demands an interpretation of these passages and the addition of much speculation on the scholar's part. Every passage is capable of differing interpretation, and the

interpretation of one passage affects the rest in a chain reaction. The history of research demonstrates the incredible range of options available in trying to define Samuel's role, his attitudes, and his activity in Israel's history. If it were really possible to reconstruct an authentic view from the textual material, we would not have had the great diversity of scholarly opinion. The plausibility of some of the more bizarre theories demonstrates the paucity of the data and the flexibility of its interpretation.

The second problem is in the nature of developing traditions. It is difficult to penetrate back through layers of tradition, for each layer is a theological filter designed to reinterpret previous ones. The interaction of traditions in their fluid oral setting and their transition into fixed written form cannot fully be discerned by scholars who sit at the end of the process. For they have only the final form and probably lack some material that has been lost in the filtering process. If they were to possess some of this material, they might alter their conclusions. An example of this filtering process with its attendant complexity is offered by the anti-monarchical source. It appears to be a continuous source, yet it also appears to be a reinterpretation of the older material which it encompasses and into which it has been inserted, and again it is like a midrash which merely supplements and explains what really happened. No reconstruction can ever be completely certain that the relocation of textual material can ascertain an original form. Lost material can be hypothesized but never can be found.

An early assumption was that the early material was more historical and would contain an authentic record. This assumption has been challenged. As material precipitates into an oral cycle of tales or into a written corpus of literature, authentic material may appear at any level of development, even the latest stages. This is why some scholars have stressed the importance of seeking historical material even in the additions of the Deuteronomistic Historian.

When one considers how the process of oral literature develops, it is fair to ask whether it is possible to develop criteria for discerning historical material in a complex of traditions. Studies in Mesopotamian literature seem to demonstrate the impossibility of this endeavor.[16] It seems that historical material is lost when later elaboration envelopes the character and events of the original historical experience. Nothing may remain of the original events, or they may be relegated to the periphery according to their potential for use in the storyteller's oral craft. The emphasis in oral literature is not upon historical accuracy, but rather narrative structure, the utilization of universal types, the general appeal of the

material to the audience, and the ability of the material to meet[17] the particular needs of the society are the important criteria. This renders the ability to discern the locus of historical material in traditions very tenuous. In reference to the Samuel traditions it is likely that the vestiges of the historical Samuel may have been lost in the ongoing theological reinterpretation of his life and accomplishments. The rediscovery of the historical Samuel in the material, if there is any such material left in the traditions, is very difficult without a more thorough knowledge of the forces operative in the oral narrative process, the nature of the particular storytellers who recounted the tales for generations, the particular social and theological needs of communities in which the tales were told, and other circumstances which might have influenced the developing traditions. The particulars of such forces may be hypothesized, but never verified, and the result will be too much uncertainty for the reconstruction of the authentic traditions of the historical Samuel.

The Samuel traditions as we now have them are a theological document. This author's consideration of the dream theophany in I Samuel 3 and the entire context of I Samuel 1-3 has indicated that this section is a late literary creation with little historical value for that early period. The roles assigned to Samuel and the actions he performed are created according to the theological intentionality of the author or authors. Concern for historical authenticity is lacking; theological concerns predominate. Every scholar who has sought to discern the role of the historical Samuel has used the material in these three chapters, and too seldom have they considered the prior theological concerns, which render the material worthless for their task. The evaluation of I Samuel 1-3 has led this author to the initial consideration of the futility of the quest for the historical Samuel. The contribution of this study for the rest of the Samuel traditions is the clear demonstration of theological agenda determining the creation of narrative material. The precipitation of old oral traditions into a fixed form and the creation of new narrative are determined by theology, and this dynamic process renders any quest for the historical kernel invalid.

Consideration of material in I Samuel 7:1-16:13, 19:18-24 yields a similar response. This material has been shaped by a definite theological perspective and literary design. Several scholars have noted throughout that Samuel seems to be cast in a composite role comparable to Moses, so that he becomes a second Moses for Israel.[18] Though many scholars have noted these comparisons, few have drawn the ultimate conclusions. Many of the Samuel traditions have been structured make him appear like Moses, but scholars still try to evaluate the traditions on their own merit, as though these parallels did not

221

exist. As is evident, the greater part of the Samuel traditions have their counterpart among Moses traditions. The probability that the oral tradition conformed these accounts is very great, and this decreases the possibility for ascertaining authentic historical remembrances. This is not to deny that there might be authentic historical memories somewhere among the Samuel traditions, but to find them would be very difficult, since stereotyping and theologizing the traditions in conformity with the Moses figure seems evident even among the earliest stages of development. The Samuel traditions betray the theological presuppositions of prophetic editors superimposed upon early traditions, which were probably already interpreted with some theological priorities. The work of the prophetic editors were in turn subsumed by the theological perspectives of the Deuteronomistic Historian. As one looks back through the layers, it becomes evident that everything was the result of someone's theological presuppositions, even the earliest memories.

The extremely critical conclusion to which this author is[19] driven is not without precedent among previous scholarship. This author concurs with these scholars. We have theologically interpreted traditions, out of which it is impossible to garner an image of the historical Samuel. This is not to deny that a real Samuel existed, for there probably had to be a figure around whom the legends first accumulated, and his eminence in so many texts and his performance of so many roles testify to the existence of a significant person by name. The significance of the deeds which he may have performed may be open to question, but later generations thought they were significant. His significance may be due to the fact that he functioned in a crucial period of Israel's history, and legends are readily created about people who live in such an era. Because of the importance of the era, many tales were told about its heroes. In recounting the events the deeds may become magnified and distorted. The original truth may be stretched beyond recognition, so that it is there, but it escapes the ability of the scientific historian to clarify it. This can be demonstrated by an analogy in Egyptian history. The Middle Kingdom Egyptian pharaoh Sesostris III made a significant raid into Palestine. Because he was one of the first pharaohs to do this, his deeds became magnified well beyond those of later pharaohs who made far greater conquests in the Palestinian theater. His exploits were eulogized and magnified until he was said to have conquered the world, and by[20] the time of Herodotus he was a great god in the pantheon. Likewise, Samuel was an early figure in Israel's history living at a time of significant changes in society. His deeds were probably magnified out of proportion with what he did by later generations, even though what he did may have been significant on the smaller scale of Israel's early history. Numerous examples can be drawn from

the folk legends and traditions of cultures everywhere. That Samuel existed is probable, that he did something for the greater good of the nation is possible, but what it was is inascertainable.

Samuel was somehow involved with the transition Israel underwent from the tribal period to the monarchy. The traditions seek to relate him to Saul and David, whether this be true, it seems likely that he had some significant contact with the affairs of state to cause such legends initially to arise. On this point this author would concur with Weiser,

> In spite of the diversity in single instances, all the traditions come down to this, that the person of Samuel exerted a varying influence in all phases of the transition of the pre-monarchical period to the kingship and on the form of the new relationship, and for that he has earned a significant memory.[21]

This author would concur with Weiser on the dynamic of traditions development, and on this statement concerning the general nature of the historical Samuel, but he would dissent from the attempt to obtain some positive historical results, as Weiser does. Whatever the significant contribution of Samuel may have been, we can never truly discover it. The biblical scholars have their texts. They may discover the theology, explicate its meaning, appreciate the literary quality, interpret the message for modern listeners, and even discover part of the traditio-historical development, but they will never perceive the actual history behind these texts.

224

CHAPTER VI

FOOTNOTES

[1] Thenius, Samuelis, pp. ix-xvii, distinguished the old Saul source (9:1-10:16, 13:1-14:51), the later Saul source (8, 10:17-27, 11-12, 15-16, 18:6-14, 17-19, 21:10-15, 23:15-18, 26, 28:3-25, 31), and the Samuel source (1-7, 14:52, 17, 18:1-5, 15-16, 20-30, 19, 21:1-9, 22:1-23:14, 19-22, 24, 27:1-28:2, 29-30). Wellhausen, Samuelis, pp. 67-101; Prolegomena to the History of Ancient Israel, trans. Allan Menzies and Sutherland Black (Edinburgh: Black, 1885; reprint. ed., Gloucester, Mass.: Peter Smith, 1973), pp. 245-262; and Composition, pp. 242-248, 253, articulated the division followed by most scholars. The older pro-monarchical source (9:1-10:16, 11:1-11, 15, 13:1-14:52) was supplemented by the later and less authentic, Deuteronomic, anti-monarchical source (8, 10:17-25, 12). Wellhausen's observations were the basis for work by Cornill, "Ein elohistischer Bericht," pp. 113-141; "Zur Quellenkritik der Bücher Samuelis," Königsberger Studien 1 (1887): 25-89; "Noch einmal Sauls Königswahl und Verwerfung," ZAW 10 (1890): 96-109; and Introduction, pp. 180-191, who viewed the sources as different editions of the Elohist. An old folktale from Benjamin (9:1-10:16, 11:1-7, 10:26-27, 11:9-13, 13:2-7a, 16-23) was taken up by the Elohist editors, who added 1:1-7:1, 8:4-5a, c, 7a, 9-22b, 10:19c-24, 15 in the first edition and 7:2-8:22, 12 in the second edition. In the first edition Samuel is a charismatic priestly prophet, but in the second edition he is recast as an institutional judge who condemns Saul and the kingship. Budde, "Sauls Königswahl und Verwerfung," ZAW 8 (1888): 223-248; Richter und Samuel, pp. 169-210; Samuel, pp. 1-14; Samuel, KHAT, pp. 1-2, 32-33, 47-114, engaged Wellhausen and Cornill in debate by maintaining there were two separate and independent sources. The older Gilgal or Yahwist account (1:1, 9:1, 10:7, 9:16, 11:1-11, 15, 13:2-7a, 15b-18, 23, 14:1-46, 52) continued the Samson sagas and portrayed Samuel as a seer to whom Saul inadvertently came. The younger Mizpah or Elohist accounts came forth in two editions (E_1 in 4:1-7:1, 15:2-23, 32-33, and E_2 in 1-3, 7:2-8:22, 10:17-24, 12:1-24, 15:1a, 24-31, 34), and Samuel is now a judge who choses Saul. These sources are independent of each other, for in the Mizpah account Samuel defeats the Philistines, whereas in the Gilgal account Saul defeats them. Most scholars followed Wellhausen and Cornill by maintaining a primary source

with a secondary interpolated source, Baudissin, Einleitung, p. 242; Steuernagel, Lehrbuch der Einleitung in das Alte Testament (Tübingen: Mohr, 1912), pp. 308-340; S. Driver, Hebrew Text, p. 88; Jepsen, Nabi, p. 107; Harold Marcus Wiener, The Composition of Judges II 11 to I Kings II 46 (Leipzig: Hinrichs, 1929), pp. 11-16, who called the pro-monarchical source a Nathan source (N) and the anti-monarchical source a Gilgal source (G); Rene Dussaud, "Israël, d'apres un livre recent," Revue de l'histoire des Religions 104 (1931): 216, who called the earlier source an Ahitub source; George, "livres de Samuel," pp. 161-184; Martin Rehm, Die Bücher Samuel, Die Heilige Schrift: Das Alte Testament, vol. 7, ed. Friedrich Nötscher (Wurzburg: Echter, 1949), p. 21; Pfeiffer, "Midrash," pp. 303, 310-311, and Introduction, pp. 131-148, who has two sources unrelated to Pentateuchal strata: an early historical source (4:1b-7:1, 9:1-10:16, 10:27b-11:11, 15, 13:2-7a, 15b-18, 23, 14:1-46), which continues the Samson cycle, and the later Deuteronomic, theologically oriented, supplement (1:1-2:26, 3, 7:3-8:22, 10:17-27a, 12, 15), which creates the image of Samuel as Nazirite, prophet, and judge; and Schulte, Geschichtsschreibung, pp. 89-90, 105-111, who built upon Richter, "Die Nagid-Formel," BZ 9 (1965): 71-84, in affirming that Samuel was present in the earliest Saul history (9:1-10:16, 11:1-11, 13:3-7a, 15b-18, 23, 14:1-31, 36-46, 52, 28:3-15, 19:a8b-25, 31, and the supplements of the Deuteronomic editor (7, 8, 10:17-27, 12, 15) altered the view of Samuel only in a minor fashion. Other scholars have followed Budde's direction of maintaining the separate existence of the two sources. Schäfers, "1 Sam. 1-15," pp. 117-132; and Schulz, Samuel, 1:132-150, spoke of the Gilgal and Mizpah sources without equating them to Pentateuchal sources. Their independence is shown by the presence of blatant contradictions (like the public election of Saul in 10:17-27 prior to his private life in 11:1-11), but the Mizpah source was aware of the existence of the Gilgal source, and thus mediating material arose (Samuel is both a seer-prophet and kingmaker in 15). Sellin, Introduction to the Old Testament, trans. W. Montgomery (New York: Doran, 1923) pp. 108-116; and Theodor Klaehn, "Die sprachliche Verwandschaft der Quelle K der Samuelisbücher mit der Quelle J des Heptateuch: Ein Beitrag zur Lösung der Frage nach der Identität beider Quellen" (Inaugural dissertation, Rostock, 1914), pp. 1-49, identified a K source from Gilgal, which had continuity with the Yahwist (1:1, 4:1-7:1, 9:1-10:16, 11:1-11, 15, 13:2-6, 15-23, 14:1-46, 52), and to this was added a K_1 source from Gibeah and Mizpah (1:2-3:21, 7:2-17, 8, 10:17-25a, 12, 15). Smith, Samuel, pp. xvii-xxxvi, 55-137, separated two sources: the older Saul source (Sl) in 9:1-10:16, 11, 13:2-14:52, which continues the book of Judges, and the younger Samuel source (Sm) in 1-3, 7:3-17, 8, 10:17-25, 12, 15, which bears similarity to the Elohist and the Deuteronomist

by virtue of its theological abstraction. The Saul source relegates Samuel to the role of seer with historical accuracy, while the theological Samuel source enlarges him with the autocratic authority of a judge. Caird, "Samuel," pp. 856, 860-864, 921-958, proposed two sources unrelated to Pentateuchal sources: the Saul source (9:1-10:16, 11, 13:1-14:46) and the later Samuel source (1:1-4:1, 7:3-8:22, 10:17-27, 12, 15), which elevated Samuel without being anti-monarchical. Deuteronomistic editors brought both sources together, added 12:11, 14:47-52, and recast 7 to make Samuel appear as a judge.

[2] Kittel, History, 2:26-33; and "Die pentateuchischen Urkunden in den Büchern Richter und Samuel," TSK 65 (1896): 44-71, returned to the three source theory of Thenius. He hypothesized the existence of the Saul source (S, 11:1-15, 13:1-14:46, to this the idyll in 9:1-10:16 was appended), which was related to the Yahwist; the Samuel source (SS, 1-3, 8, 10:17-26), which was related to the Elohist; and the Ark Narrative (4-6), which was first appended to the Samuel source. Chapters 7 and 12 are Deuteronomic additions, and 15 is independent of all sources. In the Saul source Samuel is a seer, in the Samuel source he is a prophet and priest, and with the final additions he becomes a judge. Lods, "Les sources des récits du premier livre de Samuel sur l'institution de la royauté israélite," Etudes de theologie et d'histoire: en hommage à la faculté de théologie de Montauban (Paris: Libraire Fischbacher, 1901), pp. 259-284; and Israel, pp. 352-353, divided the early pro-monarchical material into two sources: the Seer source in 9:1-10:7, 9-12, 13:3-5, 23, 14:1-14, 15a, 16-20, 23a, 24b-30, 36-46, which is prior to the Jabesh source in 11:1-11, 15, 13:2-3a, 17-18, 14:15b, 15a, 21-22, 23b-24, 31-35. When they were united, material was created in 13:7b-15a, 10:13-16, 13:1, 6-7a, 15b-16, 19-22, 9:2b, 11:7. This pro-monarchical source was later combined with the anti-monarchical source. Kennedy, Samuel, pp. 16-28, 67-110, 135, had four sources: the old and historical pro-monarchical account (M) in 9:1-10:16, 11:1-11, 15, 13:2-7, 15-18, 23, 14:1-46, 52; the ark narrative (A) in 4-6; the unhistorical Samuel material (S) in 1, 2:11-26, 3, 15:1-16:13; and the Deuteronomic, anti-monarchical source (D) in 8, 10:17-27, 12. Material in A and S was combined, D was added, and finally all three were woven in M. In M Samuel is a seer, in S he is a prophet, and in D he becomes a theocratic judge. Kennedy is followed by Anderson, Introduction, pp. 74-76, who called S and D an Elohist source, while M and A are Yahwist, and Rowley, The Growth of the Old Testament (London: Hutchinson, 1950), pp. 66-67. Smend, "JE in den geschichtlichen Büchern des Alten Testaments," ZAW 39 (1921): 192-201, postulated four successive source additions: J_1 in 10:22-27, 11:12-13, 13:1-7a, 15b-23, 14:1-23, 31-35, 46; J_2 in 9:1-10:16, 11:1-11, 15, 13:7b-15a, 14:24-30, 36-45, 15:1-11,

227

15-16, 21, 24, 27; E in 7, 8, 10:17-20, 12; and JE redaction in 15:12-14, 17-20, 22-23, 25-26, 28-35, 16:1-13. Eissfeldt, Komposition, pp. 4-14; Introduction, pp. 269-280; "Silo," pp. 417-425; and The Hebrew Kingdoms, Cambridge Ancient History Fascicles, vol. 2, chap. 34, ed. I. E. S. Edwards. Cyril Gadd, and N. G. L. Hammond (Cambridge, England: University Press, 1965), pp. 36-40, identified three sources in the narratives, which he identified as I (lay Yahwist or L), II (Yahwist or J), and III (Elohist or E). The L material, which is nomadic in origin, archaic in style, and non-cultic, is found in 10:21bβ-11:13, 13:2-3a, 6-7a, 15b-23, 14:1-46, 4:1-10, 15-16, 21, 5:2-5, 6:1-2a, 5-12a, 14a, 15, 18b-20a, 21, 7:1-2a. The archaic J material involves Samuel with Saul in 1:3b, 2:12-17, 22-25, 27-36, 9:1-10:16, 11:6aα, 13:1bα, 4b-5, 7b-15a. The E material is non-historical, critical of Saul, and elevates Samuel in 1:1-3a, 4-28, 2:11, 18b-21, 3, 7:3-17, 8, 10:17-21abα, 12, 15:1-16:13, 19:18-24. Stephen Szikszai, "Samuel," and "Samuel, I and II," IDB 4:201-202, 205-209, followed Eissfeldt's theory. Hölscher, Die Anfänge der hebräischen Geschichtsschreibung (Heidelberg: Winter, 1942), pp. 10-13, 28-30; and Geschichtsschreibung in Israel, pp. 142, 259-267, 366-372, found three sources, two of which were independent (Yahwist and Elohist$_1$) and one was a supplement (Elohist$_2$). The Yahwist source is the pro-monarchical material found in 9:1-10:16 (minus glosses in 9:2b, 9, 10:8, 9aβ, 16), 11:1-11, 14-15, 13:1-7a, 15b-23, 14:1-8, 23-46. The initial edition of the Elohist, which favors prophecy, but is not necessarily critical of kingship, includes 1:1-3a, 4-6a, 7-28, 2:11-22abα, 23-26, 3:1-11, 13, 15-18, 19abα, 20-21a, 4:1bα, 2aαb, 3αβb, 5-6a, 7a, 8-9, 10aβb, 11-12a, 13ab, 14a, 15-16aβ, 17aβb, 18a, 5:1, 6-12, 6:2b-4, 5aβbα, 6-11abα, 12-14, 16, 18b-21, 7:1, 10:17, 19b-24, 25b-27a, 11:12-13, 15:1-4a, 5-11, 12abαβ, 13-17, 18ab, 19-23, 32-35a. The anti-monarchical stress is located in the second edition of the Elohist, which serves as a bridge to later Deuteronomic thought, and it includes 7:2-17, 8:1-7, 9b-22, 12. Finally, there are Deuteronomic additions and later midrash.

[3] Douglas, Samuel, pp. iii, 69-142, 193, was an early, albeit naive, response to literary critics, which viewed the historical Samuel as prophet, priest, judge, and second Moses. Segal, "Books of Samuel," 5:201-231, 6:267-302, 555-575, 9:67-70, was the first critically to work through the texts. Contradictions in the text reflect different perspectives of the same event, and if the diversity is so great as to warrant separation into opposing sources, why did the editors bring such disparate material together in a false harmony? Segal had to admit, however, the use of pre-existing sources by the historian in 2:12-17, 22-25, 27-36, 4:1-7:1, 9:1-10:16, 13:2-14:46. James Oscar Boyd, "Monarchy in Israel, the Ideal and the Actual," Princeton Theological Review 26 (1928):

41-64; F. Langlamet, "Les récits de l'institution de la royauté, (I Sam VII-XII)," RB 77 (1970): 161-200; and Robert Martin-Achard, "L'institution de la royauté en Israël, I Sam. 8," Bulletin du Centre Protestant D'Etudes 29 (1977): 45-50, declared that the alleged two sources merely reflect two prevailing attitudes to kingship in Samuel's day, and the historian reproduced both. Edward Robertson, "Samuel and Saul," BJRL 28 (1944): 175-206 = The Old Testament Problem: A Re-Investigation, Publications of the University of Manchester, vol. 307 (Manchester, England: University Press, 1950), pp. 105-136, admitted the presence of fragments behind the present text, but he maintained they were woven together for the first time into the unified account we now have. He tried to prove the essential unity of the text by a structural analysis of the text, which discerned a balanced structure in the sethūmah and pethuhah breaks. Goldman, Samuel, pp. 1-96, maintained the unity of the material only by smoothing out the incongruities and superficially explaining the apparent seams in the literature; J. de Fraine, L'aspect religieux de la royauté israelite: L'institution monarchique dans l'Ancien Testament et dans les textes mesopotamiens, AnBib, vol. 3 (Rome: Pontifical Biblical Institute, 1954), pp. 89-112, believed there was one original account, but various editions (G_1, 9:1-10:16; M_1, 8; M_2, 10:17-27; G_2, 11; M_3, 12) caused the discrepancies to arise. But even the diverse attitudes of these editions reflect original attitudes toward kingship.

[4] Albright, Samuel, pp. 1-21; "Some Remarks on the Song of Moses in Deuteronomy XXXII," VT 9 (1959): 339-346, maintained the historicity of all of Samuel's roles, priest, judge, Nazirite, and prophet, as an appropriate response by such a significant leader to the historical crisis of that time. He hypothesized explanations for discrepancies in the sources, and he posited much of Samuel's activity as a response to the theological crisis caused by the Philistines, an idea Albright received from Eissfeldt, Das Lied Moses: Deuteronomium 32:1-43 und Das Lehrgedicht Asaphs Psalm 78 samt einer Analyse der Umgebung des Mose-Liedes, Berichte über die Verhandlungen der Sächsischen Akademie der Wissenschaften zu Leipzig, vols. 104-105 (Berlin: Akademie Verlag, 1958), pp. 21-25. Buber, "Das Volksbegehren," In Memoriam: Ernst Lohmeyer, ed. Werner Schmauch (Stuttgart: Evangelisches Verlagswerk, 1951), pp. 55-66; "Die Erzählung von Sauls Königswahl," VT 6 (1959): 113-173; and The Prophetic Faith, trans. Carlyle Witton-Davies (New York: Harper and Row, 1960), pp. 60-66, undertook the most thorough defense of unity. He declared that we have a theological interpretation instead of real history, which authentically reflects pro-Saul and pro-David traditions. Secondary material is found only in 10:8, 12:6-12, 13:7b-15, 23. Wright, "Lawsuit," p. 63; and Rolf Rendtorff, "Reflections on the Early History of Prophecy in

Israel," trans. Paul Achtemeier, History and Hermeneutic, Journal for Theology and the Church, vol. 4 (New York: Harper and Row, 1967), pp. 14-34, maintained that Samuel was a charismatic judge ruling all Israel, and in this early period such an office entailed job functions of many later institutionalized offices, such as priest, prophet, seer, and military leader. Cohen, "Shilohite Priesthood," pp. 66-67, called Samuel a priest who embodied all these other role functions. In a similar fashion several scholars have advocated Samuel was in possession of an amphictyonic league office called covenant mediator. The duties of this office included conducting covenant renewal festivals, teaching, legislating, rendering judicial decisions, officiating at major assemblies, and all of the other functions in which Samuel engaged, Kraus, Die prophetische Verkündigung des Rechts in Israel, Theologische Studien, vol. 51 (Zollikon: Evangelischer Verlag, 1957), pp. 23-25, and Worship, pp. 109-111; Muilenburg, "Covenantal Formulations," pp. 347-356; Newman, "Call of Samuel," pp. 89-95; Ritterspach, "I Samuel 1-15," pp. 121-308; Gehrke, Samuel, p. 63; Lindblom, Prophecy, p. 97; and Jenks, Elohist, pp. 86-91. Several scholars defended the historicity of the texts by maintaining that the various accounts reflect the complexity of the actual events, Christian Hauer, "Does I Samuel 9:1-11:15 Reflect the Extension of Saul's Dominions?," JBL 86 (1967): 306-310; and Jacob Weingreen, "The Theory of the Amphictyony in Pre-Monarchical Israel," Journal of the Ancient Near Eastern Society (Columbia University) 5 (1973): 431-433, postulated the various coronations of Saul reflect actual regional coronations over a period of time.

[5] Stellini, Samuel, pp. 44-63, 111-113; Karl Gutbrod, Das Buch vom König: Das erste Buch Samuel, vol. 11, pt. 1, Die Botschaft des Alten Testaments (Stuttgart: Calwer Verlag, 1959), pp. 2, 51-120; González Núñez, Profetas, sacerdotes y reges en el antiguo Israel: Problemas de adaptacion del Yahvismo en Canaan, Institutio Español de Estudios Ecclesiásticos, Monografias, vol. 1 (Madrid: n.p., 1962), pp. 129-191; Josef Scharbert, Heilsmittler im Alten Testament und im alten Orient, Questions disputatae, vols. 23-24, ed. Karl Rahner and Heinrich Schlier (Freiburg: Herder, 1964), pp. 81-89, considered the text with little or no sensitivity for textual and historical problems. Thus, Samuel was seen as prophet, priest, and judge as a matter of fact. In his era, a time of crisis, he was called upon to perform all of these functions. Stellini, Samuel, pp. 44-63, 111-113, offered the most thorough, yet uncritical work in evaluating Samuel as prophet and judge. With all of these men the role of the historical Samuel is harmonized with all of the images projected of him by the traditions.

[6] Hylander, Samuel-Saul-Komplex, pp. 26-69, 94, 99, 116, 125-154, 179-190, 201-257, 273, 291-314, described the different sections as developing stages in an ongoing process: 1) Tribal stories from Benjamin and Dan coalesce, which brings two accounts of Saul's birth (Benjaminite tale in I Samuel 1:2, 4, 5a, 6b, 7b, 9, 13-15, 17-19bα, 20aβ, 23b-26bα, 27b, and the Danite tale in I Samuel 1:6a, 5b, 11, 19a, Judges 13:3, 9bβ, 3b, 4-5aβ, 6a, 7, 6b, I Samuel 1:20-22a, Judges 13:8-9a, 11b-12, I Samuel 1:28aα, 22bα, 23aβ, 22b, 23a, Judges 13:2, I Samuel 1:28aβ, Judges 13:5b, 17-18, 21b, I Samuel 1:28b, 2:11a, Judges 13:24b) together with other Benjaminite sagas, a) I Samuel 4:1-2, 7, 9-10, 13:6-7, 17-21, b) 8:4-5, 19-21, c) 9:1-10:16, 14:1-46, d) 13:7-15, 15:10-23, and 3) 14:47-52. In this material Samuel is a seer. 2) The Abiathar strand, which comes from priestly circles at Anathoth, is part of the Yahwist, and it is taken into the earlier cycle. Material is added in 7:15-16, 8, 9:1-2, 12:1-5, and the Saul birth account is now attributed to Samuel, who is a judge in the role of establishing the kingdom. 3) The Elohist version comes forth in two editions, the former adds Danite elements, creates 1:1-3a, 4-7, 9, 11, 13-15, 17-26bα, 27b-28, 2:1-10, 11, 13-14, 18-22a, reshapes 9:1-10:16, and adds 10:27a, 11:1-13, 15:26-28; while the latter edition includes 8:6-22, 1:4-28, 2:1-21, which is now reshaped, and fragmentary additions in 3:1abα, 3-4a, 7b, 5-6, 8-11, 4:21, 13a, 2:35, 3:15a, 16-17a, 15b, 17b-18, 21, 19b, 4:2, 4b, 10a, 11a, 3:22, 4:13a, 15a, 3:2b, 4:12, 13bβ, 14abα, 14bβ, 16aα, 13bα, 16aβ, 16b, 17aαbβ, 18a, 15bα, 3:20, 7:3-4, 5-8, 9-11, 15:22-25, 29-31. Samuel is now a military leader, covenant mediator, and a priest. 4) The priestly or Zadokite edition adds 1:3b, 2:22-36 from the Nob traditions, 10:17-27, 13:7b-15, and Samuel is now idealized as the second Moses. As the core of tradition grows, Samuel is transformed from a local seer into priest, judge, and national leader. Press, "Samuel," pp. 177-225, hypothesized three layers of tradition: 1) once separate royal tales about political events and heroes, 9:1-10:16, 13:16-23, 11, 14, 2:12-17, 22-25, 4, 2) anti-Shiloh prophetic cycle, 2:13-16, 27-36, 15, and 3) anti-monarchical source, 1:1-28, 2:11, 18-21, 3, 7, 8, 10:17-27, 12, which views Samuel as priest, Nazirite and judge. Vriezen, "Samuel-Boeken," pp. 167-189, observed four levels of development: 1) Saul traditions, 9:1-10:16, 13, 14, 2) Samuel and Saul material, 7, 8, 10:17-27, 11-15, 3) Elide material 2:12-17, 22-25, 27-36, 4:1-7:1, and 4) Samuel legends, 1, 2:11, 18-21, 26, 3:1-4:1a. De Vaux, Samuel, pp. 10-75, felt there were three levels of development: 1) old material in 4-6, 9:1-10:16, 11:1-11, 13:1-14:46, where Samuel is a prophet, 2) the supplemented Samuel cycle in 1-3, 10:5-16, 13:3-15, 15:1-16:13, 19:18-24, which condemns Saul, but not kingship, and 3) unhistorical material in 7, 8, 10:17-24, 12, which is also a supplement. Segal, "The Composition of the Books of Samuel," JQR 55 (1964-1965): 318-339; 56 (1965-1966): 32-50,

137-157, observed only two layers of traditions: 1) the ark story and Saul's rise to power, 4-6, 9-11, 13-14, and 2) essentially historical material added by the Samuel editor, 7-8, 12, 15. Alberto Soggin, "Zur Enstehung des alttestamentlichen Königtums," TZ 15 (1959): 401-418; "Charisma und Institution im Königtum Sauls," ZAW 75 (1963): 54-65; and Das Königtum in Israel: Ursprünge, Spannungen, Entwicklung, BZAW, vol. 104 (Berlin: Töpelmann, 1967), pp. 29-57, maintained that Saul's kingship was charismatic rule and not an institutional office as other scholars had surmised; Hans Wildberger, "Samuel und die Entstehung des israelitischen Königtums," TZ 13 (1957): 442-469; and Walter Beyerlin, "Das Königscharisma bei Saul," ZAW 73 (1961): 186-201. Soggin thus determined that those traditions which reflected Saul's charismatic rule must be the older and more authentic. Old charismatic accounts of Saul's defensive wars are chronicled in 11, 13:1-4, 16-23, 14; a second layer of old novelistic traditions are added in 9:1-10:16, 13:5-15; and the late Deuteronomic and prophetic perspectives are provided in 7, 8, 10:17-27, 12, 15, which view Samuel as a judge. Timo Veijola, Dynastie, pp. 36-43; and Das Königtum in der Beurteilung der deuteronomistischen Historiographie: Eine redactionsgeschichtliche Untersuchung, Suomalaisen Tiedeakatemian Toimituksia, Annales Academiae scientiarum Fennicae, ser. B, vol. 198 (Helsinki: Suomalainen Tiedeakatemia, 1977), pp. 30-99, postulated that two editors supplemented an earlier collection of tales in 9:1-10:16, 13, 14. DtG added the call formula to the old version of 9:1-10:16, the framework in 10:17, 19b-27a, 11:12-14 for 11:1-11, and material in 8:1-5, 22b. DtrN added 10:18aβγ-19a, 7, 8:4-22a, 12 to give the material an anti-monarchical view.

[7] This view was advanced by Noth, Überlieferungsgeschichtliche Studien, vol. 1: Die sammelnden und bearbeitenden Geschichtswerke im Alten Testament, Schriften der Königsberger Gelehrten Gesellschaft: Geisteswissenschaftliche Klasse, vol. 18, pt. 2 (Halle: Niemeyer, 1943), pp. 55-60; "Das Amt des 'Richters Israel,'" Festschrift für Alfred Bertholet zum 80. Geburtstag, ed. Walter Baumgartner, Otto Eissfeldt, Karl Elliger, and Leonhard Rost (Tübingen: Mohr, 1950), pp. 406-417; The History of Israel, 2d ed., trans. Peter Ackroyd (New York: Harper and Row, 1960), pp. 168-176; and "Office and Vocation in the Old Testament," The Laws in the Pentateuch, pp. 243-244, who maintained that this segment is part of the larger history of the Deuteronomist, which came into its present form at the hands of one editor, who inherited old fragmented traditions. Historical traditions are found in 4:1-7:1, 9:1-10:16, 10:27b-11:15, 13:2-16:13, which were woven together with Deuteronomistic creations in 7, 8, 10:17-27a, 12, to create our present text. Noth's theory has been adopted by other scholars, Johannes Schildenberger, "Zur Einleitung in die Samuelbücher," Miscellanea biblica et orientalia, Studia

Anselmiana, vols. 27-28, ed. Athanasius Miller (Rome: Herder, 1951), pp. 130-165; Macholz, "Samuel-Überlieferungen," pp. 101-199; and Hans Jochen Boecker, Die Beurteilung der Anfänge des Königtums in den deuteronomistischen Abschnitten des 1. Samuelbuches, WMANT, vol. 31 (Neukirchen-Vluyn: Neukirchener Verlag, 1969), pp. 1-199, who has undertaken an ambitious defense of Noth's views against advocates of fragmentary traditio-historical development, like Hertzberg and Weiser. He affirmed the Deuteronomistic authorship and supplementary nature of the material in 7, 8, 10:17-27, 12, which was a free creation by the editor when the entire literary complex arose. Tsevat, "The Biblical Narrative of the Foundation of Kingship in Israel," Tarbiz 36 (1966-1967): i, 99-109; and "Samuel, I and II," IBDSup, ed. Keith Crim (Nashville: Abingdon, 1976), pp. 778-781, mediated between Noth and Weiser, but he affirmed the existence of one edition which incorporated the fragments and placed them in an ABABA pattern of positive and critical attitudes toward kingship, both of which reflected authentic early attitudes. Friedrich Mildenberger, "Die vordeuteuronomistische Saul-David-über-lieferung" (Inaugural dissertation, Tübingen, 1962), pp. vi-xi, 9-58, 122-124, 193-200; and the review in "Referate über theo-logische Dissertationen in Maschinenschrift," TLZ 87 (1962): 778-779, advocated the novel thesis that I Samuel 9 to I Kings 2 was put forth as a unified story in a pre-Deuteonomistic pro-phetic edition, which emphasized the failure or success of deliverers. There was a core of old traditions in 10:27b-11:15, 13:1-4a, 6-7a, 16-23, 14:1-46, supplemented by the prophetic editors over a long period of time with 9:1-10:16, 13:4b-5, 7b-15, 15:1-16:13, and this in turn was supplemented by Deuteronomistic material in 7, 8, 10:17-27, 12, which has some historicity behind it. This pre-Deuteronomistic prophetic edition advocated charismatic kingship with an anti-monarchical bias, it emanated from Gilgal around 750-650 B.C., and Samuel received high veneration. Rolf Knierim, "The Messianic Concept in the First Book of Samuel," Jesus and the Historian: Written in Honor of Ernest Cadman Colwell, ed. Thomas Trotter (Philadelphia: Westminster, 1968), pp. 21-41, built upon the work of Mildenberger in seeing a unifying feature in I Samuel 9-31, which is a pre-Deuteronomistic prophetic account concerning Saul's call and failure as a messianic figure.

[8] Gressmann, Geschichtsschreibung, pp. 19-52, was the first scholar to advocate a composition arising out of many small, individual stories: idylls, 1-3; late legends, 7, 8, 10:17-27, 12; historical legends, 13-15; early legends, 9:1-10:16; and history 11:1-15. The early historical material saw him as a prophet. Caspari, Samuelbücher, pp. 6-10, 14-15, 81, saw independent units coalesce into two novelistic accounts of the ark and battle narratives in 2:12-17, 22-25, 4:1b-14, 16:21a, 22b-5:1a, 5:1b-6:11a, 6:12-7:1a (ark), and

10:27-11:15, 13:2a, 3-18, 23, 14:1-4, 6-24, 14:26-47a (wars). This material was taken up by the Elohist, who added 1:1-28a, 2:11, 18-21, 3:1-18, 19b, 20b, 9:1-10:16, 14:47b, 49-50a, 15:1-7a, 8-26a, 27-35a, and he also introduced a Mizpah source in 7:2b, 5-14, 8:1-9, 21-22a, 10:17-24, 25b-27, 12:1-5. The Deuteronomist finally added 2:1-10, 27-35, 7:3, 15-17a, 8:17b, 19b, 12:6-11, 13-24. Hertzberg, "Die Kleinen Richter," TLZ 79 (1954): 285-290; and Samuel, pp. 17-20, 64-134, was the first to articulate that various traditions arose independently in specific shrines. The old pro-monarchical traditions came from Gilgal (G, 11, 15:1-16:13), the younger anti-monarchical traditions were from Mizpah (M, 7, 8, 10:17-27), and other cycles came from elsewhere, Ramah traditions in 9:1-10:16, ark traditions in 4:1-7:1, court history of the Philistine wars in 13-14, Samuel traditions in 1-3, and Deuteronomistic creations in 12. Artur Weiser, "Samuels 'Philister-Sieg,'" ZTK 56 (1959): 253-272, and "Samuel und die Vorgeschichte des israelitischen Königtums," ZTK 57 (1960): 141-161, which were subsequently used as separate chapters in Samuel: Seine geschichtliche Aufgabe und religiöse Bedeutung, FRLANT, vol. 81 (Göttingen: Vandenhoeck und Ruprecht, 1962), pp. 7-94; and The Old Testament: Its Formation and Development, trans. Dorothea Barton (New York: Association Press, 1964), pp. 162-170, located the material in the following shrines: 1) Ramah, 8, 9:1-10:16, 2) Mizpah, 7:2-17, 10:17-26, and 3) Gilgal, 10:27-11:15, 12. The oldest materials are the ark narratives (4-6) and Saul's rise to power (9:1-10:16, 11, 13:1-14:46), while the prophetic interpretations are later (7:2-17, 8, 10:17-26, 12, 15), but they also arose independently and have historical validity. By affirming especially the historical veracity of the critical speeches by Samuel in 8, 12, Weiser affirmed the position of Isaac Mendelsohn, "Samuel's Denunciation of Kingship in the Light of the Akkadian Documents from Ugarit," BASOR 143 (1956): 17-22; "On Corvee Labor in Ancient Canaan," BASOR 167 (1962): 31-35; Wildberger, "Samuel," pp. 442-469; Bernhardt, Königsideologie, p. 149; Eissfeldt, Lied Moses, pp. 21-25; Albright, "Song of Moses," pp. 339-346; Muilenburg, "Covenantal Formulations," pp. 347-356; Mauchline, Samuel, pp. 90-92; and Moriarity, Samuel, p. 19. A critical response has been given to this by Ronald Clements, "The Deuteronomistic Interpretation of the Founding of the Monarchy in I Sam. VIII," VT 24 (1974): 398-410; and Ackroyd, Samuel, p. 73, who believed that Samuel's criticism could only be articulated after Israel had experienced the evils of kingship. Weiser affirmed the historicity of the events throughout, but he indicated that the material has been colored by later interpretation. The diverse actions of Samuel are accurately reflected, but the specific roles assigned to him are projections of a later institutional age, Samuel, pp. 92-94; also Willis, "Cultic Elements," pp. 53-54; and "Anti-Elide Narrative," pp. 40-41. Weiser viewed Samuel

as primarily prophetic in his actions, but in this early era he could perform many roles according to the need of his society. Independent fragments from the various shrines were woven together into cycles about important figures like Saul (9:1-10:16, 11, 13-14), Samuel (1-3, 7-8, 12, 15), and David (I Samuel 16:14-II Samuel 5:8), the greater cycles became a continuous narrative edited by prophetic theologians, and finally the Deuteronomistic History emerged. Most subsequent scholarship has followed Weiser's approach, T. C. G. Thornton, "Charismatic Kingship in Israel and Judah," JTS 14 (1963): 1-11; and "Studies in Samuel. I. Davidic Propaganda in the Books of Samuel," CQR 168 (1967): 413-423, found inconsistency in the anti-monarchical passages, which led him to affirm their separate origin and early date. Bernhardt, Königsideologie, pp. 142-152, saw five groups of tradition: 1) ark traditions, 4:1-17, 18b-21, 5:1a-11a, 6:1-3a, 4-5a, 7-10, 11-14, 16, 19-21, 7:1, 2) Shiloh traditions, 1, 2:11-3:21, 3) Saul I traditions, 10:21bβ-11:15, 4) Saul II traditions, 9:1-10:16, 13:7b-14, 5) Saul III traditions, 13:3-7a, 15-18, 14:1-46. Critical material in 8:7, 9-10, 19-22 comparable to Hosea and material in 8:11-18, 10:17-21bα related to the Jotham cycle was added to Saul material in a nomadic-amphictyonic-prophetic source, (Stoebe, Samuelis, p. 179, affirmed the existence of such a source). After all of the fragments coalesced, Deuteronomistic material was added in 7:2-17, 12, 15. John McKenzie, "The Four Samuels," Biblical Research 7 (1961): 3-18, located the material in various shrines according to their view of Samuel as seer, prophet, priest, or judge. The oldest and most historical material in 9:1-10:16, 16:1-13, 19:18-24 (contemporary with 10:27-11:15, 13:1-14:46) views Samuel as a seer, later theological and unhistorical material in 3, 15, 28 views Samuel as a prophet, very late Deuteronomistic creations in 1:1-26, 7, 8, 10:17-27, 12 view Samuel as judge, Nazirite, and charismatic hero, and finally, fragments of a priestly image are in 1:27-28, 2:11, 18, 3:1, and I Chronicles 6:13. Unlike Weiser who attributed historicity to all the fragmentary traditions McKenzie sought to discern historical from theological traditions. A comparable approach was taken by Fohrer, Introduction, pp. 218-226, who found several layers of development, but only the early layers have historical value. In the basic stratum there were independent popular narratives, some of which were more comprehensive (ark narratives, I Samuel 4-6, II Samuel 6; rise of David, I Samuel 16:14-II Samuel 5; and the court history, II Samuel 9-20, while others were fragmentary (9:1-10:16, 11, 13:1-14:46). The Saul fragments coalesced and were supplemented by independent insertions: 1) 1-3, a collection of once loose fragments, the birth, 1:1-28, 2:11, 18-21; Elide material 2:12-17, 22-25; anti-Elide oracle, 2:27-36; and theophany, 3, 2) the victory in 7:2-17, 3) Saul's rise in 8, 10:17-27, 4) Samuel's farewell, 12, 5) Saul's rejection in 13:7b-15, 6) Saul's rejection in 15, and

7) David's anointing, 16:1-13. The Deuteronomist received this material and added only 2:22-26, 7:1. Schunck, Benjamin, pp. 80-138, believed that two successive redactors drew all the fragments together. The first redactor (R-I), who was pro-Saul, collected the Jabesh source (11, 31), Gilgal source (9:1-10:16, 13:1-6, 16-18, 23, 14:1-30, 36-46), Elide material (2:12-17, 22-25, 4:1b-7:1), family notices (14:49-51), and attached this to Judges 19-21. The second redactor (R-II) or Deuteronomist brought additions from Gilgal in 1:1-19a, 20-28, 2:18-21, 7:2-17, 8:4-17, 10:21bβ-25a, 14:31-35, 15:4a, 5, 8a, 12b, 28:3-16, 19b-25. Secondary Deuteronomistic redaction brought 10:8, 13:7b-15, 19:8-20:1a, and the rest of 15. The first redactor knew Samuel as a seer-priest from Ramathaim in Ephraim, the second knew him as a prophet-judge from Ramah of Benjamin and Mizpah. Horst Seebass, "Traditionsgeschichte von I Sam. 8, 10:17ff und 12," ZAW 77 (1965): 286-296; "I Sam. 15 als Schlüssel für das Verständnis der sogenannten Königsfreundlichen Reihe I Sam. 9:1-10:16, 11:1-15 und 13:2-14:52," ZAW 78 (1966): 148-179; and "Die Vorgeschichte der Königserhebung Sauls," ZAW 78 (1967): 155-171, postulated a very complex oral prehistory in which there were two original variants of Saul's wars: Source A consisted of 7:2b, 5-6, 8-9, 5:1-7:1, 7, 10-14a, 15-17, 8:4-7, 10, 19-22aα, 9, 22b, 10:17, 19b-24, 12:1-6a, 7a, 6b, 13bαβ, 14b, 24b-25, 10:25-27, 13:2-3a, 6-7a, 19-22, 14:2-3, 6-13a, 15, 13b, 20-22, 23b-29, 31, 36a, 37-46, 15:2a, 3-9, 12b, 13-14, 20b, 23, 29-30a, 31a, 32-35a. Source B consisted of 11:1-15, 9:1-10:16, 13:4-5, 17b-18, 14:1, 4-5, 14-15aα, 16-18, 23a, 32-35, 36b, 15:1, 11-12a, 16-19, 24-28, 47-52. The Deuteronomist drew upon Source A for his anti-monarchical view, and he added 8:1-3, 8, 11-18, 13:7b-15, 12:16-24a, reworked 7:5-12, 12:1-15, gave 10:17-27 its present form, reworked 7:5-12 to parallel 12:16-25, created 13:7b-17, turned Saul's victory in 7 into Samuel's victory, converted the issue of royal law in 8 into a rejection of God, and made 12 into a complaint rather than a clarification of divine law. After the anti-monarchical source was created, it was united with source B, the pro-monarchical source, to create our present text. Both sources A and B are valid historical memories of Saul's rise to power which Seebass reconstructed as follows: Saul defeats Ammon in 11:1-11, becomes nagid in 9:1-10:16, 11:12-15, skirmishes at Mizpah, 7:7, 10-12, receives a request to become king, 8:4-7, 10, 19-22, becomes king in 10:19b-24, 25-27, defeats the Philistines (two versions in 13:1-14:46), commits a sacrilege in 14:32-35, and is finally rejected in 15:1, 11, 16-19, 24-28. Wallis, "Die Anfänge des Königtums in Israel," and "Samuelstoff," Geschichte und Überlieferung, pp. 45-66, 70-86, assigned the independent accounts to various shrines. An Ephraimite folk tale in 1-3, 9:1-10:16 viewed Samuel as a prophet from Ramathaim in Ephraim, material from Mizpah in 7, 8, 10:17-27, 12 viewed him as a judge from Ramah of Benjamin, and 11 came from a cycle

of tales about the judges. Valid historical memories were in all the traditions, for Saul was crowned in the different locales as his rule expanded. Ludwig Schmidt, Menschlicher Erfolg und Jahwes Initiative: Studien zu Tradition, Interpretation und Historie in Überlieferungen von Gideon, Saul und David, WMANT, vol. 38 (Neukirchen: Neukirchener Verlag, 1970), pp. 58-109, 172-188, believed these accounts to be local memories of the events. The battle in 11 is a Transjordanian tradition, 9:1-10:16 comes from Ephraim, and 8, 10:17-27 is from Benjamin. The material in 9:1-10:16 is really two accounts, a call narrative and the story of the lost asses and the man of God. The early version of the lost asses and the man of God (9:1-8, 10-13aᵟᴀb, 14a, 18-19, 22a, 24b-27, 10:2-4, 7, 9) combined with material in 10:27-11:15, 13:1-14:46 to form an early Saul source (850-800 B.C.). Samuel material was added in 9:13ᵟɣ, 14b, 15-17, 20-21, 22b-24a, 10:1, 13b-16 to convert 9:1-10:16 into a call narrative like Gideon's, and further material was added in 10:5-6, 10-13a, 10:8, 13:7b-15a, 16:1-13, 19:18-24 out of theological reflection. Maxwell Miller, "Saul's Rise to Power: Some Observations Concerning I Sam. 9:1-10:16, 10:26-11:15 and 13:2-14:46, CBQ 36 (1974): 157-174, sees 1) the early version of 9:1-10:16 in which Samuel is missing, as Schmidt envisioned, which is followed by Saul's combat in 13:4-18, 14:20-23, 31-35, 2) Jonathan's victory in 13:3, 14:1, 4-9, 24, and 3) Saul's victory in 11:1-11. These three tales were united and Samuel material was inserted, so that the order of events originally was: Samuel anoints Saul and sends him to Gilgal (9:1-10:16), there Saul sacrifices and is rejected (13:7-15), Saul defeats the Philistines (13:1-6, 16-23, 14:1-46), scoffers ridicule Saul (10:26-27), he defeats Ammon after a return to private life (11:1-11), Samuel crowns Saul (11:12-15), and then Samuel replaces Saul with David (16:1-13). Later Deuteronomistic revision gave the text an anti-monarchical cast, put the Philistine wars later, harmonized the Saul and Jonathan accounts, put Jabesh after the Mizpah coronation, made Gilgal a renewal ceremony (11:2), and added elements in 10:25-26a, 10:5b-6, 10-13a. Bruce Birch, "The Development of the Tradition on the Anointing of Saul in I Sam. 9:1-10:16," JBL 90 (1971): 55-68; "The Choosing of Saul at Mizpah," CBQ 37 (1975): 447-457; and The Rise of the Israelite Monarchy: The Growth and Development of I Samuel 7-15, SBLDS, vol. 27 (Missoula, Montana: Scholars Press, 1976), pp. 141-154 et passim, gave the most thorough evaluation of this material. There are three stages of development: 1) Independent traditions ranging from archives to folktales arose, including Samuel's victory over the Philistines, 7:7-12, Samuel's circuit as a minor judge, 7:15-17, the corruption of Samuel's sons and the request of the elders, 8:1-7, the folktale of the lost asses, 9:1-14, 18-19, 22-24, 10:2-4, 9, 14-16a, the aetiology of Saul's prophecy, 10:10-13, Sauls' election, 10:20-24, opposition to Saul, 10:26-27, Ammonite

war, 11:1-11, election of Saul, 11:15, Philistine war accounts, 13:2-7a, 15b-23, Jonathan's battle, 14:1-46, and summary, 14:47-52. The only real source to arise out of these fragments was 13:1-14:46. 2) A pre-Deuteronomistic prophetic edition collected these fragments, converted Saul's anointing into a nagid call by adding 9:15-17, 20-21, 25-27, 10:1, 5-8, 16b (which Birch called a prophetic call in opposition to Richter, Richterbuch, pp. 149-155, who considered it the call narrative of a deliverer), turned the Mizpah coronation into a prophetic judgment speech by adding 10:17-19, 25, added the Gilgal coronation in 11:12-14, Samuel's defense in 12:1-5, and prophetic judgment speeches in 13:7b-15, 15. This editor gave the book its present form and converted the image of Samuel, who was probably a minor judge, into the model of a prophet like Elisha. Samuel is now seen as one who anoints kings, upholds holy war, brings judgment oracles to the nation and individuals, and dispenses divine charisma to Saul, who in turn uses it wisely in 11:1-15, but fails in 13:7b-15, 15. 3) The Deuteronomist changed this theological account by adding 7:3-4, 13-14, 8:8, 10-22, 12:6-24, 13:1, which gave the material an anti-monarchical cast. Tryggve Mettinger, King and Messiah: The Civil and Sacral Legitimation of the Israelite Kings, Coniectanea Biblica: Old Testament Series, vol. 8 (Lund: Gleerup, 1976), pp. 64-97, 175-209, built upon Seebass, Richter, and Schunck. The oldest traditions were fragments found in 9:1-14a, 18-20, 22-26, 10:2-7ab, 8, 9b-16, 11:1-15, 13:1-14:46, which were joined together and supplemented by later fragments: 1) 9:14b-17, 21, 27, 10:1, 7bβ, 9a, 10:17-27 around 900 B.C., 2) Shiloh traditions, 1-3, at the same time, 3) 16:1-13 slightly later, and 4) Mizpah traditions in 7, 12 around 850 B.C. The anti-monarchical view was then a reflection of Solomon's reign.

[9] Scholars who have affirmed the historicity of a broad range of the Samuel traditions, not just the early ones, include, Mildenberger, "Saul-David-überlieferung," pp. vi-ix, 9-58, 122-124, 193-200; Segal, "Composition of Samuel," 55:318-339, 56:32-50, 137-157; Hertzberg, Samuel, pp. 17-20, 64-134, and "Kleinen Richter," pp. 285-290; Muilenburg, "Covenantal Formulations," pp. 347-356; Weiser, Samuel, pp. 7-94; Tsevat, "Biblical Narrative," pp. 778-781; Bernhardt, Königsideologie, p. 149; Schunck, Benjamin, pp. 80-138; Wallis, Geschichte, pp. 45-66, 70-86; and Schmidt, Erfolg, pp. 58-109, 172-188. However, many traditio-historical critics attribute historicity only to the early traditions (as did literary critics), which they seek to discern by peeling away the younger traditions. Such endeavor usually reveals the historical Samuel to be a prophet or a seer for most scholars, Gressmann, Geschichtsschreibung, pp. 19-52; Hylander, Samuel-Saul-Komplex, pp. 26-69, 125-154, 179-257, 291-314; Press, "Samuel," pp. 177-225; de Vaux, Samuel, pp. 10-75;

Fohrer, Introduction, pp. 218-226; Soggin, Königtum, pp. 29-57; Miller, "Saul's Rise," pp. 157-174; and Mettinger, King and Messiah, pp. 64-97, 175-209. A few have determined that he was a minor judge, Noth, Studien, pp. 55-60, and "Richters Israel," pp. 406-417; Boecker, Beurteilung, pp. 1-99; and Birch, Monarchy, pp. 141-154, (Weiser, Samuel, pp. 7-94; and Hertzberg, "Kleinen Richter," pp. 285-290, also observed this as Samuel's primary role above all the others).

[10] Hylander, Samuel-Saul-Komplex, pp. 213-240; Hölscher, Profeten, p. 122; Press, "Samuel," pp. 221-224; and McKenzie, "Four Samuels," pp. 3-18, who offered the most thorough work. He isolated four layers of tradition, each with a separate view of Samuel's office. The youngest tradition views Samuel as a priest with Levitical genealogy (1:27-28, 2:11, 18, 3:1, I Chronicles 6:13-18), which effectively emphasizes cultic activity reflected in the earlier traditions. The late anti-monarchical layer projects the image of judge upon Samuel (1:1-26, 7:3-8:22, 10:17-25, 12), which gives the impression of covenant mediator and military leader. The prophetic traditions (3, 15, 28) are projections by the prophetic editors, who wished to view Samuel as their founder. The model which remains is the seer (9:1-10:16, 16:1-13, 19:18-24), which must be historical. Robert Bach, Die Aufforderungen zur Flucht und zum Kampf im alttestamentlichen Propheten-spruch, WMANT, vol. 9 (Neukirchen: Neukirchener Verlag, 1963), pp. 111-112; and Birch, Monarchy, pp. 19, 83-84, 96, noticed the close connections between Samuel as seer and the ancient holy war formulas, although Birch would connect the office of seer and minor judge. Jepsen, Nabi, pp. 99-114; and McKane, Samuel, pp. 63-73, viewed Samuel as a priest, who became a seer-prophet according to his peculiar circumstances, namely the destruction of Shiloh caused his slight change of vocation. Schunck, Benjamin, pp. 103-105; and Wallis, Geschichte, pp. 84-85, saw Samuel as a seer from Ephraim in one of the basic strata of the traditions, however, in the other strata he was a minor judge.

[11] The problem is rooted in questions concerning the origin of prophecy. The distinction between seer and prophet is frequently defined historically, seers were prior to prophets and the latter developed out of the former, or functionally, the seer was a mantic divinator and the prophet suppressed mantic skills in favor of proclamation. Richard Kraetzschmar, Prophet und Seher im alten Israel, Sammlung gemeinverständlicher Vorträge und Schriften aus dem Gebiet der Theologie und Religionsgeschichte, vol. 23 (Leipzig: Mohr, 1901), pp. 10-13, 17-19; Friedrich Eduard König, Der ältere Prophetismus bis auf die Heldengestalten von Elia und Elisha, Biblische Zeit- und Streitfragen, 1st ser., vol. 9, ed. Boehmer and Kropotscheck (Berlin: Lichterfelde, 1905), pp. 7-10; Hölscher, "Ursprung,"

pp. 88-100, and Profeten, 121-188; Jepsen, Nabi, pp. 8-9, 45-54, 146-151; Gressmann, Geschichtsschreibung, pp. 29-32, 52; and Schulz, Samuel, 1:132, advocated that ecstatic prophecy (as in the Wen-Amon tale) arose first among the Canaanites, and Samuel domesticated it for Israel by merging it with the calm Semitic model of the kahin, or seer, which Israel brought from the wilderness. Early Israelite prophecy thereafter had ecstatic elements, but gradually they faded with the rise of classical prophecy. Nabi meant to "rage" in the early texts (I Samuel 10:5-13, 18:10, 19:20-24, I Kings 18:29), but later it came to mean "proclaim, announce," Jepsen, Nabi, pp. 8-9. Samuel was neither an ecstatic prophet nor a seer nor even a prophet in the later classical sense. Even though Canaanite ecstasy arose in Israel under his aegis, he was a clan divinator (especially in I Samuel 9:1-10:16), which made him comparable to the bārû priest of Mesopotamia. Later prophets developed from both early ecstatic prophets and seers, but they eliminated the ecstasy of the former and the divination of the latter. Despite later criticism of this theory, scholars have affirmed its essential content in more recent work, I. H. Seeligmann, "The Problems of Prophecy in Israel, its Development and Characteristics," Eretz-Israel 3 (1954): viii, 125-132; and Ackroyd, Samuel, p. 76. This view has been effectively challenged by Hubert Junker, Prophet und Seher in Israel: Eine Untersuchung über die ältesten Erscheinungen des israelitischen Prophetentums, insbesondere der Prophetvereine (Trier: Paulinus Verlag, 1927), pp. 9-16; Meek, Hebrew Origins, p. 156; Guillaume, Prophecy and Divination, p. 292; and Lindblom, "Zur Frage des kanaanäischen Ursprungs des altisraelitischen Prophetismus," Von Ugarit nach Qumran: Beiträge zur alttestamentlichen und altorientalischen Forschung: Festschrift für Otto Eissfeldt, ed. Johannes Hempel and Leonard Rost, BZAW, vol. 77 (Berlin: Gruyter, 1958), pp. 89-104, and Prophecy, pp. 6-82, who declared that ecstasy was a general Semitic phenomena (if not universal), not limited to just the Canaanites (König, Prophetismus, pp. 7-10, also considered this as a possiblity). This demanded a new delineation between seer and prophet. Junker, Prophet, pp. 24-104, thought the prophet was an ecstatic attached to a cult site, while the seer was transient and independent, but both were authentic Israelite phenomena. Lods, Israel, p. 443, considered the seer a solitary individual, while the prophet was a guild member of a collective group. But other scholars reversed Lod's distinction by calling the seer a professional guild member, while the prophet was "called" (from the Akkadian nabû, "to call"), Mowinckel, Psalmenstudien, 3:9; Albright, From the Stone Age to Christianity: Monotheism and the Historical Process, 2d ed. (Garden City, New York: Doubleday, 1957), pp. 298-309; and Meek, Hebrew Origins, pp. 150-151. The seer divined what was hidden, but the prophet declared what was revealed. Lindblom, Prophecy, pp. 94-96, maintained both offices had

ecstasy, so the line of demarcation was fluid. A number of scholars have compared the seer to the barû priest in reference to his divinatory skills, Jastrow, "Rô'eh and Hôzeh in the Old Testament," JBL 28 (1909): 42-56; Mowinckel, "Om nebiisme og profeti," NorTT 10 (1909): 192; and Psalmen-studien, 3:9-22; Alfred Haldar, Associations of Cultic Prophets among the ancient Semites (Uppsala: Almquist und Wiksell, 1945), pp. 102-111, 122-134; Johnson, Cultic Prophet, pp. 9-15; Otto Plöger, "Priester und Prophet," ZAW 63 (1951): 165-171; G. Dossin and Adolphe Lods, "Une tablette inédite de Mari, interéssante pour l'histoire ancienne du prophétisme semitique," Studies in Old Testament Prophecy, ed. Harold Henry Rowley (Edinburgh: Clark, 1950), pp. 103-111; and Lindblom, Prophecy, pp. 94-96. Samuel was a rôeh, an itinerant seer-priest, who voluntarily divinated, and from whose early function both priest and prophet would inherit skills. Haldar, Associations, pp. 102-111, 122-124; Johnson, Cultic Prophets, pp. 9-15, both attributed seer-priests and prophets to a Mesopotamian origin, and while the former was a divinator, the latter was an ecstatic. Orlinsky, "The Seer in Ancient Israel," OrAnt 4 (1965): 153-174; and "The Seer Priest and the Prophet in Ancient Israel," Essays in Biblical Culture and Bible Translation (New York: KTAV, 1974), pp. 41-61 = The World History of the Jewish People, vol. 3: Judges, ed. Benjamin Mazar (New Brunswick, New Jersey: Rutgers, 1971), pp. 268-279, developed this theory most thoroughly by advocating that both Samuel and Eli were seer-priests, a divinatory professional comparable to the barû priests of Mesopotamia, who also wielded political power in pre-monarchical Israel. While prophets were an Israelite phenomena, seer-priests were universal, although only in Israel did they actively control national destinies. Cohen, "Shilohite Priesthood," pp. 69-82, built on this idea.

[12] Noth, Studien, pp. 96-97; "Richters Israel," pp. 406-417; "Office and Vocation," pp. 243-244; and "Samuel und Silo," pp. 396-397, compared lists of minor judges in Judges 10:1-5, 12:7-15, and I Samuel 7:15-17, and he concluded the historical Samuel was an amphictyonic league official who traveled a judge's circuit to render legal decision, interpret the law, and teach. Only the later Deuteronomistic Historian enlarged this judicial tradition to become a charismatic warrior judge image and merged the old but less authentic prophetic traditions into this new construct. Noth built upon the earlier work of Kittel, History, 2:31-32; Klostermann, Samuelis, pp. xviii-xix, xxviii-xxxvi; and Hertzberg, "Entwicklung des Begriffes špṭ im Alten Testament," ZAW 40 (1922): 256-287; 41 (1923): 16-76, who formulated this idea in various forms, but they never developed it. Noth's concept of Samuel as a judge has been utilized by Hertzberg, "Kleinen Richter," pp. 285-290; Wildberger, "Entstehung," pp. 455-468, who viewed Samuel as a

charismatic and Saul as institutional in the performance of their roles, and Samuel performed both functions of the later prophets and kings; Werner Vollborn, "Der Richter Israels," Sammlung und Sendung: Vom Auftrag der Kirche in der Welt: Eine Festgabe für Heinrich Rendtorff zu seinem 70. Geburtstag am 9, April 1958, ed. Joachim Heubach and Heinrich-Hermann Ulrich (Berlin: Christlicher Zeitschriftenverlag, 1958), pp. 21-31; Bright, A History of Israel (Philadelphia: Westminster, 1959), pp. 165-166; Beyerlin, "Königscharisma," pp. 186-201, who agreed with Wildberger in viewing Samuel as a charismatic leader and Saul as an institutional leader; Weiser, Samuel, pp. 10-12, 92-94; McKane, Samuel, p. 64; Hertzberg, Samuel, p. 138; von Rad, Old Testament Theology, 1:33; Schunck, "Die Richter in Israel und ihr Amt," VTSup,vol. 15 (Leiden: Brill, 1965), pp. 252-262; Richter, "Zu den 'Richter Israels,'" ZAW 77 (1965): 40-72; Segal, "Composition of Samuel," p. 149; Friedrich Horst, "Recht und Religion im Bereich des Alten Testaments," EvT 16 (1966): 49-75; Donald McKenzie, "The Judge of Israel," VT 17 (1967): 118-121; Soggin, Königtum, p. 31; Ritterspach, "Samuel Traditions," pp. 285-288, who called Samuel a covenant mediator grounded in the cult; Rendtorff, "Reflections," pp. 31-32, who agreed with Wildberger that Samuel as a judge embodied the functions of later prophets and kings; Bardkte, "Samuel und Saul," pp. 289-302; Boecker, Beurteilung, pp. 1-99; Cody, Priesthood, p. 79; and Schulte, Geschichtsschreibung, pp. 106-107. Utilization of Noth's model has produced interesting historical reconstructions. Eli has been presented as a minor judge also, Cody, Priesthood, pp. 71-79; but this has been challenged by Brinker, Sanctuaries, p. 168. Kurt Möhlenbrink, "Sauls Ammoniterfeldzug und Samuels Beitrag zum Königtum des Saul," ZAW 58 (1940-1941): 66-69, believed Samuel was an amphictyonic leader over the central tribes in Shiloh, while Saul was an amphictyonic leader over the Gilgal amphictyony, which included the tribes of Gad, Reuben, and Benjamin. Saul assumed rule of both leagues as a compromise move in the Philistine crisis, and Gibeah became the compromise capital. Ishida, "Leaders," pp. 528-530; and Royal Dynasties, p. 33, believed the amphictyonic league was led by charismatic judges until the Philistine crisis, at which time leadership was given to a hereditary priest-judge office, filled first by Eli, then Samuel. Dus, "Die 'Sufeten' Israels," Archiv Orientali 31 (1963): 444-469, constructed the most unusual theory -- Samuel was an amphictyonic ruler like the later Carthaginian sufete, and he headed a democratic assembly with authority over twelve princes from each tribe and seventy senior legislators.

[13] Even the meaning of the word judge has engendered a debate, which prevents Noth's hypothetical reconstruction from attaining any consensus. Noth's definition of a minor judge was given its basis by Oskar Grether, "Die Bezeichnung 'Richter'"

für die charismatischen Helden der vorstaatlichen Zeit," ZAW 57 (1939): 110-121, who found a two-fold distinction in the word špṭ according to Phoenician and Punic sources, "to give judgment," and "to rule, have jurisdiction." Samuel was seen to have both functions as a minor judge, and major judges had their military activity projected onto them by the Deuteronomist. This evaluation was disputed by F. C. Fensham, "The Judges and Ancient Israelite Jurisprudence," and A. van Selms, "The Title 'Judge,'" Die Ou Testamentiese Werkgemeenskap in Suid Afrika, 2d Congress, 1959 Papers, Papers read at the 2d meeting held at Potschefstroom 2-5 February, 1959 (Potschefstroom: Pro Rege-Pers Beperk, 1959), pp. 15-22, 41-50, whose study of Phoenician, Ugaritic, and Punic material indicated that a judge was a wealthy landowner. They maintained this was the basis of Samuel's authority, not his possession of a hypothetic amphictyonic office. But their work may actually reinforce Noth's hypothesis by defining what constituted the qualifications for a person who held office as minor judge. Ownership of land may have been the basis of a minor judge's authority, as Richter, "Richter Israels," pp. 40-72, has maintained. Dus, "Sufeten," pp. 444-469, has used this observation to build his theory about the pre-monarchical democratic assembly of which Samuel was appointed leader. Utilizing form critical analysis McKenzie, "Judge," pp. 118-121; and Richter, "Richter Israels," pp. 40-72, attempted to demonstrate the age and authenticity of I Samuel 7:15, which would undergird Samuel's role as a minor judge. Noth's concept has received strong criticism for being based on too little data. Samuel appears to fulfill a charismatic role not an institutional office, Macholz, "Samuel-Überlieferungen," pp. 58, 99, 123-126, 201-213; and Rendtorff, "Reflections," pp. 31-32. Samuel's affiliation with the rise of kingship caused the Deuteronomist to enlarge his role of minor judge (dispenser of law) and major judge (military deliverer). Stoebe, Samuelis, pp. 85-86; and Birch, Monarchy, p. 19, questioned the methodology behind elevating a few verses in I Samuel 7 to become the starting point for defining Samuel's historical role, especially when they may reflect a particular office unknown to us.

[14] Noth, Das System der zwölf Stämme Israel (Darmstadt: Wissenschaftliche Buchgesellschaft, 1930), passim, articulated this view, which has been accepted by many. The office of minor judge is contingent upon the existence of such a league, without it the office of minor judge is homeless. Only Richter, "Richter Israels," pp. 40-72, worked without this theory by calling the minor judge a local municipal office, and Samuel had authority only in those towns which he visited. Noth's theory has been effectively challenged by Orlinsky, "The Tribal System of Israel and Related Groups in the Period of the Judges," OrAnt 1 (1962): 11-20 = Studies and Essays in Honor of Abraham A. Neuman (Leiden: Brill, 1962), pp. 375-387 =

Essays, pp. 66-77; C. H. J. de Geus, "De Rechters van Israël," Nieuw Theologische Tijdschrift 20 (1965-1966): 81-100; B. D. Rahtjen, "Philistine and Hebrew Amphictyonies," JNES 24 (1965): 100-104; Fohrer, "Altes Testament -- 'Amphiktyonie' und 'Bund,'" Studien zur alttestamentlichen Theologie und Geschichte, BZAW, vol. 115 (Berlin: Gruyter, 1969), pp. 84-119 = TLZ 91 (1966): 801-816, 893-904, and Israelite Religion, pp. 87-96; Anderson, "Israel: Amphictyony: ʿAM; KAHAL; ʿEDAH," Translating and Understanding the Old Testament: Essays in Honor of Herbert G. May, ed. Harry Thomas Frank and William Reed (Nashville: Abingdon, 1970), pp. 135-151; and de Vaux, The Early History of Israel, trans. David Smith (Philadelphia: Westminster, 1978), pp. 695-715.

[15] Martin Kessler, "Narrative Technique in I Sam. 16: 1-13," CBQ 32 (1970): 547.

[16] Thorkild Jacobsen, The Treasures of Darkness: A History of the Mesopotamian Religion (New Haven: Yale University Press, 1976), pp. 195-219, has shown how the evolution of the Gilgamesh Epic tended to elaborate on narrative accounts, dialogues, folkloristic motifs, and theological agenda, while authentic historical memories were relegated to the periphery of the epic, separated from the main plot, or even lost. Allusions to the real Gilgamesh and his activity are often found in fragmentary accounts that are not part of the epic, the war with Agga king of Kish, forced labor of the men in Uruk, and building the walls of Uruk, while the epic may contain historical allusions only insofar as the real Gilgamesh may have obtained wood from the cedar forest. J. V. Kinnier-Wilson, The Rebel Lands: An investigation into the origins of the early Mesopotamian mythology, University of Cambridge Oriental Publications, vol. 29 (Cambridge, England: University Press, 1979), pp. 1-133, produced a provocative and speculative theory of how actual history may have given rise to not only legend and saga, but also mythology. He demonstrated the continued existence of a geological land fault and accompanying seismic disturbance from proto-literate down into historical periods, which may have given rise not only to archival reports, but also affected the development of mythology concerning the nature of the gods and the activity of epic heroes like Lugalbanda and Gilgamesh. He wisely refrained from establishing any criteria to discern the historical evidence, for the textual evidence demonstrated increased complexity and confusion which arose over the years in various myths and legends. In Mesopotamian studies one dare not establish criteria to discern the core of traditions, for the oral process of elaboration is too unpredictable. Outside archaeological or geological research might give insight into the original history, and only then may the historian observe how the later legends and myths have elaborated and deviated from the original

event. But one might never discern that event merely from the narrative material itself.

[17] Albert Lord, The Singer of Tales, Harvard Studies in Comparative Literature, vol. 24 (Cambridge: Harvard University Press, 1960), pp. 30-138; Robert Culley, Studies in the Structure of Hebrew Narrative (Missoula, Montana: Scholars Press, 1976) pp. 1-115; and Culley, ed., Oral Tradition and Old Testament Studies, Semeia, vol. 5 (Missoula, Montana: Scholars Press, 1976), pp. 1-163.

[18] The literary affinities are great. Samuel's birth is humble, he is raised by a stranger, Eli, just as Moses is reared in Pharaoh's house. His encounter with the divine has some formal similarities, the double vocative and human response, "behold, here I am." Samuel's victory over the Philistines is like Moses' victory over Amalek in Exodus 17:9-13. Both men give a condemnation of kings, I Samuel 8:11-18, Deuteronomy 17:16-17. Both men mediate covenants for the people. The Covenant Code has similarities with material in I Samuel 12:3-5; the covenantal obligations of Exodus 23:22 and Deuteronomy 28:1 are found in I Samuel 12. Samuel and Moses both intercede for the people. Moses parts the sea, Samuel brings a storm in I Samuel 12:16. The rîb formula is found in Deuteronomy 32:1-3, I Samuel 8:7-9, 10:17-19, and in various parts of 7:3-17, 12:1-25. Moses has a priestly function in Exodus 24:3-8, 35:12-14, Numbers 11:24-25, and Samuel has them in I Samuel 2:11, 3:1, 7:3-17, 9:1-10:16. Moses has prophetic functions in Exodus, 33:7-11, Numbers 12:5-8, and Samuel has them in I Samuel 3:19-21, 9:9, 13:7-15, 15:1-35, 19:18-24. Moses is the great intercessor in Exodus 20:18-21, Numbers 21:7, like Samuel in I Samuel 12:18-20, Jeremiah 15:1, Psalm 99:6. Moses is a covenant mediator in Exodus 19:3-6, Samuel is such in I Samuel 12:18-20. Both receive the Word of the Lord directly, Exodus 20:18-21, Numbers 12:5-8, I Samuel 3:11-14. Moses exercises judicial function in Exodus 18:13-27, as does Samuel in I Samuel 7:15-17. Samuel proclaims the law to the people in I Samuel 7 as Moses did in Exodus 20:2-23:19, Deuteronomy 5-26. Samuel is a leader of Israel like Moses. He leads the battle against the Philistines in I Samuel 7:13, the elders come to him for a king in 8:4-5, he anoints leaders in 9:1-10:16, 16:1-13, he officiates at coronations in 10:17-27, 11:11-15, and he undertakes censure of the leader in 15:1-35. Ritterspach, "Samuel traditions," pp. 226-279, who made most of the observations listed above, concluded the anti-monarchical source used authentic traditions, but the material was molded strongly by the theological intention of the editor, who portrayed Samuel as a second Moses. Albright, Samuel, p. 18, called Samuel the "first great religious reformer after Moses," on the basis of observations like these. Jenks, Elohist, p. 91,

even suggested that the traditions about Moses may have been influenced by the more authentic traditions about Samuel.

[19] William Irwin, "Samuel and the Rise of the Monarchy," AJSLL 58 (1941): 132-134, concluded that there was not one "single narrative of Samuel's activity that merits respect as good source material," and Irwin doubts whether Saul or David had any contact with the historical Samuel. Hylander, Samuel-Saul-Komplex, pp. 206-207, clearly affirmed the difficulty of historical reconstruction when working with theological traditions. Elias Auerbach, Wüste und Gelobtes Land: Geschichte Israels von den Anfängen bis zum Tode Salomos (Berlin: Wolff, 1932), p. 178, considered the material to be a good reflection of the era, but as a historical romance specific details cannot be drawn from it. Merrill, "I Samuel 1-12," pp. 126-134, 196-203, called this material a northern prophetic cultic legend, which was created to parallel other literature, and he gave an example of the strong similarity in form and structure between Genesis 35 and I Samuel 7:3-17, which were both calls to give up old idols. Macholz, "Samuel-Überlieferungen," pp. 99-213, considered the material to be a theological projection by the Deuteronomist, who sought to submerge Saul by creating the figure of Samuel. V. Fritz, "Die Deutungen der Königtums Sauls in den Überlieferungen von seiner Entstehung I Sam. 9-11," ZAW 88 (1976): 346-362, also considered the image of Samuel to be a projection from a later period.

[20] Alan Gardiner, Egypt of the Pharaohs (New York: Oxford, 1966), p. 136; and William C. Hayes, "The Middle Kingdom in Egypt: Internal History from the Rise of the Heracleopolitans to the Death of Ammenemes III," The Cambridge Ancient History, vol. 1, pt. 2, 3d ed., edited by I. E. S. Edwards, Cyril Gadd, N. G. L. Hammond (Cambridge, England: University Press, 1971), pp. 505-509.

[21] Weiser, Samuel, p. 92.

CHAPTER VII

CONCLUSION

The scope of this work has included a number of topics, but their elucidation of the dream experience of Samuel has been the point of convergence.

Dreams are phenomena which have intrigued both primitive and technologically advanced people. Among primitive societies dreams are viewed as contact with another realm, which enable the dreamer to perceive the future and obtain insights otherwise unavailable to mortals. Modern societies view the origin of dreams to lie within the dreamer, the product of the subconscious working out stress, anxiety, anticipations, and expectations. Like primitive understandings, modern explanations also see dreams as future oriented. They prepare the dreamer for the future by either relieving frustrations or creating an individualized life-world wherein the dreamer can perform in advance actions intended for the waking world. Fascination with dreams remains undiminished from primitive to modern societies, and the role of dreams in the psychological and social structures of both societies continues, if only in a new and modified fashion.

Ancient Near Eastern and Old Testament people, though not primitive in the totality of their thought structures, still shared with their primitive counterparts the belief that dreams could be an avenue to the divine realm. As such, dreams functioned as formal messages by which the gods might communicate their will or give advice to their human servants. Because dreams were a contact with the divine realm, dreams needed to be treated in a very circumspect fashion. Thus formal literary genres arose for the purpose of reporting and recording such dreams, perhaps lest the dream defile the dreamer and the listener by disrespectful treatment. Such forms or structures began to arise at the earliest stage of development, for among primitive peoples such well-structured oral forms for retelling dreams may be found. Those dream reports and dream references which have come into our hands from the ancient Near East clearly bear the marks of such formal structure and stylized expression. Because this is so, we may classify ancient Near Eastern dreams into four

247

categories: 1) auditory message dreams, wherein little or no visual image is perceived, and auditory communication is the primary revelation; 2) symbolic message dreams, wherein a visual image is perceived, and auditory communication may be lacking; 3) mantic dreams, a complex revelatory experience composed of several visual images or symbols capable of prognosticating the future when decoded; and 4) psychological status dreams, those non-recorded experiences which, if recorded, defile the dreamer and reader, yet which reflect the physical or psychological status of the dreamer. Modern concern for dreams would emphasize only this latter category, while the first three categories would be considered more important by ancient Near Eastern standards due to the revelatory nature of such experiences. The common dream report format, as we have discerned it, includes mention of the setting, recipient, time, theophany by the deity, awakening of the recipient, introduction, message, and formal termination. This format was the literary convention used to handle such sacred experiences, and its stylized expression renders the task of perceiving the original experience very difficult.

Biblical dream reports share much with their ancient Near Eastern counterparts. Dream reports in epic literature and historical narratives conform to ancient Near Eastern dreams in several respects. Dreams are a mode of revelation by which God communicates to His servants in order to assure them of His continued presence and impart to them special directions for the future. Thus the purpose and content of dreams in the Old Testament correspond to other ancient dream reports. Similarity also extends to structure and expression. Biblical dream reports record setting, recipient, time, theophany, address, message, and formal termination. It is evident that biblical writers utilized a ready made literary convention to describe an important aspect of divine communication.

Throughout the developing biblical tradition evidence of changing attitudes exists. Early traditions preserved in the epic literature and historical narratives attest a positive attitude toward dreams as a source of divine revelation. But with the later classical prophets, Isaiah and especially Jeremiah, this attitude changed. Perhaps the conflict with false prophecy caused dreams to be discredited gradually as a valid source of revelation. This critical attitude continued into the post-exilic period and manifested itself most clearly in the Wisdom tradition. However, when prophecy began to decline as a living theological movement, dreams began to regain their popularity in apocalyptic literature and post-exilic novel forms like Daniel and the Joseph cycle. Dreams again became an acceptable mode of revelation, but the emphasis moved from auditory dream theophanies to symbolic and mantic dreams, which required the dream interpreter. Finally, in the New

Testament dreams were a mode of revelation, but they were subordinated to the central revelation in the person of Jesus of Nazareth.

The consideration of biblical dreams has been undertaken in the past, but ancient Near Eastern dream reports have not been used comprehensively in the ensuing evaluations. Psychoanalytic categories have been forced on biblical dreams, but this procedure failed because of the very different attitudes toward dreams held by the biblical authors and modern people. Biblical literary dream reports are not conducive to modern psychoanalytic penetration, but biblical dream reports lend themselves to ready comparison with literary structures of contemporary dream reports in the ancient Near East. Bringing ancient Near Eastern categories to biblical accounts produces several insights, but the most significant results come out of a consideration of I Samuel 3. The similarity of this chapter with ancient Near Eastern auditory message dreams becomes quite apparent. Without such a comparison the scholar might not be able even to identify Samuel's experience as a dream; indeed, many have erroneously disclaimed it as such due to their lack of familiarity with ancient Near Eastern dreams. Whereas formerly this text was perceived form critically as a prophetic call narrative, the application of ancient Near Eastern textual data has led us to redefine the form of I Samuel 3 as an auditory message dream. Samuel's experience shares several characteristics in its structure with other ancient Near Eastern dreams: 1) setting in a sanctuary, 2) the recipient is near a holy object, 3) night theophany, 4) the recipient is awakened by the deity in order to receive the message, 5) the recipient is called by name, 6) the recipient responds to the deity, 7) an introductory word is spoken by the deity, 8) auditory message, 9) the message conveys the information of future actions intended by the deity, and 10) the recipient remains in the shrine until morning. There are some dissimilarities between Samuel's experience and the ancient Near Eastern format, but then no one dream contains all of the formal elements. Samuel does not pray, sacrifice, or perform ritual actions as do his ancient counterparts, including Solomon in I Kings 3. But Samuel's dream experience is not an intentional incubation dream, an activity which would be repugnant to the biblical author; accordingly, such details are missing. There is no self-identification of the deity, but Eli has already identified Him for Samuel in the narrative. The dream theophany contains no mention of deeds to be performed directly for Samuel's benefit, but the unfolding narrative reveals the implications for Samuel's future. Therefore, the central conclusion of this work is that Samuel's experience is form critically an auditory message dream theophany and not a prophetic call narrative.

249

This conclusion may subsequently be applied to the context in which this pericope is located. This auditory message dream form has been placed into its present context by the editor for theological reasons. The dream as a theological motif is a mode of revelation for a distant deity to communicate to His prophetic spokesmen. This God, whose word has been rare according to the text in I Samuel 3, now speaks through the mouth of a small child, and the divine silence and distance created by human sin are ended in a theophanic word of judgment. The dream as a literary motif may have had an increased popularity at this time, for there seems to be an abundance of dream reports in the contemporary Assyrian world. This may be another reason why the Deuteronomistic Historian or a pre-prophetic Deuteronomic Historian would have chosen this format (even though the prophetic critique against dreams was arising at this time). The text in I Samuel 3 and the greater context of I Samuel 1-3 bring condemnation upon the Elide priesthood and the shrine at Shiloh. I Samuel 3 is the conclusion, the response of God to the sinful human situation. God works through the prophetic ministry of the great Samuel, who is prophet, seer, priest, judge, Levite, and covenant mediator according to the various traditions. But God works through Samuel, not as an adult, but as a little boy, and this testifies not only to the importance of Samuel who begins his great career as a child, but it shows that indeed the condemnation of Shiloh and the Elide priesthood is the work of God and not men. The reader of the Deuteronomistic History is thus prepared for the eventual transition of religious authority from Shiloh to Jerusalem, an act to be accomplished by David in the next generation.

The text of I Samuel 3 seems to be a literary creation imposed upon possible earlier traditions in I Samuel 1-3. This dream theophany may have displaced an earlier prophetic call narrative, if such a form did exist prior to the creation of this text. The present text as it stands is a late literary creation. Consideration of the childhood narratives about Samuel in I Samuel 1-3 further supports this conclusion. Not only is I Samuel 3 a fitting theological conclusion to the entire childhood account, but the whole structure of the material in I Samuel 1-3 betrays late editorial work. The present structure seems to be a late creation with much inserted material. The purpose of the present text is to discredit the Elide family of priests in favor of the new priestly structures in Jerusalem, which will arise later in the books of Samuel. There are historical memories in the text, but they are subordinate to theological concerns of editors and authors of the text that lies before us.

When we compare I Samuel 1-3 to the traditions gathered about the adult figure of Samuel in I Samuel 7:1-16:13,

19:18-24, we discover that the same conclusions may be made concerning the latter corpus of literature. Theological concerns predominate in the creation of all these narratives, as they do most clearly in I Samuel 3. This is not to deny the historicity behind the text; rather such history lies beyond the ability of the scientific historian to recover it definitively. The nature of developing oral traditions in their complex social matrix is difficult to reconstruct and discover. Samuel is theologically portrayed by the prophetic editor and the Deuteronomistic Historian as the great paradigm for Israel. He is the model seer, prophet, judge, war leader, and priest for Israel in time of great distress. The need to project Samuel as such a great moral leader of the nation transcends any need merely to repeat the existing traditions or record a simple history. Such was not the procedure for Israel's theological historians. The original role of the historical Samuel becomes unimportant in the light of the theological needs to which the authors address their message. Thus we stand at the end of a great theological and literary process. The oral traditions have developed and interwoven in an exceedingly complex fashion. We have only the final product, the written corpus. Any attempt to dissect that corpus will produce as many theories as there are scholars, for each scholar will see and emphasize part of that very complex process. The total process can never be recovered, only conjectured. Dissection will not only fail to produce results, it does a disservice to the theology of the text by destroying the choral harmony of the various traditions.

I Samuel 3 shows the little boy Samuel receiving divine revelation in the midst of immoral chaos, and it foreshadows the religious and political leadership the adult Samuel will render in an era of national crisis. As a small child he was already a bulwark of faithfulness to God in a deteriorating situation. From this particular text we may perceive Samuel functioning primarily as a prophet and also as a priest or seer-priest, but the text is not trying to make such nice institutional distinctions. Samuel is a man of faith given to Israel by God in a period of crisis who can perform many roles according to his charismatic personality. These may be the particular projections of the author in this chapter, but their melodies merge into the greater choral harmony of the total corpus of Samuel traditions. The final picture of Samuel cannot be dissected into various component parts; rather, Samuel was a man for all seasons whose actions cut across institutional lines. For this reason the author of I Samuel 3 was perfectly justified in utilizing an ancient Near Eastern message dream formula to mold a beautiful literary creation about the young boy Samuel. Even as a little boy the great Samuel was about the task to which God had ultimately assigned him.

SELECTED BIBLIOGRAPHY

Ackroyd, Peter. The First Book of Samuel. CBC. Cambridge, England: Cambridge University Press, 1971.

Albright, William Foxwell. Samuel and the Beginnings of the Prophetic Movement. The Goldenson Lecture for 1961. Cincinnati: Hebrew Union College Press, 1961.

Alster, Bendt. Dumuzi's Dream. Aspects of Oral Poetry in a Sumerian Myth. Mesopotamia. Copenhagen Studies in Assyriology, vol. 1. Copenhagen: Akademisch Forlag, 1972.

Anderson, George W. A Critical Introduction to the Old Testament. Studies in Theology. London: Duckworth, 1959.

Artemidorus, Daldianus. The Interpretation of Dreams: Oneirocritica. Translated by Robert J. White. Noyes Classical Studies. Park Ridge, New Jersey: Noyes, 1975.

Baltzer, Klaus. "Considerations Concerning the Office and Calling of the Prophet." HTR 61 (1968): 567-581.

Batten, Loring Woart. "The Sanctuary at Shiloh, and Samuel's Sleeping therein." JBL 19 (1900): 29-33.

Bentzen, Aage. Introduction to the Old Testament. 2 vols. Copenhagen: Gads, 1948.

Bernhardt, Karl-Heinz. Das Problem der altorientalischen Königsideologie im Alten Testament: unter besonderer Berücksichtigung der Geschichte der Psalmenexegese dargestellt und kritisch gewurdigt. VTSup, vol. 8. Leiden: Brill, 1961.

Bertram, Georg. "Berufung II. Biblisch." RGG, vol. 1. 2d ed. Edited by Hermann Gunkel and Leopold Zscharnack. Tübingen: Mohr, 1927.

Birch, Bruce C. The Rise of the Israelite Monarchy: The

253

Growth and Development of 1 Samuel 7-15. SBLDS, vol. 27. Missoula, Montana: Scholars Press, 1976.

Boecker, Hans Jochen. Die Beurteilung der Anfänge des Königtums in den deuteronomistischen Abschnitten des 1. Samuelbuches. WMANT, vol. 31. Neukirchen: Neukirchener Verlag, 1969.

de Boer, Pieter Aric Hendrik. Research into the Text of I Samuel 1-16; a Contribution to the Study of the Books of Samuel. Amsterdam: Paris, 1938.

Bourke, Joseph. "Samuel and the Ark." Dominican Studies 7 (1954): 73-103.

Brinker, R. The Influence of Sanctuaries in Early Israel. Manchester, England: Manchester University Press, 1946.

Budde, Karl. The Books of Samuel: A Critical Edition of the Hebrew Text. Translated by B. W. Bacon. Leipzig: Hinrichs, 1894.

Budde, Karl. Die Bücher Richter und Samuel, ihre Quellen und ihr Aufbau. Giessen: Ricker, 1890.

Budde, Karl. Die Bücher Samuel. KHAT, vol. 8. Tübingen and Leipzig: Mohr, 1902.

Buhl, Marie-Louise, and Holm-Nielsen, Svend, eds. Shiloh: The Danish Excavations at Tall Sailūn, Palestine, in 1926, 1932, and 1963. Copenhagen: National Museum of Denmark, 1969.

Buttrick, George Arthur, ed. IB. 12 vols. Nashville: Abingdon, 1952-1956.

Buttrick, George Arthur, ed. IDB. 4 vols. Nashville: Abingdon, 1962.

Campbell, Joseph, ed. Myths, Dreams, and Religion. New York: Dutton, 1970.

Carlson, R. A. David, The chosen King: A Traditio-historical Approach to the Second Book of Samuel. Translated by Eric Sharpe and Stanley Rudman. Uppsala: Almquist und Wiksell, 1964.

Caspari, Wilhelm. Die Samuelbücher. KAT, vol. 7. Leipzig: Scholl, 1926.

Cody, Aelred. A History of Old Testament Priesthood. AnBib, vol. 35. Rome: Pontifical Biblical Institute, 1969.

Cornill, Carl. "Ein elohistischer Bericht über die Entstehung des israelitischen Königtums in 1 Samuelis 1-15 aufgezeigt." Zeitschrift für kirchliche Wissenschaft und kirchliche Leben 6 (1885): 113-141.

Dhorme, Edouard Paul, ed. La Bible: Ancien Testament. 2 vols. Paris: Gallimard, 1956.

Dhorme, Edouard Paul. L'evolution religieuse d'Israel. Vol. 1: La religion des Hebreux nomades. Brussels: Nouvelle Societe d'editions, 1937.

Dhorme, Edouard Paul. Les livres de Samuel. Etudes Bibliques, vol. 9. Paris: Gabalda, 1910.

Driver, Godfrey Rolles. Canaanite Myths and Legends. Old Testament Studies, vol. 3. Edinburgh: Clark, 1956.

Driver, Samuel Rolles. Notes on the Hebrew Text and the Topography of the Books of Samuel. 2d ed. Oxford: Clarendon, 1913.

Dus, Jan. "Die Geburtslegende Samuel I Sam. 1: Eine traditionsgeschichtliche Untersuchung zu I Sam. 1-3." RSO 43 (1969): 163-194.

Edelstein, Ludwig and E. J., eds. Asclepius: A Collection and Interpretation of the Testimonies. 2 vols. Baltimore: Johns Hopkins Press, 1945.

Ehrlich, Arnold B. Randglossen zur Hebräischen Bibel: Textkritisches, Sprachliches und Sachliches. 7 vols. Hildesheim: Georg Olms, 1968.

Ehrlich, Ernst Ludwig. Der Traum im Alten Testament. BZAW, vol. 73. Berlin: Gruyter, 1953.

Eichrodt, Walther. Theology of the Old Testament. 2 vols. Translated by James A. Baker. Philadelphia: Westminster, 1961.

Eissfeldt, Otto. Die Komposition der Samuelisbücher. Leipzig: Hinrichs, 1931.

Eissfeldt, Otto. "Silo und Jerusalem." Kleine Schriften, vol. 3. Edited by Rudolf Sellheim and Fritz Maas. Tübingen: Mohr, 1966.

Eliade, Mircea. Myths, Dreams, and Mysteries. Translated by
Philip Mairet. New York: Harper and Brothers, 1960.

Encyclopaedia Britannica, 1972 ed. S.v. "Dreams and
Dreaming," by David Ballin Klein.

Encyclopaedia of Religion and Ethics, 1922 ed. S.v. "Dreams
and Sleep," by various authors.

Fichtner, Johannes. "Berufung II. Im Alten Testament."
RGG, vol. 1. 3d ed. Edited by Kurt Galling.
Tübingen: Mohr, 1957.

Finkel, Asher. "The Pesher of Dreams and Scriptures." RevQ
(1963-1964): 357-370.

Fohrer, Georg. "Die Gattung der Berichte über symbolische
Handlungen der Propheten." ZAW 64 (1952): 101-120.

Frankfort, Henry, ed. Before Philosophy. Baltimore: Penguin, 1966.

Frazer, James George. The Golden Bough: A Study in Magic
and Religion. 12 vols. 3d ed. New York: Macmillan,
1935.

Freud, Sigmund. An Outline of Psychoanalysis. Translated by
James Strachey. New York: Norton, 1949.

Freud, Sigmund. The Standard Edition of the Complete Works
of Sigmund Freud. Vols. 4-5: The Interpretation of
Dreams. Translated and edited by James Strachey,
Anna Freud, Alix Strachey, and Alan Tyson. London:
Hogarth, 1953.

Garbini, Giovanni. "Osservazioni linguistiche a I Sam cap.
1-3." Bibbia e Oriente 5 (1963): 47-52.

Gaster, Theodor H. "Dreams: In the Bible." EncJud, vol. 6.
Jerusalem: Keter, 1971.

Gaster, Theodor H. The Oldest Stories in the World. Boston:
Beacon Press, 1952.

Gaster, Theodor H. Thespis: Ritual, Myth and Drama in the
Ancient Near East. New York: Schuman, 1950.

Gehrke, Ralph David. 1 and 2 Samuel. Concordia
Commentary. St. Louis: Concordia, 1968.

Gnuse, Robert Karl. "The Dream Motif in the Theology of the

Elohist: An Investigation into the Relationship of
Dreams in the "E" Source to the overall Theology of the
Elohist, other Old Testament Theologica, and the
Cultural Milieu of that Day." S.T.M. Thesis, Joint
Project for Theological Education, St. Louis and
University of Chicago, 1975.

Goldman, Solomon. Samuel. Soncino Books of the Bible.
London: Soncino, 1951.

Gordon, Cyrus. UT. AnOr, vol. 38. Rome: Pontifical Biblical Institute, 1965.

Gray, John. The KRT Text in the Literature of Ras Shamra:
A Social Myth of Ancient Canaan. Leiden: Brill, 1955.

Gressmann, Hugo. Die Schriften des Alten Testaments. Vol.
2: Die älteste Geschichtsschreibung und Prophetie
Israels. Göttingen: Vandenhoeck und Ruprecht, 1910.

von Grunebaum, Gustave Edmund, and Callois, Roger, eds.
The Dream and Human Societies. Berkeley, California:
University of California Press, 1966.

Guillaume, Alfred. Prophecy and Divination among the Hebrews
and other Semites. London: Hodder, 1938.

Habel, Norman. "The Form and Significance of the Call
Narratives." ZAW 77 (1965): 297-323.

Haran, Menahem. "Shiloh and Jerusalem: The Origin of the
Priestly Tradition in the Pentateuch." JBL 81 (1962):
14-24.

Heidel, Alexander. The Gilgamesh Epic and Old Testament
Parallels. Chicago: University of Chicago Press, 1949.

Herrmann, Siegfried. "Die Königsnovelle in Ägypten und in
Israel. Ein Beitrag zur Gattungsgeschichte in den
Geschichtsbüchern des Alten Testaments."
Wissenschaftliche Zeitschrift der Karl-Marx Universität,
Leipzig 3 (1953-1954): 51-62.

Hertzberg, Hans Wilhelm. I and II Samuel. Translated by J.
S. Bowden. OTL. Philadelphia: Westminster, 1964.

Hölscher, Gustav. Geschichtsschreibung in Israel. Acta
Regulatis Societatis Humaniorum Litterarum Lundensis,
vol. 50. Lund: Gleerup, 1952.

Hölscher, Gustav. Die Profeten. Untersuchungen zur

Religionsgeschichte Israels. Leipzig: Hinrichs, 1914.

Hölscher, Gustav. "Zum Ursprung des israelitischen Prophetentums." Alttestamentliche Studien für Rudolf Kittel zum 60. Geburtstag. BWAT, vol. 13. Leipzig: Hinrichs, 1913.

Hubbard, Benjamin. "Commissioning Stories in Luke-Acts: A Study of their Antecedents, Form and Content." Semeia, vol. 8. Edited by Robert Funk. Missoula, Montana: Scholars Press, 1977.

Hylander, Ivar. Der Literarische Samuel-Saul-Komplex (I Sam. 1-15) Traditionsgeschichtlich untersucht. Uppsala: Almquist und Wiksell, 1932.

Jenks, Alan W. The Elohist and North Israelite Traditions. SBLMS, vol. 22. Missoula, Montana: Scholars Press, 1977.

Jepsen, Alfred. Nabi. Soziologische Studien zur alttestamentlichen Literatur und Religionsgeschichte. Munich: Beck, 1934.

Jirku, Anton. "Ein Fall von Inkubation im Alten Testament (Ex 38:8)." ZAW 33 (1913): 151-153.

Jung, Carl Gustav. Psychological Types or the Psychology of Individuation. Translated by Godwin Baynes. New York: Random House, 1962.

Kaufmann, Yehezkel. The Religion of Israel. From its Beginnings to the Babylonian Exile. Translated by Moshe Greenberg. New York: Schocken, 1972.

Kenik, Helen Ann. "The Design for Kingship in I Kings 3:4-15: A Study in the Deuteronomistic Narrative Technique and Theology of Kingship." Ph.D. dissertation, St. Louis University, 1978.

Kennedy, Archibald Robert Sterling. Samuel: Introduction Revised Version with notes, index and maps. The Century Bible. Edinburgh: Jack, 1905.

Kittel, Rudolf. "Bücher Richter und Samuel." Die Heilige Schrift, Das Alte Testament. 3d ed. Tübingen: Mohr, 1909.

Kittel, Rudolf. "Die pentateuchischen Urkunden in den Büchern Richter und Samuel." TSK 65 (1896): 44-71.

Kittel, Rudolf. "I and II Samuel." Die Heilige Schrift des
Alten Testaments. Edited by E. Kautzsch. Freiburg:
Mohr, 1894.

Kjaer, Hans. The Excavation of Shilo, the Place of Eli and
Samuel. Jerusalem: Beyl-Ul-Makdes, 1930. = JPOS 10
(1930): 87-174.

Kjaer, Hans. "Shiloh. A Summary Report of the Second
Danish Expedition, 1929." PEQ 63 (1931): 71-88.

Klostermann, August. Die Bücher Samuelis und der Könige.
Kurzgefasster Kommentar zu den Heiligen Schriften
Alten und Neuen Testaments, vol. 3. Nördlingen:
Beck, 1887.

Kraus, Hans Joachim. Worship in Israel: A Cultic History of
the Old Testament. Translated by Geoffrey Buswell.
Richmond: John Knox, 1965.

Kutsch, Ernst. "Gideon's Berufung und Altarbau Jdc.
6:11-24." TLZ 81 (1956): 75-84.

Laufer, Berthold. "Inspirational Dreams in Eastern Asia."
Journal of American Folk Lore 44 (1931): 208-216.

Lichtenstein, Murray. "Dream Theophany and the E
Document." Journal of Ancient Near Eastern Society
(Columbia University) 1-2 (1969): 45-54.

Lindblom, Johannes. Prophecy in Ancient Israel. Philadelphia:
Fortress, 1973.

Lindblom, Johannes. "Theophanies in Holy Places in Hebrew
Religion." HUCA 32 (1961): 91-106.

Long, Burke. "Prophetic Call Traditions and Reports of
Visions." ZAW 84 (1972): 494-500.

McCarter, P. Kyle. I Samuel. AB, vol. 8. Garden City, New
York: Doubleday, 1980.

MacDermot, Violet. The Cult of the Seer in the Ancient Middle
East. Berkeley and Los Angeles: University of California Press, 1971.

Macholz, Georg Christian. "Untersuchungen zur Geschichte der
Samuel-Überlieferungen." Th.D. dissertation,
Heidelberg, 1966.

McKane, William. I and II Samuel. Torch Bible Commentary.

London: SCM Press, 1963.

McKenzie, John. "The Four Samuels." Biblical Research 7 (1962): 3-18.

MacLaurin, E. C. B. The Hebrew Theocracy in the Tenth to the Sixth Centuries B.C. London: Angus and Robertson, 1959.

Macrobius, Ambrosius Aurelius. Commentary on the Dream of Scipio. Translated by William Harris Stahl. New York: Columbia University Press, 1952.

Mauchline, John. 1 and 2 Samuel. New Century Bible. London: Oliphants, 1971.

Mazar, Benjamin, ed. The World History of the Jewish People. Ser. 1, vol. 3: Judges. New Brunswick, New Jersey: Rutgers University Press, 1971.

Meek, Theophile James. Hebrew Origins. Rev. ed. New York: Harper and Brothers, 1950.

Merrill, Arthur L. "I Sam 1-12: A Traditio-historical Study." Ph.D. dissertation, University of Chicago, 1962.

Mettinger, Tryggve. King and Messiah: The Civil and Sacral Legitimation of the Israelite Kings. Coniectanea Biblica: Old Testament Series, vol. 8. Lund: Gleerup, 1976.

Miller, Patrick, and Roberts, J. J. M. The Hand of the Lord: A Reassessment of the "Ark Narrative" of I Samuel. The Johns Hopkins Near Eastern Studies. Baltimore: The Johns Hopkins University Press, 1977.

Muilenburg, James. "The Form and Structure of the Covenantal Formulations." VT 9 (1959): 347-356.

New Encyclopaedia Britannica Macropaedia, 1974 ed. S.v. "Dreams," by Wilse Webb.

Newman, Murray. "The Prophetic Call of Samuel." Israel's Prophetic Heritage: Essays in honor of James Muilenburg. Edited by Bernhard Anderson and Walter Harrelson. New York: Harper and Brothers, 1962.

Noth, Martin. "Samuel und Silo." VT 13 (1963): 390-400.

Noth, Martin. Überlieferungsgeschichtliche Studien. Vol. 1:

Die sammelnden und bearbeitenden Geschichtswerke im Alten Testament. Schriften der Königsberger Gelehrten Gesellschaft, vol. 18, pt. 2. Halle: Niemeyer, 1943.

Nowack, Wilhelm. Richter, Ruth und Bücher Samuelis übersetzt und erklärt. HKAT, vol. 4. Göttingen: Vandenhoeck und Ruprecht, 1902.

Obermann, Julian. How Daniel was blessed with a Son: An Incubation Scene in Ugarit. Publications of the American Oriental Society, vol. 20. = JAOS Supplement 66, pt. 2 (1946): 1-30.

Oepke, Albrecht. "Onar." TDNT, vol. 5. Edited by Gerhard Kittel and Gerhard Friedrich. Translated by Geoffrey Bromiley. Grand Rapids, Michigan: Eerdmans, 1973.

Oppenheim, A. Leo. The Interpretation of Dreams in the Ancient Near East: With a Translation of an Assyrian Dream Book. Transactions of the American Philosophical Society, New Series, vol. 46. Philadelphia: American Philosophical Society, 1956.

Oppenheim, A. Leo. "New Fragments of the Assyrian Dream-Book." Iraq 31 (1969): 153-165.

Orlinsky, Harry. "The Seer in Ancient Israel." OrAnt 4 (1965): 153-174.

Peters, Norbertus. Beiträge zur Text- und Literarkritik, sowie zur Erklärung der Bücher Samuel. Freiburg: Herder, 1899.

Pfeiffer, Robert. "Midrash in the Books of Samuel." Quantulacumque: Studies presented to Kirsopp Lake. Edited by Robert Casey, Silva Lake, and Agnes Lake. London: Christophers, 1937.

Plöger, Otto. "Die Prophetengeschichten der Samuel- und Königsbücher." Th.D. dissertation, Greifswald, 1937.

Press, Richard. "Der Prophet Samuel. Eine traditionsgeschichtliche Untersuchung." ZAW 56 (1938): 177-225.

Pritchard, James B., ed. ANET. 3d ed. Princeton: Princeton University Press, 1969.

von Rad, Gerhard. Old Testament Theology. 2 vols. Translated by D. M. G. Stalker. New York: Harper and Row, 1965.

Resch, Andreas. Der Traum in Heilsplan Gottes: Deutung und Bedeutung des Traums im Alten Testament. Freiburg: Herder, 1964.

Richter, Wolfgang. Die sogenannten vorprophetischen Berufsberichte: Eine literaturwissenschaftliche Studie zu 1 Sam 9,1-10,16, Ex 3f, und Ri 6, 11b-17. FRLANT, vol. 101. Göttingen: Vandenhoeck und Ruprecht, 1970.

Richter, Wolfgang. Traditionsgeschichtliche Untersuchungen zum Richterbuch. BBB, vol. 18. Bonn: Hanstein, 1963.

Richter, Wolfgang. "Traum und Traumdeutung im Alten Testament." BZ 7 (1963): 202-220.

Ritterspach, Austin D. "The Samuel Traditions: An Analysis of the Anti-Monarchical Source in I Samuel 1-15." Ph.D. dissertation, Graduate Theological Union and San Francisco Theological Seminary, 1967.

Robertson, Edward. "Samuel and Saul." BJRL 28 (1944): 175-206. = The Old Testament Problem: A Re-investigation. The Publications of the University of Manchester, vol. 307. Manchester, England: University of Manchester Press, 1950.

Schäfers, Joseph. "1 Sam. 1-15 literarkritisch untersucht." BZ 5 (1907): 1-21, 126-145, 235-257, 359-380; 6 (1908): 117-132.

Schlögl, Nivard. Die Bücher Samuelis oder erstes und zweites Buch der Könige übersetzt und erklärt. Kurzgefasster Wissenschaftlicher Commentar zu den Heiligen Schriften des Alten Testaments, vol. 3. Vienna: Mayer, 1904.

Schmidt, Ludwig. Menschlicher Erfolg und Jahwes Initiative: Studien zu Tradition, Interpretation und Historie in Überlieferungen von Gideon, Saul und David. WMANT, vol. 38. Neukirchen: Neukirchener, 1970.

Schmidtke, Friedrich. "Träume, Orakel und Totengeister als Künder der Zukunft in Israel und Babylonien." BZ 11 (1967): 240-246.

Schulte, Hannelis. Die Entstehung der Geschichtsschreibung im Alten Israel. BZAW, vol. 128. Berlin: Gruyter, 1972.

Schulz, Alfons. Die Bücher Samuel. Übersetzt und erklärt. 2

vols. EHAT, vol. 8. Münster: Aschendorff, 1919-1920.

Schulz, Alfons. Erzählungskunst in den Samuel-Büchern. Biblische Zeitfragen, vol. 11. Münster: Aschendorff, 1923.

Schunck, Klaus-Dietrich. Benjamin. Untersuchungen zur Entstehung und Geschichte eines israelitischen Stammes. BZAW, vol. 86. Berlin: Töpelmann, 1963.

Segal, M. H. "The Composition of the Books of Samuel." JQR 55 (1964-1965): 318-339; 56, (1956-1966): 32-50, 137-157.

Segal, M. H. "Studies in the Books of Samuel." JQR 5 (1914-1915): 201-231; 6 (1915-1916): 267-302, 555-587; 8 (1917-1918): 75-100; 9 (1918-1919): 43-70.

Shulman, Sandra. The Interpretation of Dreams and Nightmares. New York: Ottenheimer, 1973.

Smith, Henry Preserved. A Critical and Exegetical Commentary on the Books of Samuel. ICC. New York: Scribners, 1899.

Soggin, J. Alberto. Das Königtum in Israel: Ursprünge, Spannungen, Entwicklung. BZAW, vol. 104. Berlin: Töpelmann, 1967.

Stekel, Wilhelm. The Interpretation of Dreams: New Developments and Techniques. 2 vols. Translated by Eden and Cedar Paul. New York: Livergith, 1943.

Stellini, Angelus. Samuel propheta (1 Sam 3, 20) et iudex (1 Sam 7, 16) in Israel. Pontificium Athenaeum Antonianum, Facultas Theologica (Sectio Biblica), Theses ad Lauream, vol. 113. Rome: Novara, 1957.

Steuernagel, Carl. "Die Weissagung über den Eliden." Alttestamentliche Studien für Rudolf Kittel zum 60. Geburtstag. BWAT, vol. 13. Leipzig: Hinrichs, 1913.

Stoebe, Hans Joachim. Das erste Buch Samuelis. KAT, vol. 8, pt. 1. Gütersloh: Mohn 1973.

Thenius, Otto. Die Bücher Samuelis. Kurzgefasstes Exegetisches Handbuch zum Alten Testament, vol. 4. 2d ed. Leipzig: Hirzel, 1864.

Tiktin, Hariton. Kritische Untersuchungen zu den Büchern

Samuelis. FRLANT, vol. 16. Göttingen: Vandenhoeck und Ruprecht, 1922.

Tsevat, Matitiahu. "Studies in the Book of Samuel I. Interpretation of 1 Sam. 2:27-36: The Narrative of Kareth." HUCA 32 (1961): 191-216.

de Vaux, Roland. Les livres de Samuel. La Sainte Bible. Paris: Cerf, 1953.

Veijola, Timo. Die Ewige Dynastie: David und die Entstehung seiner Dynastie nach der deuteronomistischen Darstellung. Suomalaisen Tiedeakatemian Toimituksia, Annales academiae scientiarum Fennicae, ser. 2, vol. 193. Helsinki: Suomalainen Tiedeakatemia, 1975.

Vogt, Ernst. "Novae inscriptiones Nabonidi." Bib 40 (1959): 88-102.

Wallis, Gerhard. Geschichte und Überlieferung: Gedanken über alttestamentliche Darstellungen der Frühgeschichte Israels und der Anfänge seines Königtums. Arbeiten zur Theologie, ser. 2, vol. 13. Stuttgart: Calwer, 1968.

Weiser, Artur. Samuel: Seine geschichtliche Aufgabe und religiöse Bedeutung. FRLANT, vol. 81. Göttingen: Vandenhoeck und Ruprecht, 1962.

Wellhausen, Julius. Die Composition des Hexateuchs und der historischen Bücher des Alten Testaments. Berlin: Reimer, 1889.

Wellhausen, Julius. Der Text der Bücher Samuelis. Göttingen: Vandenhoeck und Ruprecht, 1871.

Wikenhauser, Alfred. "Doppelträume." Bib 29 (1948): 100-111.

Willis, John. "An Anti-Elide Narrative Tradition." JBL 90 (1971): 288-308.

Willis, John. "Cultic Elements in the story of Samuel's birth and dedication." ST 26 (1972): 33-61.

Woods, Ralph Louis, ed. The World of Dreams: An Anthology. New York: Random House, 1947.

Zannoni, Arthur Edward. "An Investigation of the Call and Dedication of the Prophet Samuel: I Samuel 1:1-4:1a." Ph.D. dissertation, Marquette University, 1975.